Psychotherapy Case Formulation

D1557562

Theories of Psychotherapy Series

Theories of Psychotherapy Series
Jon Carlson and Matt Englar-Carlson, Series Editors

Psychotherapy Case Formulation

Tracy D. Eells

American Psychological Association

Washington, DC

Published by
American Psychological Association
750 First Street, NE
Washington, DC 20002
www.apa.org

To order
APA Order Department
P.O. Box 92984
Washington, DC 20090-2984
Tel: (800) 374-2721; Direct: (202) 336-5510
Fax: (202) 336-5502; TDD/TTY: (202) 336-6123
Online: www.apa.org/pubs/books
E-mail: order@apa.org

In the U.K., Europe, Africa, and the Middle East, copies may be ordered from
American Psychological Association
3 Henrietta Street
Covent Garden, London
WC2E 8LU England

Typeset in Minion by Circle Graphics, Inc., Columbia, MD

Printer: Edwards Brothers, Inc., Lillington, NC
Cover Designer: Minker Design, Sarasota, FL
Cover Art: Lily Rising, 2005, oil and mixed media on panel on craquelure frame, by Betsy Bauer

The opinions and statements published are the responsibility of the authors, and such opinions and statements do not necessarily represent the policies of the American Psychological Association.

Library of Congress Cataloging-in-Publication Data

Eells, Tracy D., author.
  Psychotherapy case formulation / Tracy D. Eells. — First edition.
    p. ; cm. — (Theories of psychotherapy series)
  Includes bibliographical references and index.
  ISBN 978-1-4338-2010-6 — ISBN 1-4338-2010-2
  I. American Psychological Association, issuing body. II. Title. III. Series: Theories of psychotherapy series.
  [DNLM: 1. Patient Care Planning—Case Reports. 2. Psychotherapy—methods—Case Reports. 3. Evidence-Based Practice—methods—Case Reports. WM 420]
  RC465
  616.89'14—dc23
                              2014045845

British Library Cataloguing-in-Publication Data
A CIP record is available from the British Library.

Printed in the United States of America
First Edition

http://dx.doi.org/10.1037/14667-000

To Bernadette, who has made everything possible.

He who would do good to another must do it in Minute Particulars.
General Good is the plea of the scoundrel, hypocrite, and flatterer;
For Art and Science cannot exist but in minutely organized Particulars,

—William Blake, Jerusalem: *The Emanation of the Giant Albion*

Contents

CONTENTS

Series Preface

Some might argue that in the contemporary clinical practice of psycho-therapy, evidence-based intervention and effective outcome have over-shadowed theory in importance. Maybe. But, as the editors of this series, we don't propose to take up that controversy here. We do know that psycho-therapists adopt and practice according to one theory or another because their experience, and decades of good evidence, suggests that having a sound theory of psychotherapy leads to greater therapeutic success. Still, the role of theory in the helping process can be hard to explain. This narrative about solving problems helps convey theory's importance:

> Aesop tells the fable of the sun and wind having a contest to decide who was the most powerful. From above the earth, they spotted a man walking down the street, and the wind said that he bet he could get his coat off. The sun agreed to the contest. The wind blew, and the man held on tightly to his coat. The more the wind blew, the tighter he held. The sun said it was his turn. He put all of his energy into creating warm sunshine, and soon the man took off his coat.

What does a competition between the sun and the wind to remove a man's coat have to do with theories of psychotherapy? We think this decep-tively simple story highlights the importance of theory as the precursor to any effective intervention—and hence to a favorable outcome. With-out a guiding theory we might treat the symptom without understanding the role of the individual. Or we might create power conflicts with our clients and not understand that, at times, indirect means of helping (sunshine) are often as effective—if not more so—than direct ones (wind). In the absence of theory, we might lose track of the treatment rationale and instead get caught up in, for example, social correctness and not wanting to do something that looks too simple.

What exactly *is* theory? The *APA Dictionary of Psychology* defines theory as "a principle or body of interrelated principles that purports to explain or predict a number of interrelated phenomena." In psychotherapy, a theory is a set of principles used to explain human thought and behavior, including what causes people to change. In practice, a theory creates the goals of therapy and specifies how to pursue them. Haley (1997) noted that a theory of psychotherapy ought to be simple enough for the average therapist to understand, but comprehensive enough to account for a wide range of eventualities. Furthermore, a theory guides action toward successful outcomes while generating hope in both the therapist and client that recovery is possible.

Theory is the compass that allows psychotherapists to navigate the vast territory of clinical practice. In the same ways that navigational tools have been modified to adapt to advances in thinking and ever-expanding territories to explore, theories of psychotherapy have changed over time. The different schools of theories are commonly referred to as waves, the first wave being psychodynamic theories (i.e., Adlerian, psychoanalytic), the second wave learning theories (i.e., behavioral, cognitive–behavioral), the third wave humanistic theories (person-centered, gestalt, existential), the fourth wave feminist and multicultural theories, and the fifth wave postmodern and constructivist theories. In many ways, these waves represent how psychotherapy has adapted and responded to changes in psychology, society, and epistemology as well as to changes in the nature of psychotherapy itself. Psychotherapy and the theories that guide it are dynamic and responsive. The wide variety of theories is also a testament to the different ways in which the same human behavior can be conceptualized (Frew & Spiegler, 2008).

It is with these two concepts in mind—the central importance of theory and the natural evolution of theoretical thinking—that we developed the APA Theories of Psychotherapy Series. Both of us are thoroughly fascinated by theory and the range of complex ideas that drive each model. As university faculty members who teach courses on the theories of psychotherapy, we wanted to create learning materials that not only highlight the essence of the major theories for professionals and professionals in training but also clearly bring the reader up to date on the current status of the models. Often in books on theory, the biography of the original theorist overshadows the evolution of the model. In contrast, our intent is to highlight the contemporary uses of the theories as well as their history and context.

As this project began, we faced two immediate decisions: which theories to address and who best to present them. We looked at graduate-level theories of psychotherapy courses to see which theories are being taught, and we explored popular scholarly books, articles, and conferences to determine which theories draw the most interest. We then developed a dream list of authors from among the best minds in contemporary theoretical practice. Each author is one of the leading proponents of that approach as well as a knowledgeable practitioner. We asked each author to review the core constructs of the theory, bring the theory into the modern sphere of clinical practice by looking at it through a context of evidence-based practice, and clearly illustrate how the theory looks in action.

There are 24 titles planned for the series. Each title can stand alone or can be put together with a few other titles to create materials for a course in psychotherapy theories. This option allows instructors to create a course featuring the approaches they believe are the most salient today. To support this end, APA Books has also developed a DVD for each of the approaches that demonstrates the theory in practice with a real client. Many of the DVDs show therapy over six sessions. Contact APA Books for a complete list of available DVD programs (http://www.apa.org/pubs/videos).

Case formulation is an important component of psychotherapy training and practice. The case formulation process presented by Dr. Tracy Eells guides the psychotherapist in applying theory to practice. This book describes a general formulation model that is both fundamentally integrative and takes an evidence-based approach to formulation. The model is designed to adapt to any theory in the Theories of Psychotherapy Series, any specific treatment manual, or any component of a theory or manual. Dr. Eells has created a masterpiece that should find a home in the library of all clinicians. From the onset, we wanted the Theories of Psychotherapy Series to be a pragmatic tool that all clinicians and students could use to deepen their understanding of theory. *Psychotherapy Case Formulation*, along with Dr. Bruce Wampold's (2010) *The Basics of Psychotherapy*, will give readers the additional tools needed to understand and apply all the major theories of psychotherapy. These two books can be combined with other titles in the series to create a complete textbook that is tailored for a course in psychotherapy theory.

—Jon Carlson and Matt Englar-Carlson

REFERENCES

Frew, J., & Spiegler, M. (2008). *Contemporary psychotherapies for a diverse world.* Boston, MA: Lahaska Press.

Haley, J. (1997). *Leaving home: The therapy of disturbed young people.* New York, NY: Routledge.

Wampold, B. E. (2010). *The basics of psychotherapy: An introduction to theory and practice.* Washington DC: American Psychological Association.

How to Use This Book
With APA Psychotherapy Videos

Each book in the Theories of Psychotherapy Series is specifically paired with a DVD that demonstrates the theory applied in actual therapy with a real client. Many DVDs feature the author of the book as the guest therapist, allowing students to see an eminent scholar and practitioner putting the theory they write about into action.

The DVDs have a number of features that make them excellent tools for learning more about theoretical concepts:

- Many DVDs contain six full sessions of psychotherapy over time, giving viewers a chance to see how clients respond to the application of the theory over the course of several sessions.
- Each DVD has a brief introductory discussion recapping the basic features of the theory behind the approach demonstrated. This allows viewers to review the key aspects of the approach about which they have just read.
- DVDs feature actual clients in unedited psychotherapy sessions. This provides a unique opportunity to get a sense of the look and feel of real psychotherapy, something that written case examples and transcripts sometimes cannot convey.
- There is a therapist commentary track that viewers may choose to play during the psychotherapy sessions. This track gives unique insight into why therapists do what they do in a session. Further it provides an in vivo opportunity to see how the therapist uses the model to conceptualize the client.

The books and DVDs together make a powerful teaching tool for showing how theoretical principles affect practice. In the case of this book, the DVD *Case Formulation in Psychotherapy*, which features the author as the guest expert, provides a robust example of how this approach looks in practice.

Acknowledgments

There are so many to thank that it is hard to know where to begin. This book would not be possible were it not for, in some semblance of chronological order, of course, my parents; my siblings; professors who made a difference, changed my life, and inspired me to an academic life, including Mel Gurtov, Frank Barron, Chalsa Loo, George Welsh, Lon Ussery, Jaan Valsiner, John Weisz, Don Baucom, Ray Schmidt, and Mardi Horowitz; research colleagues, including Ed Kendjelic, Cynthia Lucas, Carolyn Schneiderman, Nick Salsman, Andrew Brothers, Camille Frey, Katie Hoover, Greg Lynch, Maryrose Manshadi, Lisa Milliner, Richard Morris, Diane Taylor, Troy Raffield, Julia Ward, and above all, with deepest thanks, Ken Lombart; my friends and colleagues at the Society for Psychotherapy Research; Bahr Weiss for his friendship and the opportunity to coteach case formulation with him in Vietnam; and, each for something special, Chuck Fauteaux, John Curtis, Devora Depper, Allan Tasman, and Dan Fishman. I thank Susan Reynolds at APA for her gentle perseverance, kindness, and patience. Above all, this would not be possible without my family: Bernadette, Elias, Aidan, and Lillian.

Psychotherapy Case Formulation

Introduction

My first exposure to psychotherapy case formulation came as a graduate student at the University of North Carolina, Chapel Hill. I remember my first adult practicum experience. The client arrived, a man in his 30s who had been referred for possible depression. Before meeting him, I sat with my supervisor and we reviewed the referral information. He then suggested I "go in and get the lay of the land." Not knowing quite what that meant, I went in and followed an outline. I asked the man what brought him to the clinic, what his symptoms were, and when he started feeling badly. We talked about his past mental health care, medical history, and developmental, social, and occupational history. After an hour, we agreed to meet again and concluded the interview. My supervisor, who had observed the entire exchange, described my effort as "yeoman's work," which I took to mean, "Not artful, but good enough for a first time."

http://dx.doi.org/10.1037/14667-001
Psychotherapy Case Formulation, by T. D. Eells

Afterward, I was expected to complete an intake form. Most of the form was straightforward, requiring a summary of the information I had collected under the headings just described: presenting complaint, a history of mental health care, and so on. But then I came to a section labeled "Formulation." I had little idea what to do with this. None of my course work had explicitly covered case formulation. I assumed that formulation was part of psychiatric training, since my practicum was at a hospital, but I later learned my counterparts in psychiatry were as puzzled as I was about what to do with this section. I wrote a few lines, drawing loosely from psychodynamic theory, and signed the form. Receiving no comment afterward, I assumed it was okay.

Reflecting back on this first interview, I see that while the instruction to "get the lay of the land" puzzled me then, it was wise advice. I understand it to mean, "Get an understanding of the unique psychological landscape of an individual, attempt to see the world as they do, and draw a map of that landscape to help guide treatment." Yet, I also see the value in providing more explicit direction, both in interviewing and in drawing that map.

This and similar practicum experiences marked the beginning of what turned out to be a career-long interest in and study of individual psychological processes and psychotherapy case formulation as a vehicle to understanding the individual in distress. My interest in individual psychological functioning took the early form of a case study dissertation on the development of Franz Kafka's capacity for intimate relationships, advised by Jaan Valsiner, a developmental psychologist with vast knowledge of, and even vaster curiosity about, individual psychological development. Later, I pursued a postdoctoral fellowship at the Program on Conscious and Unconscious Mental Processes at the University of California, San Francisco, mentored by Mardi Horowitz. That work involved conducting intensive studies of individuals in psychotherapy for posttraumatic stress disorder or pathological grief. I learned Configurational Analysis (Horowitz, 2005), which shed a great deal of light on the value of formulation.

As a result of these experiences, I have come to see psychotherapy case formulation as an essential component of psychotherapy training and practice. Experts from virtually all theories of therapy describe formulation using terms such as a "linchpin concept" (Bergner, 1998), "the heart of evidence-based treatment" (Bieling & Kuyken, 2003), the "first principle" underlying therapy (J. S. Beck, 1995), and as filling "a gap that would otherwise exist between diagnosis and treatment" (Horowitz, 1997, p. 1). Similarly, professional organizations in the mental health fields identify case formulation as a "core competency" (American Board of Psychiatry & Neurology, 2009), "core skill" (Division of Clinical Psychology, 2001), and as a key component of evidence-based practice (APA Presidential Task Force on Evidence-Based Practice, 2006). The recognition given to case formulation is reflected in the publication of multiple books and journal articles on the topic in recent years (e.g., Eells, 2007a; Goldfried, 1995; Horowitz, 2005; Ingram, 2012; Kuyken, Padesky, & Dudley, 2009; Persons, 2008; Sperry & Sperry, 2012; Sturmey, 2008). Most of these works present case formulation from a single theoretical perspective and apply that theory to formulation; only a few are explicitly integrative (e.g., Caspar, 2007; Goldfried, 1995; Jose & Goldfried, 2008; Sperry & Sperry, 2012).

This book describes a general formulation model that is both fundamentally integrative and takes an evidence-based approach to formulation. The model is designed to adapt to any theory of therapy, any specific treatment manual, or any component of a theory or manual. It works for simple and straightforward cases, as well as those involving many problems in many spheres of life and multiple diagnostic comorbidities. The book is evidence based in three ways. First, it emphasizes case formulation inferences that are based on theories with supporting evidence. Second, the formulation process described incorporates both expert knowledge about formulation and steps to enhance sound reasoning in case formulation. Third, the model incorporates evidence in psychological science beyond theories of psychotherapy. This evidence includes findings from developmental psychology, psychopathology research, epidemiology, and cognitive science that may help explain a client's presenting problems and guide treatment. The approach taken in the book is consistent with the perspective on evidence-based practice in psychology as adopted by the American Psychological Association (APA Presidential Task Force on Evidence-Based Practice, 2006), which is "the integration of the best available research with clinical expertise in the context of patient characteristics, culture, and preference" (p. 273).

The genesis of this book came from years of teaching psychotherapy case formulation to clinical psychology graduate students and psychiatry residents. Initially, I taught multiple models of case formulation, assuming that students would pick and choose from the methods that best suited the needs of their clients, the evidence, and the theoretical interest of the student. On occasion, however, at the end of the course a student would approach me and ask, "Okay, I now know several models of case formulation, but which one should I use?" I also observed that beginning therapists struggle to apply theory to the individual case and frequently have a range of ideas about clients, but struggle to organize and order those ideas. I am asked, "How do I begin my formulation?" and "Where do I put the ideas I have about my client's problems?" This book is my answer to these questions.

The primary audience for the book is graduate-level trainees who are learning psychotherapy. These include clinical and counseling psychology graduate students, psychiatry residents, social work students, and anyone else who is learning psychotherapy. I hope more experienced therapists will also find value in the book, and that those reading other volumes in the *Theories of Psychotherapy Series* will find that it complements those works.

In writing the book, I found it helpful to imagine a particular type of reader. Whether or not this is you, I thought it might be of interest to describe my "ideal reader." It is a reader with broad interests and a curious and skeptical disposition who values simple formulations when they provide enough direction, complexity to the extent necessary, and tools that guide one in determining how much information is enough. This reader values the full range of perspectives on why clients come to therapy, why they are having problems, and what may help them; this reader may not want to choose a single set of lenses through which to view their clients. This reader values a broad foundation in psychological science, including the science of psychotherapy, the insights this work provides about process and outcome, and the value of prescribed, empirically supported treatments; yet this reader also values the art that is gained through practice, study, feedback, and reflection. This reader is looking for a basic model for organizing knowledge they can use in treating their clients. That is the person I have in mind.

To all readers, I have a note of caution: Many details are covered in the book, and as you read it you may wonder whether case formulation is too onerous and time consuming. With practice, however, the method is not daunting to use. It is not necessary to produce a lengthy, written formulation for every client or to consider every detail that is described. Rather, a more important goal is to develop a systematic case formulation frame of mind as a guide to treatment.

ORGANIZATION

The book is organized into nine chapters in two parts that together provide a foundation in evidence-based, integrative psychotherapy case formulation, including specific formulation steps and criteria for evaluating a formulation. Part I sets the context for the description of the general case formulation model and Part II describes the model.

Chapter 1 defines case formulation, describes its benefits, and suggests goals to seek when formulating. It continues with a brief history of formulation and a discussion of contemporary influences on case formulation. I introduce a case that I will use as an example in Part II. Chapter 1 closes with a discussion of tensions inherent in formulation that therapists must navigate.

Chapter 2 focuses on sound reasoning in case formulation. It draws heavily from cognitive-science research on decision making. Scholars have taken two general perspectives in regard to decision making. One perspective, led by Kahneman and colleagues (Kahneman, 2011; Kahneman, Slovic, & Tversky, 1982) as well as Meehl (1954, 1973a, 1973b), is highly skeptical of expert and clinical opinion in predicting outcomes and the ability of experts to perform better than nonexperts or statistical formulas. The other, summarized most comprehensively by Ericsson, Charness, Feltovich, and Hoffman (2006), recognizes expert performance in naturalistic settings and seeks to understand how these experts perform so well. The aim of Chapter 2 is to encourage readers to think in a sound and sophisticated way when developing explanatory hypotheses or making other inferences and predictions about clients.

Chapter 3 addresses culturally responsive case formulation. After defining key terms, it presents a cultural perspective on case formulation and suggests areas to consider when incorporating culture into a case conceptualization. This chapter also considers a client's religion and spiritual orientation in case formulation. Suggestions are offered to help the therapist develop a formulation that is culturally, religiously, and spiritually responsive. Specific steps for incorporating culture in case formulation are deferred until Chapter 7.

Chapter 4 introduces the general case formulation model and places it in the context of an evidence-based integrative approach to psychotherapy. It provides a rationale for thinking integratively and contrasts a case formulation approach to treatment with an approach that is not case formulation based. The chapter presents an overview of the four basic, action-oriented components of the case formulation model. These components are: create a problem list, diagnose, develop an explanatory hypothesis, and plan treatment. The chapter continues with a discussion of how and what type of information to gather when developing a formulation, both in regard to the type of information needed and the process by which it may be gathered. I describe basic principles for applying a formulation to treatment and why it is critical to empirically monitor progress on a session-by-session basis.

Part II provides a detailed description of the integrative, evidence-based case formulation model. It opens with Chapter 5, which focuses on creating a comprehensive problem list. The chapter describes how to do so and why. It discusses what a problem is, suggests ways to select and organize problems, and offers suggestions on problem formulation.

Chapter 6 attempts to put psychiatric diagnosis in perspective, showing the limitations of diagnosis as well as why it is nevertheless useful to include in a case formulation. It discusses what a mental disorder is, what role psychiatric diagnosis plays in psychotherapy, its societal impacts, and what it contributes uniquely to case formulation.

Chapter 7 addresses developing an explanatory hypothesis. Since many students find this to be the most challenging part of case formulation, I describe the process in step-by-step detail. The chapter shows how to develop an account of why the client is having problems, what triggers the problems, and what is maintaining them. It begins by proposing the diathesis-stress model of psychopathology as a powerful, enduring, and overarching integrative explanatory framework. It continues with a review of primary theories of psychotherapy and sources of evidence for formulation, expanding upon the historical and contemporary influences on case formulation presented in Chapter 1. The chapter concludes with a discussion of five steps to follow when developing the explanatory hypothesis. These are to identify (a) precipitants, (b) origins of problems, (c) client resources, (d) client obstacles, and finally, (e) a core hypothesis.

Chapter 8 presents a three-step model of treatment planning: assessing the set point for treatment, identifying treatment objectives, and selecting interventions to achieve those objectives. *Set point* refers to habitual psychological and interpersonal states that foreshadow and constrain treatment. Specific aspects of the set point discussed are reactance, client preferences, cultural and religious/spiritual considerations, and readiness for change. Regarding treatment objectives, I distinguish between end-point, outcome goals and short-term and intermediate-term process goals, which are designed to lead to the desired outcomes. Three approaches to organizing treatment interventions will be described.

Finally, Chapter 9 presents criteria for evaluating the quality of a case formulation and describes how to apply the criteria. These criteria emphasize the form and content of the formulation and the formulation's grounding in theory and evidence.

I hope you find this book engaging and readable, and that it provides you with a useful framework for conceptualizing your clients and planning treatment, regardless of your specific theoretical orientation. Above all, I hope it helps you serve your clients well by enhancing therapy outcomes.

UNDERSTANDING PSYCHOTHERAPY CASE FORMULATION IN CONTEXT

Defining Formulation: Benefits, Goals, History, and Influences

How do you know what to do in psychotherapy? In the concrete situation in which you are sitting across from a suffering individual who is seeking your help, who indeed may be relying on you to show them a way into the future, how do you know what to do? This is the question I ask psychotherapy students when I teach case formulation. Before reading any further, you might want to do what I ask students in my classes to do, which is to take a minute or two and write your answer.

What did you come up with? My answer is that we never know for sure what the best thing to do next is, whether it is to ask a question, listen empathically, suggest an exercise, offer an observation, give advice, ask for clarification, or any of a number of other possibilities. Although we cannot know for sure what to do, we can nevertheless always have a plan. Planning is preparation, and I am convinced that preparation increases the chances of doing something useful in therapy. Planning is where case

http://dx.doi.org/10.1037/14667-002
Psychotherapy Case Formulation, by T. D. Eells

formulation comes into play. But what goes into the plan, that is, where does the plan come from? I suggest three sources of information for plans: theory, evidence, and expert practice. In this book, I describe each of these sources. For now, consider the following case, which is a composite of cases presented by 4th-year psychiatry residents in a class on formulation. Imagine what you would do, and why, if you were treating the client:

Rochelle is a 41-year-old married White woman with 2 years of college who is not currently employed but worked previously as a nurse's aide. She has two living children: a 16-year-old daughter and a 7-year-old son, both by men other than her current husband. Her firstborn child, a son, died 5 years ago in a car accident at the age of 20. She tells you that the son was the product of sexual abuse she experienced when she was 16 years old.

Rochelle is currently living with her third husband, a man who works part-time and has chemical dependency problems. They jointly own a home with her husband's sister, who also lives with them, and Rochelle's two surviving children.

The client was referred to you by her primary care physician with complaints of depression, anxiety in many situations, difficulty sleeping, exhaustion, and chronic headaches. She also has poorly controlled diabetes.

She is tearful as she relates her suspicion that her husband is having an affair and reports that in a rage she scratched the length of his car with a key. She also mentions that her sister-in-law plans to move in with a new boyfriend and will no longer be contributing to house payments.

Rochelle has a history of suicidal ideation that she says did not lead to an attempt. She has had two psychiatric hospitalizations, both more than 10 years ago and both following threatened overdoses.

She was raised in an intact, Catholic home and there was considerable marital turmoil throughout her childhood. Her father had relatively stable employment in a factory and made enough to support the family. Her mother was a homemaker. Rochelle recalled that alcohol was pervasively present in the home. Currently, she has few friends, but feels close to those she does have. She complains that she does not see them often because her husband likes her to stay at home.

In her first session, Rochelle reports she is motivated for treatment, but she does not come to her second appointment and does not call ahead to cancel.

Rochelle's case raises many questions about her symptoms, problems, diagnosis, what explains her behavior, and what treatment approach to choose. Regarding *symptoms and problems*, questions include: What are her main problems, and how are they interrelated? Is she still grieving the loss of her son? Are there problems that if successfully treated would also solve others? What triggers her symptoms? Why did she scratch her husband's car instead of seeking better solutions?

Diagnostic questions include: What is Rochelle's diagnosis? Does she have major depression or another mood disorder? Does she have an anxiety disorder or a personality disorder? Does she meet criteria for more than one diagnosis? If so, which diagnosis should be the primary focus in therapy? What are her psychosocial stressors? What is her overall level of functioning?

Questions surrounding possible *explanations* of her behavior include: What is her self-concept? How does she view others? What are her wishes and fears? What are her primary coping strategies? How well integrated is her personality? How strong is her sense of identity? What automatic thoughts does she have? What factors influence her mood regulation? What are her goals and why is she not able to achieve them? How is her environment, both interpersonal and physical, affecting her behavior? How are her current and past family dynamics influencing her current functioning? Is diabetes contributing to her mood? What role are finances playing? What are her strengths? What is her risk for suicide? How are cultural factors and social role expectations affecting her behavior?

Questions focusing on *treatment planning* include: Are there evidence-based treatments or treatment processes that can help Rochelle? Does she need behavioral therapy? Cognitive–behavioral? Psychodynamic? Supportive? Some other modality? How long does she need to be in treatment? What short-term and long-term goals would be most helpful? Which problem or problems should we start with? Will she be able to form a therapeutic alliance with me? How motivated is she? Above all, will she or can she come for treatment?

These are questions anyone treating Rochelle might consider, regardless of theoretical orientation. People often look to diagnosis to explain and give direction. This is common in general medicine. Psychiatric diagnoses, however, are descriptive and do not address etiology in most cases, and they provide limited guidance on choosing type of treatment, let alone the specifics of a treatment plan. Clearly, something more than diagnosis is needed, which is where case formulation becomes relevant. Case formulation provides a framework to begin organizing answers to questions such as those posed above.

The reason for describing Rochelle and for raising these questions is to demonstrate the need for case formulation in practical terms. With this purpose served, we will leave Rochelle now but return to her in Part II. At this point, I continue by defining case formulation and discussing further why it is worth taking the time to formulate.

WHAT IS A PSYCHOTHERAPY CASE FORMULATION?

Here is a working definition: *Psychotherapy case formulation* is a process for developing a hypothesis about, and a plan to address, the causes, precipitants, and maintaining influences of a person's psychological, interpersonal, and behavioral problems in the context of that individual's culture and environment. As a hypothesis, a case formulation is the therapist's best account of the client's problems: why the client is experiencing them, what precipitates symptom onset, and why symptoms continue to occur instead of resolving. Formulation includes consideration of within-person factors, such as the person's learning history, style of interpreting information, coping style, self-concept, core beliefs, and basic, axiomatic assumptions about the world. A formulation attends to an individual's behavior, including whether it is under- or overexpressed, normative or nonnormative, and adaptive or maladaptive. It includes consideration of how the person interacts with others, what basic or automatic beliefs the person has about the intentions and wishes of others and what the responses are to those expectations. A formulation also takes into account the individual's environment, including cultural influences, social roles and whether they conflict with each other, and the potential influence of the physical environment on functioning, such as the safety of the neighborhood, socioeconomic factors, and education and work opportunities.

A formulation is more than a summary of history and presenting problems. It explains *why* the individual has problems. Some explanatory account is therefore necessarily a component of formulation. Since a formulation is pragmatic in focus, it includes a treatment plan. The treatment plan flows from the explanatory hypothesis, translating the conceptualization of the client's problems into a proposal for addressing them that includes goals and the client's preferences and readiness to change.

A formulation is a plan, but also a tool for planning. To serve well as a tool, it is preferable to articulate the formulation in terms that are testable. When a test fails, a formulation should be revised. Regular progress monitoring, easily done by way of symptom and problem measures, is a straightforward way of testing the formulation and its implementation. Revision may be necessary not only because a client is not responding but also because new information constantly emerges, new problems develop, and new insights are gained, and these developments may need to be incorporated into the formulation. As we will see in Chapter 4, the case formulation model described in this book includes a progress-monitoring step to facilitate evaluation of treatment response.

Process and Content Aspects of Formulation

A case formulation has both process and content aspects (Eells, 2007b; Eells & Lombart, 2004). *Process aspects* refer to the therapist's activities involved in eliciting the information necessary to formulate. I discuss this step in Chapter 4. *Content aspects* refer to the problems identified, the diagnosis, the explanation of the problem, and the treatment. I focus on these steps in Chapters 5 through 8.

Case, Event, and Prototype Formulations

A case formulation can be distinguished from the formulation of an event in psychotherapy and from a prototype formulation. An event formulation seeks to explain a particular episode or event in therapy, not the entire treatment. It is the therapist's attempt in treatment to understand unfolding events. Ideally, an event formulation fits with the case formulation, is guided by it, and either confirms or disconfirms it. Luborsky (1996) gave several examples of how in-session events, such as sudden shifts in depressed mood or onset of tears, can be understood in terms of interpersonal conflicts reflected in the case formulation. Some approaches to case formulation, such as that of Greenberg and Goldman (2007), emphasize the moment-to-moment emotional experience of clients, thus blending the idea of an event formulation with that of a case formulation.

A *prototype formulation* of a psychological disorder is based on a theoretical conception of that disorder. For example, Beck and colleagues conceptualized depression as characterized by negative views about oneself, others, and the world, and as marked by characteristic automatic thoughts, negative emotions, and problem behaviors flowing from the activation of negative schemas by stressful life events (A. T. Beck, Rush, Shaw, & Emery, 1979). Alternatively, the learned helplessness model of depression proposes that repeated noncontingent reinforcing experiences lead to depression and a pattern of attributions in which negative events are interpreted as due to internal personality flaws that are global and stable, whereas positive events are interpreted as due to external factors (Abramson, Seligman, & Teasdale, 1978). Another prototype formulation of depression is that of Lewinsohn and Shaffer (1971; Lewinsohn, Antonuccio, Breckenridge, & Teri, 1987) who proposed that a low rate of positive reinforcement is an antecedent to depression. A prototype formulation of depression based on attachment theory is that vulnerability to the condition is due to failure early in life to attain a secure, stable relationship with caretakers, repeated messages of one's unlovability, or the experience of genuine loss (Bowlby, 1969). Similar prototype formulations could be offered for other conditions such as generalized anxiety disorder (Behar & Borkovec, 2006), social phobia (Clark & Wells, 1995), posttraumatic stress disorder (Ehlers & Clark, 2000), and borderline personality disorder (Koerner, 2007). These prototype formulations can serve as starting points for developing an idiographic case formulation (Persons, 2008). With this introduction to the concept of case formulation, I now turn to reasons why formulation is useful.

WHY FORMULATE?

The presentation of Rochelle illustrated concretely why one would want to formulate a case. There are strong conceptual reasons to engage in formulation as well. Since formulation takes time and effort that the therapist could spend on other activities, it is worthwhile to understand why a therapist should take time to formulate. I propose four reasons. First, a case formulation guides treatment by helping the therapist stay on track from one session to the next, monitor progress, and be alert when a change of direction is indicated. It provides the therapist with an overarching perspective of the treatment. It is due to this planning and guiding function that formulation has been compared to a "map," a "blueprint," a "north star," and as the "heart" of evidence-based treatment. Second, a formulation increases treatment efficiency. Because the therapist has a plan, a time-effective, evidence-based route can be developed from the beginning to the end of treatment. Third, formulation tailors treatment to the specific circumstances a client is facing. By being client centered rather than treatment centered, a tailored formulation can take into account the problems and range of diagnoses being addressed, and the context of treatment; for example, whether multiple providers are being seen and whether there is a history of previous, possibly failed treatment. Fourth, a well-crafted formulation should enhance therapist empathy, an attribute that contributes to treatment outcome (Elliott, Bohart, Watson, & Greenberg, 2011). Since case formulation is designed to help a therapist understand a client better, it follows that case formulation contributes to empathy.

HISTORICAL AND CONTEMPORARY INFLUENCES ON CASE FORMULATION

Just as the practice of psychotherapy grew out of medicine, so can the modern psychotherapy case formulation be traced to the medical examination, which is rooted in Hippocratic and Galenic medicine (Eells, 2007b). Hippocratic physicians viewed the individual as a whole when considering a diagnosis and encouraged the client's active participation in the cure (Nuland, 1995). In contrast to their forebears' beliefs in polytheism and mythological causes of disease, they based conclusions on observation, reason, and the conviction that natural forces alone are responsible for disease. Hippocratic case reports provided many observable details about physical functioning and drew inferences from these observations before prescribing treatment. Galen's contribution to modern medicine was his emphasis on experimentation and a focus on physical structure and function as the foundation of disease.

In accord with these early medical traditions, psychotherapy case formulation depends on close observation, takes a holistic perspective, and considers multiple facets of functioning, including biological, psychological, and social facets. Galenic influences are seen in inferences about psychological structures, such as the schema concept from the cognitive perspective, traits from trait theory, and the psychoanalytic concepts of id, ego, and superego. Galenic influences are also seen in the emphasis on testing and experimentation seen in some case formulation approaches.

At least four contemporary developments in psychology have influenced psychotherapy case formulation. These are conceptions of the nature and classification of psychopathology, theories of psychotherapy, the psychometric tradition, and the advent of structured case formulation models. I now review each of these.

Nature and Classification of Psychopathology

Psychopathology is, to a large degree, the "stuff" of case formulation. A first step in defining and classifying psychopathology is to define what is abnormal. This concept is discussed in some detail in Chapter 6 when considering the role of diagnosis in case formulation. For now, note only that defining abnormality is a socially constructed task, and common criteria include personal distress, behavior that causes distress in others, capacity to adapt to stress, deviation from an ideal of normality, personality inflexibility, and irrationality. Decisions about normality and abnormality are central to the case formulation task. They shape the identification of problems and symptoms, explanations of those problems, treatment goals, and intervention strategies. They provide a reference point for understanding clients in a particular culture; for example, they enable the therapist to compare stress responses with what normatively would be expected under the circumstances.

Prevailing perspectives on psychopathology are categorized in the fifth edition of the American Psychiatric Association's (2013b) *Diagnostic and Statistical Manual of Mental Disorders (DSM–5)*, the World Health Organization's (1992) *International Classification of Diseases and Related Health Problems (ICD–10)*, and their predecessors. Historically, nosological systems have oscillated between those that are descriptive and those that are etiological (Mack, Forman, Brown, & Frances, 1994). This oscillation reflects dissatisfaction with descriptive models and the scientific shortcomings of etiological models. During the 20th century, this trend was seen as Kraepelin's descriptive psychiatry gave way to a biopsychosocial focus inspired by Adolf Meyer and Karl Menninger as well as a Freudian emphasis on unconscious determinants of behavior. A focus on description to the virtual exclusion of etiology was revived in 1980 with the publication of the third edition of the *DSM* (American Psychiatric Association, 1980), and continues to this day. The absence of etiological considerations creates a need that case formulation attempts to fill.

A question that has bedeviled psychopathologists for many years is whether psychopathology lies on a continuum or is a discontinuous set of distinct states. Consider an individual who is anxious, depressed, or hears voices. Is this person qualitatively different from individuals who are not anxious, depressed, or hearing voices, or are the differences one of degree? Your answer to this question places you either in the categoricalist or the dimensionalist camp (Blashfield & Burgess, 2007). The *categorical* view holds that mental disorders are syndromal and qualitatively distinct from each other as well as from normal states. It is the "medical model" view of mental disorders, which makes several assumptions: Diseases have predictable causes, courses and outcomes; symptoms are expressions of underlying pathogenic structures and processes; the primary but not exclusive province of medicine is disease, not health; and disease is fundamentally an individual phenomenon, not a social or cultural one. It is the dominant model embedded in the *DSM–5*, the *ICD–10*, and their predecessors, although the *DSM–5* has taken steps to incorporate a dimensionalist perspective. A drawback to the syndromal model is that therapists encounter clients who are disordered, but do not meet any of the diagnostic categories, or meet some criteria of a disorder but not enough to be diagnosed with a disorder (Angst, 2009). However, many find the categorical approach easier to use than the dimensional approach because clinical decisions are often categorical in nature (e.g., treat or not, use intervention A or B).

The *dimensionalist* view is that psychopathology lies along a set of continua from normal to abnormal. The difference between normal and abnormal behavior is one of degree, not quality. Dimensionalists assert that viewing psychopathology along continua better reflects psychopathology as it exists in nature and that the descriptive goals of any nomenclature are better served by a dimensional approach than by a categorical one (Blashfield & Burgess, 2007). Other advantages claimed for the dimensionalist perspective are that dimensions can be measured more easily, better capture subclinical phenomena, and are a more parsimonious way of understanding psychopathology. Trull and Durrett (2005), for example, asserted that much of the variability in personality can be understood in terms of only four dimensions: neuroticism/negative affectivity/emotional dysregulation; extraversion/positive emotionality; dissocial/antagonistic behavior; and constraint/compulsivity/conscientiousness. These four dimensions are rooted in decades of research on human personality and are deeply embedded in theory about personality (Blashfield & Burgess, 2007).

Thinking categorically or dimensionally affects how one explains problems and plans treatment in case formulation. Dimensionalists think in terms of a relatively small set of uncorrelated personality dimensions developed by administering psychological instruments to large numbers of people and measuring individual differences. Consequently, they are viewing psychopathology within an interindividual frame of reference (Valsiner, 1986). From this perspective, emphasis is placed on how individuals differ on dimensions of interest and understanding where a client is situated on a dimension is meaningful primarily in reference to where others fall on that trait. A therapist working from a dimensionalist perspective might be more likely to use well-normed personality tests as part of an assessment, might propose a set of cardinal traits as composing the core of a case formulation, and might develop treatment plans that aim at modifying maladaptive traits. On the other hand, categoricalists use a broader range of terms to describe psychopathology, including criteria of disorders listed in the *DSM–5*. Categoricalists may also be more prone to stigmatize clients by reifying what is actually a social construct. For example, being told one "has" a personality disorder may have the adverse effect of demoralizing an individual and confirming pathogenic beliefs. On the other hand, diagnostic categories may be framed in a contextual, transactional, and functional manner that aids in formulation and is useful for planning interventions. For example, instead of simply diagnosing someone with a borderline personality disorder, one might formulate that the individual misinterprets social cues as abandonment, leading to panic, helplessness and hopelessness, rage, and suicidal ideation. The treatment plan could therefore include reviewing episodes in which the above phenomena occur and considering more adaptive interpretations and solutions.

Can these two perspectives be reconciled? In my view, a therapist need not choose between the categorical and dimensional lenses, and it is helpful to be familiar with both modes of thinking. Cognitive scientists have found that we think more easily in terms of categories; it feels natural and is quick. Yet, dimensional approaches are parsimonious and address shortcomings of categorical systems. Each is a valid perspective, and one can learn to view clients alternately using either approach.

Theories of Psychotherapy

A therapist's theoretical orientation to psychotherapy provides a framework for explanation in case formulation. I will examine this proposition by looking briefly and selectively at four major models of psychotherapy: psychodynamic, cognitive, behavioral, and humanistic and phenomenological.

Psychoanalysis and psychodynamic psychotherapy have had a pervasive effect on views of personality and psychopathology and have contributed a wealth of constructs that are routinely incorporated into understanding psychotherapy clients. These include the notion of an active unconscious that determines much of conscious content; basic mental structures such as the id, superego, and ego; the role of reality-mediating processes, specifically the defense mechanisms; views on the role of sexuality, aggression, and human attachment in our lives; and a theory of psychological development. Freud also contributed to our understanding of symptom formation and of specific mental conditions such as depression, grief, and anxiety. Psychodynamic theory changed our understanding of the psychiatric interview. Before Freud, the psychiatric interview was viewed simply as an opportunity for the client to report his or her symptoms. Now, we recognize the interview as a vehicle through which the client's interpersonal and other problems outside of therapy may be enacted within the therapy.

Like psychoanalysis, cognitive therapy has provided a lexicon for case formulation and sets of standardized formulations of psychopathology, including for depression, anxiety, substance abuse, and personality disorders. These formulations emphasize cognitive patterns, schemas, faulty reasoning processes, and core beliefs, each specific to particular disorders. In addition, a massive amount of research has shown this method's efficacy across a broad range of disorders (Nathan & Gorman, 2007). Cognitive therapy research has demonstrated the wisdom in Shakespeare's lines from Hamlet: "For there is nothing either good or bad, but thinking makes it so."

Behavior therapy has historically not emphasized diagnosis or formulation, but nevertheless has influenced the case formulation process through its emphasis on symptoms, skepticism toward mental representations, and a focus on empiricism. Behaviorists strive to understand the topography of symptomatology, including stimulus-response connections, behavioral chains, and contingencies of reinforcement. Behaviorists have also focused on the role that environmental conditions play in maladaptive behavior. Consequently, behavioral formulations include analysis of the environment and how it might be changed to help an individual. A new "third wave" of behavioral theory has grown in significance in recent years (e.g., Hayes & Strosahl, 2004). It emphasizes the role of mindfulness, acceptance of one's past and current realities, and a commitment to awareness.

Phenomenological and humanistic psychotherapy has also influenced case formulation. Like behaviorists, adherents have traditionally rejected case formulation, although on the grounds that it can position the therapist in a superior relationship to the client and foster an unhealthy dependency. The contributions of humanistic thought to case formulation are an emphasis on the person as a whole instead of a disorder, a focus on the here-and-now experiencing of the therapist and client, and the view of the client and therapist as equals who are both focused on enabling the client to achieve greater self-awareness and congruence within the self.

The Psychometric Tradition

One of the "brightest jewels in the crown of clinical psychology" (Wood, Garb, & Nezworski, 2007, p. 72) is psychological testing, including the development of reliable and valid personality tests, standards for constructing and administering these tests, and the application of probability theory to assessment. The psychometric tradition involves a statistically informed frame of mind that is useful for case formulation. Awareness of concepts such as norming, reliability, validity, and standard administration of a measure may improve the quality of a case formulation. Some evidence of the value of the psychometric frame of mind in case formulation may be provided by one study, which found that undergraduates who were asked to think like a clinician were less likely to consider base rates than those asked to think like a scientist (Schwarz, Strack, Hilton, & Naderer, 1991). The psychometric tradition is reflected in the efforts of some to assess the reliability and validity of some methods of case formulation (Ghaderi, 2011; Mumma, 2011). The psychometric tradition is also evident in the American Psychological Association Presidential Task Force on Evidence-Based Practice (2006) recommendation that evidence-based practice include progress monitoring, which relies on psychometrically sound instruments. Nevertheless, the contribution of psychometric assessment to case formulation has been limited, perhaps because many psychologists see psychotherapy and psychometric assessment as not closely related. For example, Nelson-Gray (2003) questioned whether psychometric assessment contributes to beneficial treatment outcome in psychotherapy. The influence of the psychometric tradition may also be limited due to the configurational or narrative structure of some case formulations, which differs from the itemized structure of most psychometric instruments.

Structured Case Formulation Models

A final influence on case formulation is the advent of structured case formulation models. Beginning in the 1960s and 1970s, concern arose when therapists with similar theoretical orientations disagreed more than they agreed when formulating clients, even when using the same clinical material (e.g., Caston, 1993; Caston & Martin, 1993; Eells, 2007b; Seitz, 1966). It was also concerning that therapists, especially psychodynamic therapists, tended to infer psychological structures that seemed only distantly connected to observable clinical phenomena. In response, several formal methods for constructing case formulations have been developed and empirically tested in recent decades (Eells, 2007a). These methods have been generated primarily from the psychodynamic perspective; for example, Luborsky's core conflictual relationship theme (CCRT; Luborsky & Barrett, 2007), Horowitz's configurational analysis (Horowitz & Eells, 2007), and Silberschatz and Curtis's plan formulation method (Curtis & Silberschatz, 2007). However, some are cognitive–behavioral (e.g., Kuyken et al., 2009; Persons, 2008), some are behavioral (e.g., Nezu, Nezu, & Cos, 2007), and others are integrative (Bennett & Parry, 1998; Caspar, 1995, 2007; Ryle & Bennett, 1997). Most of these methods share common features: They identify problems; infer maladaptive relationship transactions and concepts of self, others, and the world; and rely primarily on clinical observation. In addition, they involve relatively low-level inferences, they structure the formulation task into components and sequences, and they reveal a trend toward psychotherapy integration.

The first and most researched of these methods is the CCRT (Luborsky, 1977), which aims to reliably and validly identify a client's central problematic relationship pattern. The CCRT focuses on narratives a client tells in therapy, identifying three key components within those narratives: an individual's wishes, expected responses of others, and responses of the self. The method is based on Freud's concept of transference, which holds that innate characteristics and early interpersonal experiences predispose a person to initiate and conduct close relationships in particular ways and in a repeated fashion later in life. A common CCRT may be that a person wishes to be close and accepting, expects rejection from others, and then becomes depressed or angry (Luborsky & Barrett, 2007). Research on the CCRT has demonstrated that narratives about relationship episodes are routinely told in psychotherapy; that CCRTs are consistent over the course of treatment, different relationships, and the life span; and that CCRTs differ by diagnosis (Luborsky & Barrett, 2007).

TENSIONS INHERENT IN CASE FORMULATION

In many ways, case formulation is a balancing act. The therapist has multiple concerns when applying theory and evidence to a case and must balance five basic tensions (Eells, 2007b). The first is that of immediacy versus comprehensiveness. Case formulation is fundamentally a pragmatic task; the therapist has limited time to gather information, formulate a case, and then implement it. The therapist must work with partial and often one-sided information when more comprehensive knowledge would be better. Following a rule of parsimony can help reconcile this tension. This means deciding how much information is enough to formulate and determining when more information is needed and of what type. The therapist should avoid being drawn into topics that do not use time well, yet she or he must also judge whether a topic will be fruitful or not. A balance must be struck between demands of pragmatism and the need for sufficient information.

A second tension is between complexity and simplicity. Human behavior is complex and difficult to predict. A therapist cannot hope to fully capture that complexity in a case formulation, nor is there a need to do so, since a formulation is about a limited range of problems. At the same time, sufficient complexity is needed to serve the goals of treatment. By *complexity*, I mean the extent to which multiple aspects of the client's problems are integrated into a meaningful presentation. A highly complex formulation may integrate several problems into a single theme and show how that theme triggers problematic responses; how those responses affect relationships, including, potentially, the therapy relationship; how the client copes; and how problems might be addressed in treatment. In other cases, there may be no need for the same level of complexity; for example, someone with high premorbid functioning and a strong support system who becomes overwhelmed with the stress of work or school due to a time-limited increase in responsibility. In short, a formulation should be as simple as possible and as complex as necessary.

Third is the tension between therapist bias and objectivity. No therapist can enter a course of psychotherapy free of bias from personal values, feelings, judgments, the influence of stereotypes, and the therapist's own personal and cultural history. Further, a persuasive body of research has demonstrated that we are all subject to systematic errors in judgment and reasoning, as discussed more fully in the next chapter. In addition, a long tradition exists in the clinical literature about therapist bias. Examples include the concept of countertransference, the therapist's response to interpersonal distortions on the part of the client, the therapist's personal problems, and therapeutic ruptures (Benjamin, 2003; Henry, Schacht, & Strupp, 1990; Levenson, 1995; Ogden, 1979; Safran, Muran, & Eubanks-Carter, 2011). Another way therapist bias comes into play is by relying too heavily on personal experience. As Ruscio (2007, p. 38) wrote, "To grant center stage to one's personal experience . . . can be to devalue the more informative collective experience of many other therapists who have worked with a much larger and broader sample of clients." Personal experience is invariably selective and subject to the judgment and reasoning biases noted above. Ruscio noted that a double standard of evidence is applied to one's own experiences versus information from other sources. To illustrate, he challenged readers to describe how they might evaluate evidence drawn from personal experience if that evidence retained all its characteristics, except the fact that it came from personal experience. He suggests it could be described as follows: The evidence is unsystematically sampled; lacks completeness and context due to the effects of selective memory; is not from a study in which clients were randomly assigned to condition; and is based on measures with unknown reliability and validity. Would you give this information privileged status compared with that resulting from large, well-controlled, and replicated studies, from metanalytic studies, or from a series of rigorous and systematic case studies? The point is not to devalue personal experience, but rather to view it in context as just one source of information in a field with many sources. In sum, therapists are inevitably pulled in the direction of making biased judgments yet must strive to manage this tendency and potentially even use it to benefit therapy.

A fourth tension is between observation and inference. By *observation*, I mean theory-free descriptive evidence gathered by careful watching and listening. An *inference* is a conclusion formed on the basis of observation; it may logically or reasonably follow from an observation, and it may be guided by theory. A therapist may observe tears flowing down a client's face and infer that the client is sad, or depending on the context, is guilty, feels unlovable, or is histrionic. A formulation draws from both observation and inference, and it is important to balance the two. If a therapist relies too heavily on observation, patterns will be missed and the formulation becomes merely a collection of facts. If the therapist's inferences stray too far from descriptive evidence, the connections back to observable phenomena are missed, inferences are more likely to be incorrect, and reliability of the formulation will suffer. Low-level inferences are often the most useful because they are more closely tied to empirical evidence and to the client's experience.

A final tension is between individual and general formulations. A case formulation is always, by definition, about a specific individual. It should take into account that individual's unique problems, life circumstances, learning history, stressors, wishes, hopes, goals, and so on. Yet, a wealth of information has been generated about the causes, characteristics, and course of specific psychological disorders, problems, and stressors. As noted above, prototype formulations provide useful hypotheses about the causes and maintaining influences in psychological disorders. An expert therapist has knowledge of relevant theories and research, yet the fit between the theory and the individual is always approximate. The therapist should be careful not to err on the side of being overly nomothetic and thus overlooking important unique aspects of a client's presenting problems. Conversely, he or she should be careful not to be overly idiographic in developing a formulation and thus disregard the collection of research that can help in treating the client. Again, as with the other tensions described, the right balance should be sought.

CONCLUSION

In this chapter, I defined psychotherapy case formulation and elaborated on the meaning of the term. I discussed why case formulation is important, both in concrete and conceptual terms. The history of case formulation was traced, and contemporary influences and tensions inherent to the case formulation process were discussed. With this background, I now continue with a discussion of how to think soundly when making decisions in case formulation.

2

Sound Decision Making in Case Formulation

In the mid-1990s, a psychiatrist colleague referred a client to me whom I will call Angela. Angela was a divorced Caucasian woman in her early 50s who was on disability for depression and dissociative identity disorder. She lived alone in a small, unkempt apartment that she rarely left. The only company she kept was with her adult son and an ex-boyfriend who occasionally called or visited. Angela was seeing the referring psychiatrist every 3 months for a medication check. In the initial session, Angela reported that she was sexually abused as a child on multiple occasions, beginning at age 3, and that she was also a victim of satanic ritual abuse. She claimed she had been awakened in the middle of the night by her parents, taken to a secret location, and forced to witness ritualistic killings of animals and, on some occasions, killings of infant children. The reported perpetrators of the sexual abuse were her father and friends of his. Angela was distressed as she recounted her story. A cycle occurred in

http://dx.doi.org/10.1037/14667-003
Psychotherapy Case Formulation, by T. D. Eells

that initial session. Her voice rose to a loud pitch, then she burst into tears, and finally regained her composure only to repeat the pattern two or three times. She reported that these incidents of abuse continued until her early adolescence, at which point she forgot them. In her 30s Angela entered therapy and gradually recovered the memories. She initially recalled only fragments, but with the encouragement of the therapist, more details emerged until coherent narratives were formed. Angela grew attached to her therapist, but after 2 years the therapist abruptly terminated treatment and left the counseling center. Angela continued to see a psychiatrist but had not seen any other counselor until I met with her. My psychiatrist colleague was concerned primarily about Angela's social isolation and lack of improvement in depression symptoms. Angela was not psychotic, had never been hospitalized for psychiatric reasons, and was convinced that her experiences of sexual and satanic ritual abuse were at the root of her problems. Imagine you are formulating her case and need to develop an explanatory hypothesis of her problems, which you see primarily as depression, social isolation, poor self-care, and emotional instability. Do you agree that sexual and satanic ritual abuse is the root of her problems?

You may be moved by Angela's vivid and detailed account of her abuse and by the conviction with which she tells her story. You may be aware that in the mid-1990s many stories and claims about recovered repressed memories, satanic ritual abuse, and multiple personality disorder were in the national news and popular press (ABC News, 1993; Achenbach, 1995; CNN, 1993; Thomas, 1994). You may feel Angela is one of those rare cases of satanic ritual abuse or one of those many previously unappreciated cases of multiple personality disorder, and that these events indeed lie at the heart of her problems. However, I hope you are as skeptical about this formulation as I was. In fact, it contains several clues that these may be false memories of abuse. These include the vividness of her recall, how well elaborated her accounts of abuse are, her conviction in the truthfulness of her account, and the story of repression and recovery of memories with therapist assistance. This is not to say that these events did not happen. It is possible that Angela has a repressive personality style (Bonanno & Singer, 1990) and through a process of memory blocking such as directed forgetting or retrieval inhibition (Schacter, 2001), events transpired as she recounted them. Nor is it to say that if they did not happen, the therapist's role is to disabuse Angela of her account of her own history. Rather, it is to suggest that the therapist should have a thorough grounding in relevant psychological research to be able to put such accounts into perspective and to use that knowledge to benefit the client in therapy.

The goal of this chapter is to provide you with tools to make sound decisions as a psychotherapy case formulator. Decision making is a major component of case formulation. In the last 30 years, our knowledge of decision making has advanced considerably. I discuss the implications of this research for case formulation, and then examine systematic errors in reasoning that can affect case formulation and the role of intuition in expert judgment. I conclude with suggestions for sound decision making in the case formulation process.

SYSTEM 1 AND SYSTEM 2

Perhaps the most powerful idea in the last 30 years of cognitive science, and one with considerable empirical support, is that cognitive processes in judgment and decision making are organized into two systems, each with distinct characteristics (Evans, 2008; Kahneman, 2011; Stanovich, 2009), and each existing in "uneasy interaction" with the other (Kahneman, 2011, p. 415). These systems have enormous relevance to decision making in psychotherapy case formulation. Following Kahneman (2011), I summarize characteristics of these two systems in a personified way to aid explication, labeling them as *System 1* and *System 2*, with the understanding that they are processes not personalities.

Kahneman (2011) described System 1 as automatic, effortless, quick, impulsive, and intuitive. System 1 is in charge when you are offered a piece of chocolate cake and immediately accept and indulge in it, forgetting about prior resolutions to lose weight. System 1 hits the snooze button in the morning, rolls you over, and puts you back to sleep when the alarm sounds, notwithstanding intentions the night before to get up early to study or exercise. System 1 leads you to decide whether you like a person within the first few minutes of meeting that individual. System 1 is affected by mood, is associated with good feelings, responds to intensity and vividness, and seeks easy solutions to problems. It provides impressions and is the source of impulses that lead to beliefs, thus allowing us to make sense of a complex world with only partial information. It scans the environment for threats and new information one may need to respond to. Its main function is "to maintain and update a model of your personal world, which represents what is normal in it" (Kahneman, 2011, p. 71). As Kahneman wrote, "If System 1 is involved, the conclusion comes first and the arguments follow" (p. 45).

In case formulation, System 1 is involved when a new client cries and the therapist automatically thinks "depression." It is involved when the word "borderline" flashes into the therapist's mind as a client becomes angry and demanding, threatens suicide, and then no-shows for the next appointment. It may be involved when a client appears sad and dejected and describes lack of success in finding a partner, and the therapist infers that the client has a self-schema of being unlovable. System 1 is involved when a client bursts into tears on the first visit, explains that their spouse has left them and they can't live without that person, and the therapist concludes that the problem has been identified and stops asking about other problems the client may have, such as those related to functioning at work, parenting, use of leisure time, finances, physical health, substance abuse, history of mental health care and need, and the potential role of cultural factors. In short, System 1 is involved when the therapist recognizes a pattern based on partial information.

System 1 operates according to well-established principles of associative activation. When an idea is primed or otherwise activated, it triggers a spreading cascade of other ideas with which it is connected in varying degrees of strength; multiple nodes in an associative network are activated, mostly occurring outside of conscious awareness. Kahneman (2011) noted, "The essential feature of this complex set of mental events is coherence" (p. 51). Each element in the network is connected and each reinforces the other, evoking memories that evoke other memories that together can also affect facial expressions, emotional responses, and events such as muscle tension and approach or avoidance tendencies. These ideas may be linked causally, by temporal or spatial contiguity, or by similarity.

System 1 is thought to arise from our evolutionary heritage. In order to survive, it was more important to think quickly and to find a good-enough-for-the-moment outcome to a problem than to think slowly and systematically until an optimal solution was determined (Stanovich, 2009). As Taleb (2007) wrote, "My counterfactual, introspective, and hard-thinking ancestor would have been eaten by a lion while his nonthinking but faster-reacting cousin would have run for cover" (p. xii).

Because the quick solutions that System 1 produces are a first approximation to an optimal response, System 1 sometimes makes mistakes. As it interprets the world to satisfy its need for coherence, it may see causal connections that are illusory. In this sense, System 1 is gullible, biased to believe, and jumps to conclusions even on weak evidence. It is insensitive to the quantity and quality of evidence that give rise to its conclusions. Stanovich (2009) went so far as to say that System 1 thinking threatens our autonomy as independent thinkers.

In contrast to System 1, System 2 is effortful, deliberative, orderly, rule-following, and slow. System 2 can solve demanding problems with great accuracy, but the power comes at a cost. System 2 places high demands on cognitive resources, requires a great deal of attention and concentration, and interferes with other thoughts and actions being carried out. When attention is withdrawn, System 2 processes are disrupted.

System 2 is algorithmic. It involves intentional efforts to apply inductive or deductive reasoning and logic in a stepwise fashion to solve problems. System 2 is involved in working memory when you attempt to recall in alphabetical order the names of the last five people you have spoken with. It is involved when you multiply 23×17. It is involved when you feel an impulse but resist it. System 2 is associated with the experience of agency, choice, and self-monitoring. System 2 is involved when you consider two options, weigh their respective advantages and disadvantages, and choose between them. It is oriented toward fulfilling our goals as people rather than fulfilling genetic goals that are based on our evolutionary heritage and that might not be personal goals.

System 2 has also been described as "lazy" (Kahneman, 2011; Stanovich, 2009). It is reluctant to invest more effort than is necessary to solve a problem. Due to the exertion it demands, exercising System 2 can be experienced as aversive and can easily lead to cognitive depletion. A common way that System 2 exhibits laziness is by substituting an easier question for a more difficult one. In one study, participants estimated the number of murders in Michigan during a given year. This is a difficult task because it requires one to recall information about a state's population, the distribution of population into urban and rural communities, wealth distribution, crime rates generally, news reports of crime in that state, and other predictors and evidence of violent crime. In another version of the study, participants estimated the number of murders in Detroit, and reported a number that on average was more than twice that estimated for Michigan (Kahneman & Frederick, 2002). This result violates what is called a dominance relationship and is not logical since any murder in Detroit is also a murder in Michigan, as Detroit is located in Michigan. Question substitution may explain the result. Instead of answering the question, "How many people were murdered in Detroit last year?" these participants may have answered the easier affect-laden question, "How safe is Detroit?" Later in this chapter, I give examples of how question substitution can occur when formulating cases.

System 2 is involved in case formulation when the therapist follows a step-by-step, systematic process to develop the formulation. It is involved when the therapist reviews and asks about the criteria for disorders when determining a client's diagnosis. System 2 is involved when the therapist reviews key domains of life and functioning when developing a comprehensive problem list. System 2 is involved when the therapist develops a treatment plan by identifying goals and specific interventions that will maximize goal attainment. In short, System 2 is involved whenever the therapist follows deliberate, goal-oriented, and effortful processes.

System 1 and System 2 interact in an alliance that is uneasy but usually works well. System 2 monitors System 1. It tells you to focus when your attention drifts in a meeting; it keeps you polite when you are angry, and instructs you to slow down when red lights flash ahead as you drive. System 1 continuously generates suggestions, impressions, impulses, and feelings about the state of the world. System 2 ordinarily accepts these suggestions with little or no change, and converts them to beliefs, attitudes, actions, and intentions. System 2 is alerted when an event occurs that does not fit the model of the world System 1 has created or when it detects that System 1 is leading one to err. System 2 believes it is in charge and believes it knows the reasons for our decisions; however, it is not and usually does not. It is akin to the metaphor of the elephant and the rider that social psychologist Jonathan Haidt (2006) described as he tried to understand why he struggled to muster the willpower to keep resolutions and act as rationally as he aspired to act:

> I was a rider on the back of an elephant. I'm holding the reins in my hands, and by pulling one way or the other, I can tell the elephant to turn, to stop, or to go. I can direct things but only when the elephant doesn't have desire of his own. When the elephant really wants to do something, I'm no match for him. (p. 4)

This is the dilemma faced by System 2, the rider, when trying to manage System 1, the elephant.

COGNITIVE HEURISTICS THAT COULD AFFECT CASE FORMULATION

In this section, I describe some case formulation thinking errors that are primarily due to System 1, but also to the laziness of System 2. The errors are based on *heuristic thinking*, which is an automatic and relatively effortless shorthand way of finding adequate, although often nonoptimal, answers to difficult questions. Heuristics involve a great deal of System 1 thinking, and they help explain why "a remarkable aspect of your mental life is that you are rarely stumped" (Kahneman, 2011, p. 97). While we may struggle with questions like "What is 23×17?" we usually have immediate and intuitive opinions about much of what we are asked. We form quick impressions about whether we like someone, whether that person is competent, why someone did or did not do something, what cardinal attributes characterize a person, whether a project will succeed, and whether we can trust someone. These conclusions are often based on thought processes that are outside our awareness and that we cannot explain or support with evidence.

In the past 30 years of cognitive science research, several thinking heuristics have been identified. Although individual differences exist in the use of these heuristics (Stanovich, 2009), they are characteristic of human thinking and are used by people regardless of level of intelligence. Heuristics do not always lead us to errors. In fact, they are usually useful and adaptive (Gigerenzer, Todd, & ABC Research Group, 1999). Later in this chapter I discuss conditions under which heuristics are adaptive and when they lead us astray. In this section, however, I review several heuristics that are relevant to psychotherapy case formulation. I provide a brief explanation and examples of relevance to case formulation. Readers interested in understanding the research supporting the heuristics are encouraged to consult Kahneman (2011), Stanovich (2009), Faust (2007), and Ruscio (2007).

Availability Heuristic

The *availability heuristic* is based on the principle that people make judgments based on "the ease with which instances come to mind" (Kahneman, 2011, p. 128). If asked to estimate the association between violence and mental illness, chances are you will overestimate the association after a high-profile violent incident involving a mentally ill individual receives national media attention than you would prior to the incident being reported. The reason is that instances of a class (mentally ill individuals who are violent) are more easily activated in associative memory in the former scenario and thus more easily recalled. Similarly, the more individuals with bipolar disorder in your case load, the more likely you are to see bipolar disorder in your next case. The availability heuristic is also likely to lead mental health professionals to see mental illness generally when it does not exist; similarly, the availability heuristic may lead psychologists to overestimate the role of psychological factors when explaining a psychological disorder, and psychiatrists to overestimate the role of biological factors. The availability heuristic is also at play when therapists give disproportionate influence to their own personal experience when making judgments, as discussed in Chapter 1 (Ruscio, 2007). One way to understand the availability heuristic is that it involves question substitution. When you wish to report the frequency of violence among the mentally ill, the likelihood that your client is bipolar, or the percentage of household tasks you perform, you instead report an impression based on the ease with which instances come to mind (Kahneman, 2011).

System 2 is required to resist the availability heuristic. One must make the effort to reconsider the immediate estimate that comes to mind; for example, by asking, "Is my estimate of the association between violence and mental illness inflated because of the recent case in the news?" Or, one might reflect, "My practice is heavily weighted toward bipolar clients, so I must be careful not to presume that every new client has bipolar disorder." In the case of Angela, recent media coverage of claims of recovered repressed memories and of satanic ritual abuse could lead, through the availability heuristic, to an overestimate of the likelihood that events of this type explain her problems.

It is useful to be aware of the availability heuristic when planning and implementing treatment. One of the better-known studies of the availability heuristic asked married couples to estimate what percentage of household activities they performed themselves. Consistent with the availability heuristic, the sum of percentages from the spouses exceeded 100. Each spouse is more aware of their own contributions to household upkeep than their partner's contribution, leading to an overestimate of their own contribution and an underestimate of their partner's contribution (M. Ross & Sicoly, 1979). A psychoeducation intervention explaining this common phenomenon might be helpful in marital and family counseling, as well as in individual therapy when discussing relationship conflicts. Research also shows that the more powerful one is or perceives oneself to be, the more vulnerable one is to the availability heuristic, and thus to accept hunches uncritically and without review by System 2 (Kahneman, 2011). This is relevant to case formulation since therapists are relatively more powerful than their clients in the context of therapy.

Affect Heuristic

The *affect heuristic* is related to the availability heuristic. It states that "people form opinions and make choices that directly express their feelings and their basic tendency to approach or avoid, often without knowing that they are doing so" (Kahneman, 2011, p. 139). The affect heuristic involves judging an idea as important to the extent that it is emotionally charged and readily comes to mind. It is involved when System 1 makes unconscious judgments based on feelings and then System 2 generates reasons to justify these judgments. The more novel, vivid, poignant, frightening, and unusual a phenomenon is, the greater the ease with which it is accessed in memory, and the greater the likelihood that it will shape decision making. In many situations, affect is an effective guide to judgments, leading to an adaptive weighing of cost and benefit, and ultimately good outcomes. A large body of evidence, however, shows that affect can sometimes replace better judgment that involves analysis, consideration of evidence quality, perspective taking, and other System 2 processes. This assertion should come as no surprise to mental health therapists, who regularly meet with people who make decisions based on impulse and immediate emotional reaction rather than what their better judgment tells them when emotion has cooled.

When asked whether you prefer an 8% or a 10% chance to win $100, you, like nearly everyone, will choose a 10% chance. Yet, when the same odds are presented in a more vivid and colorful way that activates System 1 and the affect heuristic, results change. In one study, students were offered the opportunity to win $100 by drawing a red marble from one of two jars. One jar contained 10 marbles; one was red and nine were white. The other jar contained 100 marbles: eight red ones and 92 white ones. A sizable minority (30%–40%) chose the jar with the greater number of red marbles, but an 8% chance of winning rather than the 10% chance (Kahneman, 2011). This result has been explained in terms of the affect heuristic. The vivid appearance of eight red marbles, an appealing image compared with dry percentages, appears to lead many people to make a decision that reduces their chances of winning $100, sometimes when knowing full well what they are doing. Obviously, this study does not involve the level of affect encountered in psychotherapy, but it does illustrate the role that vividness can play in decision making.

The affect heuristic is another example of substitution. In the study just reported, participants were asked about probabilities, but in the marble variation they may have substituted the question "How do you feel about those eight red marbles as opposed to that single red marble?" In the case of Angela, instead of answering the question "How likely is it that she is a victim of satanic ritual abuse?" we may substitute, "How do I feel about satanic ritual abuse?" and answer based on the vividness and horror of imagining satanic ritual abuse, thus overestimating its likelihood. The vividness of her description might lead one to agree with her formulation, even if one knew that the chances of her being a victim of satanic ritual abuse were extremely small. Similarly, a client's attractiveness may lead a therapist to draw immediate but incorrect inferences about that person's personality functioning. Further, liking a client may lead us to underpathologize and underpredict the obstacles that must be overcome to achieve a good outcome. Dislike of a client may lead us unconsciously to reject the client, predict a poor outcome, and conduct ourselves in ways that produce a self-fulfilling prophecy. These latter phenomena are well described by Freud's concept of countertransference, although the explanatory mechanism is quite different.

Representative Heuristic

The *representative heuristic* is a mental shortcut that is based on the principle of "like goes with like." It involves making judgments according to how well a situation matches a prototype of that or similar situations that we have stored in memory, without regard to other important relationships and probabilities. To illustrate, consider a client named Henry who sought psychotherapy because his wife found out he was having affairs and moved out of the house. Henry wanted her back because he felt it was important in his profession to project an image of stability. Henry described multiple relationships in which he was deceptive and showed utter disregard for how his lying affected others; he regularly engaged in impulsive, reckless behavior and demonstrated a seemingly complete lack of remorse for having failed to honor financial obligations that he could well afford. When asked about goals for therapy, he replied that he wanted his wife to accept his affairs in exchange for the affluent lifestyle he could provide her. Now, rank order the likelihood of the following statements:

1. Henry has an arrest record for speeding and drinking while driving.
2. Henry enjoys reading classical literature at home in the evenings.
3. Henry enjoys reading classical literature at home in the evenings and has an arrest record for drinking while driving.

If you are like many people presented with similar scenarios, you probably evaluated the first statement as most likely, the second statement as least likely, and the third as somewhere in between. If you did, then you committed a logical fallacy that can be understood in terms of the representative heuristic. The description of Henry fits criteria for an individual with antisocial personality disorder (ASPD). It is common for individuals with ASPD to have arrest records and substance abuse, hence the likely high rating of Statement 1. It is not likely that many with ASPD enjoy reading classical literature at home in the evenings, since those with ASPD tend to be impulsive, experience-seeking extraverts. However, since the set of individuals who enjoy reading classical literature includes literature-loving individuals who have arrest records for speeding and drinking while driving, as well as those who do not have such records, the second statement logically must be more probable than the third statement, which includes only those who enjoy classical literature and also have arrest records for speeding and drinking while driving. If you ranked Statement 3 as more likely than Statement 2, it is probably because drinking and an arrest record is representative of antisocial behavior and its representativeness guided your judgment and led you to disregard the logic relationship among the options. Again, question substitution helps explain the representative heuristic. Instead of asking the more difficult question of the logical likelihood of the three statements, which invokes System 2 processing, you likely substituted an easier question that System 1 can handle, such as, "How similar is drinking and speeding to people like Henry?"

I learned an important lesson about the representative heuristic when volunteering at a halfway house for clients with schizophrenia many years ago. One day, a young man who had recently been released from the psychiatric hospital asked me if I would like to see his Jaguar. Immediately assuming this would be my first opportunity to observe delusional behavior, I indulged him and said yes, whereupon he walked me down the street and showed me his Jaguar. My internal representation of an individual with schizophrenia fit well with delusional behavior but not with ownership of an expensive sports car; thus, I was misled by my System 1.

To be sure, the representative heuristic is often useful in decision making. The immediate first impressions that it generates often aid judgment. Clients who have borderline personality disorder may also have been sexually abused. Clients with more education likely are more verbally articulate than others. But the representative heuristic is something to be aware of when formulating cases. For example, when a client reports she was sexually abused as a child, the representative heuristic may lead the therapist to conclude, based on this single disclosure, that the client is intensely and pervasively damaged; scarred for life; vulnerable to depression, anxiety, and alcohol abuse; has poor self-esteem; is sexually maladjusted; and is unable to form healthy adult intimate relationships. This conclusion could be based on similarities between the client's report of sexual abuse and the therapist's mental prototype that child sexual abuse causes severe and pervasive harm to virtually all its victims. In fact, there is strong empirical evidence that the degree and pervasiveness of harm caused by child sexual abuse may be overstated in some populations (Rind, Tromovitch, & Bauserman, 1998, 2001). This evidence suggests much more resilience than the stereotype suggests, although it does not deny that some individuals do experience severe, pervasive, and lasting harm from child sexual abuse. The finding was so contrary to the stereotypical, vivid image of the child sexual abuse victim that the original research report stirred up considerable controversy, including attacks by radio talk-show hosts, congressional committees, a variety of academics and practitioners, and conservative groups (Ondersma et al., 2001). In the example just given, an alternative inference may be that the client is remarkably resilient as evidenced by her success in resolving a painful childhood experience. The point with regard to psychotherapy case formulation is that one should avoid easy conclusions and inferences based solely on similarities between a client's descriptions of events and the stereotype of an individual with similar experiences.

Neglect of Base Rates

Suppose you have a chronically depressed client who threatens suicide. Imagine further that one in a thousand persons with chronic depression successfully commits suicide in their lifetime and that there is a psychological test that correctly diagnoses intent to commit suicide 100% of the time when the person actually intends to commit suicide. Finally, assume that the test has a false-positive rate of 5%; that is, the test wrongly indicates intent to commit suicide in 5% of cases in which the person does not intend to commit suicide. Now, imagine your chronically depressed client takes the test and it indicates suicide intent. Assume we know nothing more about the client other than the test score and that the individual is chronically depressed. What are the chances the client will commit suicide, and how will your treatment plan be affected?

The most common answer given to questions of this type is 95% (Stanovich, 2009). In fact, the odds are about 2%, or 1 in 51 persons. It is easy to calculate this result: The false-positive rate of 5% means that of 1,000 persons taking the test, about 50 will be falsely identified as suicidal. The sensitivity of the test is 100%; so, if 1 in 1,000 is the base rate for successful suicide, we can add one person to the 50 who are false positives, giving us 51 persons identified by the test as suicidal among our sample of 1,000. Thus, the odds of a positive test result leading to a successful suicide are 1 in 51, or approximately 2%.

Neglect of base rates has enormous significance in case formulation and, particularly, treatment planning. Your treatment plan will presumably differ when based on an inference of a 95% chance of suicide versus a 2% chance. If everyone who scored a positive on this test were hospitalized for safety, 50 people would be hospitalized who would not have committed suicide for every 1 that would have. The point is not that a therapist should disregard the risk of suicide even if it is only a 2% chance, but rather that the treatment plan should take into account the actual risk based on epidemiology and the appropriate application of base-rate information.

Considering base rates is helpful in trying to understand whether Angela was actually the victim of satanic ritual abuse. Although base rates of this activity are not known, it is reasonable to assume they are quite low. Assuming the base rate is 1 in 10,000 persons, and assuming that Angela has a mental disorder of some type, which has a 1-year prevalence in the United States of about 25% (Kessler, Chiu, Demler, Merikangas, & Walters, 2005), the odds of Angela actually being a victim of satanic ritual abuse are approximately .03% or 3 in 10,000.

Overconfidence

Another well-documented error in thinking is *overconfidence.* Numerous studies show that we overestimate our confidence about what we know and the likelihood of future events occurring. When people report answering all items on a questionnaire correctly, they actually answer about 88% correctly. Similarly, when people say they are 70% to 80% confident of decisions in a dichotomous choice situation, actual performance is often only chance; that is, 50% (Stanovich, 2009). Another example is the observation that while hypnosis does not improve accuracy of memories, it does increase one's confidence in the accuracy of memories (Krass, Kinoshita, & McConkey, 1989; Steblay & Bothwell, 1994). One explanation for these phenomena is that we tend to accept the quick answer to questions that System 1 generates and not think of reasons those answers might be wrong. In effect, System 1 generates a response and System 2 confirms it by generating selective evidence and neglecting disconfirming evidence.

Overconfidence takes different forms. One is the planning fallacy (Kahneman, 2011; Stanovich, 2009), which is the ubiquitous tendency to underestimate the time it will take to complete projects. Another is *hindsight bias*, in which people consistently overestimate in hindsight what they believe they knew in foresight (Fischhoff, 1975, 1982). In one study, a group of neuropsychologists read a case history and were then asked to estimate the probability of three different diagnoses. Others were told that one of the diagnoses was correct and were asked what probability they would have assigned to each of the diagnostic possibilities had they not known the diagnosis. Those in the hindsight condition were much more likely to assign a greater probability to the ostensibly correct diagnosis than were those in the foresight group (Arkes, Faust, Guilmette, & Hart, 1988). This phenomenon has also been called the "I knew it all along effect" (Fischhoff, 1975).

Overconfidence can have damaging effects on clinical decision making. Potchen (2006) compared radiologists who demonstrated high diagnostic accuracy (95%) with others who demonstrated low accuracy (75%). He found that while the accuracy of the two groups differed, the confidence of each group in its diagnostic accuracy did not differ. Confidence did not predict accuracy. Groopman (2007) described several case studies in which harm occurred due to overconfidence in medical diagnostic reasoning. Because overconfidence tells us we know more than we do, we tend not to critique our thinking, and not to learn from mistakes or appreciate when our predictions are incorrect. Further, misdiagnosis can lead to mistreatment.

WHEN CAN WE TRUST OUR INTUITION?

In the previous section, I focused on decision-making errors that pose risks for psychotherapy case formulators. Many of these errors grow from uncritical reliance on intuition flowing from System 1 processes. Yet, it is well documented that experts in a variety of skill domains are capable of accurate, insightful, and intuitive judgment (Chi, Glaser, & Farr, 1988; Ericsson, Charness, Feltovich, & Hoffman, 2006; Klein, 1998). Accounts have been written about remarkable feats performed by chess players, athletes, musicians, mathematicians, physicists, and physicians, among others. Within their area of expertise, these individuals quickly perceive large meaningful patterns, are faster than novices at performing the skill in question, and quickly solve problems with little error (Chi, 2006).

Some writers highlight intuition as important in psychotherapy. Reik (1948) extolled the experienced psychotherapist's ability to "listen with the third ear" to gain insight into areas of conflict of which the client is unaware: "One of the peculiarities of this third ear is that it works two ways. It can catch what other people do not say, but only feel and think; and it can also be turned inward. It can hear voices from within the self that are otherwise not audible because they are drowned out by the noise of our conscious thought processes" (pp. 146–147). Similarly, Benjamin (1996b) compared the skill of a therapist conducting a diagnostic interview to that of a hound following a scent:

> The interviewer follows the tracks of the unconscious as the hound follows the scent of the fox. The hound does not cut up the field into sections and search systematically. Rather, it puts its nose to the ground and follows the trail, circling back and going every which way, if that is where the scent goes. The scent is laid down by the unconscious. (p. 79)

Researchers have also identified intuition as a significant component of therapist activity. Caspar's (1997) research on "what goes on in a psychotherapist's mind" shows that therapists engage in a great deal of intuitive as well as rational-analytic thinking. Charman (2004) found that therapists include the word *intuitive* when describing the skills of effective psychotherapists. In my own research, which is described further in Chapter 9, expert case formulators developed higher quality case formulations than nonexperts and did so using a mix of cognitive processes involving short-term, data-near, intuitive leaps as well as effortful deductive and inductive processes (Eells, 2010; Eells, Lombart, Kendjelic, Turner, & Lucas, 2005; Eells et al., 2011).

Thus, two views of intuition exist in the literature—one praising it and the other panning it. Taleb (2007) captured the perspectives with two examples:

> Would you rather have your upcoming brain surgery performed by a newspaper's science reporter or by a certified brain surgeon? On the other hand, would you prefer to listen to an economic forecast by someone with a PhD in finance from some 'prominent' institution such as the Wharton School, or by a newspaper's business writer?

While the answer to the first question is empirically obvious, the answer to the second one isn't at all. (p. 146)

In this section, I attempt to reconcile these two views of expert behavior and intuition. I begin by defining the term and continue by considering conditions that allow for accurate intuition.

Cognitive scientists agree that *intuition* is a mode of thought that is fast, automatic, largely unconscious, and provides a solution to a problem or an answer to a question; usually the individual cannot explain how the solution came to mind (Gigerenzer, 2007; Hogarth, 2001; Kahneman & Klein, 2009; Myers, 2002). Simon (1992) put recognition at the center of his view of intuition: "The situation has provided a cue; this cue has given the expert access to information stored in memory, and the information provides the answer. Intuition is nothing more and nothing less than recognition" (p. 155). A major advantage of Simon's definition is that it demystifies the term and places it squarely in the realm of ordinary psychological processes. Thus, intuition is a process not unlike that of recognizing when a friend is upset simply by looking at his or her face. You may not know how you know; you just accept it as natural. Similarly, you may not know why a client's story of relationship problems fits a familiar pattern; it just does.

Kahneman and Klein (2009) suggested that two conditions must be met in order to acquire genuine expertise. First, the learning environment must be regular, predictable, and highly valid; to use Hogarth's (2001) terminology, it must be "kind." The game of basketball is an example of a kind learning environment. It has clear rules and boundaries; and play provides feedback that is immediate, relevant, unambiguous, consistent, and accurate. Baskets are made or missed; passes are completed or not; rebounds are caught or not; and ultimately, the game is won or lost. Adjustments are made on the basis of this feedback to improve performance, and those adjustments can then be subject to further feedback. These characteristics facilitate the acquisition of skill in recognizing and responding effectively to tacit cues as they unfold on the basketball court. In contrast, irregular, inconsistent, and low-validity environments are not conducive to the acquisition of accurate intuition. One example might be leadership of a large and complex organization. In these environments, causal connections between actions taken by leadership and the effects of these actions are often not clear; feedback may come slowly, irregularly, ambiguously, inaccurately, or not at all; the environment is influenced by powerful and difficult to control forces both within and outside the organization; and the problems faced are often novel rather than familiar (P. Rosenzweig, 2007).

It is important to be aware of "wicked" environments in which consistencies provide misleading feedback (Hogarth, 2001). Hogarth cited as an example Lewis Thomas's account of a physician who developed a reputation for accurately diagnosing typhoid in patients who had not yet developed symptoms of the disease. The physician's method was to walk from bed to bed and palpate the tongue of each patient, examining that organ for its texture and irregularities. As predicted, within a week or two these patients exhibited florid symptoms of typhoid fever. Feedback in this environment was consistent, regular, unambiguous, predictable, and reinforcing of the physician's diagnoses; but it was terribly misleading, since the physician himself was infecting his patients.

Fortunately, competently delivered psychotherapy occurs in a relatively kind environment. The respective roles of the therapist and client are well defined. The therapist aims to provide a facilitating environment, and to behave in a manner that is stable, consistent, and predictable. The client is educated about his or her role and the expectations therapy involves. Collaborative agreement is sought on identifying problems, causes, and maintaining influences; and the two decide upon a course of action to address them. The setting in which therapy unfolds is stable in that sessions usually have a predictable length and structure, and session tasks are usually defined. In addition, the events that occur in therapy are relatively limited in scope. Near-term feedback is provided to therapists after every intervention, and on a session-by-session basis when progress is monitored. While the feedback may not be as explicit as a made or missed shot in a game of basketball, therapists can learn to tune in to the cues clients give after interventions. Other skills performed by mental health professionals do not occur in such kind environments. These include predicting suicidality or violence; offering forensic opinions related to criminal responsibility, competency, or disability; predicting academic or job performance; and evaluating one's success rate as a therapist (due to overconfidence and hindsight bias). These activities involve predictions well into the future, so feedback is significantly delayed, if it comes at all.

The second condition that must be met to acquire genuine expertise is adequate opportunity to practice the skill. Ericsson (2006) found that extensive experience is necessary to acquire expertise in a domain, as much as 10,000 hours; further, the skills are acquired gradually and after exposure to a vast repertoire of examples within the domain in which one aspires to achieve expertise. But experience alone is not sufficient. Deliberate practice is also necessary, and it involves sustained levels of concentration and effort; suitable training tasks that isolate components of the skills desired; and explicit, detailed feedback and monitoring from a coach or teacher.

Psychotherapy and psychotherapy case formulation appear to be skill domains suitable to deliberate practice, although Tracey, Wampold, Lichtenberg, and Goodyear (2014) suggested that therapists rarely capitalize on the opportunity. Supervision is a core component of training in psychotherapy and ordinarily includes feedback. In addition, feedback comes from clients directly and through progress monitoring. It is possible to decompose therapy and case formulation skills into specific components, and evidence suggests that doing so may facilitate learning more than a global approach to supervision (Henry, Schacht, Strupp, Butler, & Binder, 1993). Caspar, Berger, and Hautle (2004) demonstrated that an individualized, computer-assisted training program that provides concise and intensive feedback is well accepted by trainees and improves their ability to cover relevant aspects of case formulation.

Another advantage of psychotherapy in facilitating the development of expert intuition is that it provides many opportunities for learning because it is a frequently occurring event. It differs in this respect from other areas in which expertise might be sought, such as in responding to natural or man-made disasters.

The main lesson in this section is that you as a therapist should be wary of hunches, gut feelings, and intuitions unless they are made in a highly regular and valid environment; involve temporally short-term predictions; and you have engaged in many hours of deliberate practice in which complex tasks have been broken down into component parts and specific, timely feedback has been given.

SUGGESTIONS FOR SOUND DECISION MAKING IN CASE FORMULATION

On the basis of the research reported in this chapter, several suggestions are offered to aid in sound decision making when formulating cases.

First, do not be overly persuaded by vivid, coherent accounts of events. Monitor your inferences, especially those that come easily, and consider whether you are engaging in question substitution.

Second, use research, base rates, and other nomothetic evidence as counterbiasing tools. Toward this end, when considering probabilities, convert percentages to actual numbers; that is, instead of asking, "What percent?" ask "How many out of 1,000?"

Third, remain aware of what types of judgments therapists excel in and what types they do not. Know your limits: The further into the future you predict, the less you should trust your intuition and the more you should trust statistical predictions and, in general, the nomothetic literature.

Fourth, guard against overconfidence. Your confidence that the case formulation is sound is not good evidence that it actually is sound. Instead, challenge your formulation by creating an alternative and comparing the two. It is helpful to critique your formulation with colleagues and to use a checklist to ensure basic components of the formulation are present. Croskerry and Norman (2008) offered several specific strategies to correct for overconfidence.

Fifth, ensure that the environment you provide in therapy is kind, not wicked. By structuring the psychotherapy experience, therapists can facilitate the creation of a predictable, consistent, and stable environment that will facilitate accurate intuition. Obtaining feedback and challenging your intuitions will help ensure that they are accurate.

Sixth, tell yourself to perform better. As we have seen, effort makes a difference in exercising sound clinical judgment.

CONCLUSION

This chapter began with a description of Angela, a psychotherapy client who felt she had been victimized by satanic ritual abuse and sexual abuse since the age of 3. I discussed various aspects of her presentation that cast skepticism on her account. I discussed two modes of thinking that have emerged in cognitive science: System 1, which is automatic, low resource, fast, and intuitive; and System 2, which is effortful, high resource, slow, and systematic. I reviewed errors in thinking that these two systems, led primarily by System 1, can lead us into, showing how these errors might play out in case formulation. I also addressed conditions under which intuition, guided primarily by System 1, aids in case formulation, and when it does not. Finally, tips were offered to aid therapists in thinking soundly when developing case formulations. It is important for the therapist to have a thorough grounding in relevant psychological research to be able to put accounts such as that of Angela into perspective and to use that knowledge in therapy. With these caveats in mind, I now move to another critical aspect of case formulation: taking into account the cultural context of the client and in which the formulation occurs.

3

Developing a Culturally Responsive Formulation

Relatively little has been written about culture in psychotherapy case formulation. This is unfortunate because culture pervades and informs, often silently, every aspect of case formulation (Ridley & Kelly, 2007). During my clinical training at the University of North Carolina, Chapel Hill, one psychiatrist made a lasting impression on me regarding the power of culture in clinical work. During one of my practicum placements, we spent a morning each week assessing families who had been referred to us because a child in the family was identified as having a problem. Ordinarily, the psychiatry resident started by gathering signs and symptoms, followed by the social work student who obtained a psychosocial history, then the clinical psychology student (myself) did some psychological testing. One lower income, rural North Carolina family that lacked formal education seemed particularly uncomfortable during their morning assessment. It was a father, mother, and a son who was

http://dx.doi.org/10.1037/14667-004
Psychotherapy Case Formulation, by T. D. Eells

about 8 years old. They spoke almost inaudibly, responded to questions with as few words as possible, and then sat in silence. After enduring the probing and prodding from the students, they were met by the attending psychiatrist. I knew him as a well-spoken, sophisticated, and much-respected senior professor at the medical school. When he entered the room, he walked slowly to a chair, sat down, leaned forward, and in a soft, rural North Carolina accent (thicker than in conversations I had with him), he introduced himself and spoke as if he were an interested neighbor. He asked short questions and used simple language and rural idioms. Within minutes, the family had visibly relaxed and become much more self-disclosing. The psychiatrist had the benefit of coming from rural North Carolina, the same culture the family was from. That gave him genuineness and an inroad we students lacked. Nevertheless, the incident illustrated for me the power of making an immediate cultural connection.

In this chapter, I make a case for applying a cultural lens to every formulation. I set the context by reviewing key definitions, discussing cultural universalism versus relativism, and articulating reasons why a cultural perspective on case formulation is critical. I continue by reviewing how culture affects the expression of some major psychological disorders, and then consider religion and spirituality as aspects of culture in case formulation. I discuss common features of various approaches to incorporate culture into formulation. Finally, I offer suggestions for developing a culturally sensitive formulation.

DEFINITIONS: CULTURE, RACE, ETHNICITY, AND MINORITY

Defining the word *culture* has proven to be difficult for scholars. Kroeber and Kluckhohn (1952) reviewed more than 150 scholarly definitions and developed a definition of their own that has stood the test of time:

> Culture consists of patterns, explicit and implicit, of and for behavior acquired and transmitted by symbols, constituting the distinctive achievement of human groups, including their embodiments in arti-

facts; the essential core of culture consists of traditional (i.e., historically derived and selected) ideas and especially their attached values; culture systems may, on the one hand, be considered as products of action, on the other as conditioning elements of further action. (p. 181)

At the core of this definition is the idea that culture is a collection of ideas and associated values that are reflected in individual and group behavior and that over time have acquired stabilizing power in a personality and a society. Culture binds people together in ways they are often not aware of. As the writer Samuel Johnson said of habit, the ties of culture are "too weak to be felt until they are too strong to be broken."

Ridley and Kelly (2007) identified several characteristics of culture that are relevant to case formulation. First, culture permeates all of human experience and thus is present throughout the formulation process. Second, culture is experienced internally and also has external referents. A Hispanic man, for example, may feel anger, resentment, and guilt related to cultural norms to care for adult family members who are unemployed, all leading to a clinical presentation of anxiety. A third characteristic is that cultural influences vary among people from similar cultural backgrounds. Culture is only one of many factors that shape an individual's identity. How culture affects one person will differ from how it affects another. Finally, culture is a broad and multidimensional term that distinguishes groups of people not only by race and ethnicity but also by age, socioeconomic status, sexual orientation, gender identity, religion, occupation, and education, among other characteristics. Culture contains many ingredients that express themselves uniquely in each individual.

The word *culture* is sometimes used interchangeably with terms like *race*, *ethnicity*, and *minority*, but each has distinct meanings that are helpful to keep in mind. *Race* is a term originally developed by European scientists to differentiate people on the basis of physical characteristics such as skin color, facial features, hair type, and geographical origin (Betancourt & López, 1993; Hays, 2008). It is problematic as a scientific concept, however, since many groups identified on the basis of race have more within-group heterogeneity than between-group heterogeneity. For example, Asian American is a term used for individuals tracing their heritage to any of several Asian countries, each with its own dominant culture and set of subcultures. For this reason, the term is better construed as a social construct than as a scientific one (Hays, 2008). As a construct, race has social meaning that is often important to people in terms of identity, values, priorities, and social roles. For this reason, it may be important for the therapist to understand that meaning for a specific individual when formulating.

Ethnicity overlaps in meaning with culture and is considered to provide more information about a person than race. Ethnicity refers to historical and social patterns and collective identities shared by people from a specific region of the world (Duckworth, 2009). It conveys the notion of "peoplehood" and common ancestry (McGoldrick, Giordano, & Garcia-Preto, 2005), including the beliefs, norms, behaviors, language, and institutions connected to that ancestry (Hays, 2008). To illustrate, one patient understood her anxiety in terms of her parents' European roots. Her mother was from ethnically Russian eastern Ukraine, which the patient connected to her mother's high-strung emotionality. Her father was from Scandinavia, which the patient connected with her ability to remain outwardly calm despite inward anxiety. As can be seen, ethnicity is a more nuanced concept than race, and is another component of identity that may be important in case formulation.

The term *minority* has more political meaning than either *race* or *ethnicity;* it has been used in reference to groups whose access to power is limited by a dominant culture (Wang & Sue, 2005). Minority status is not necessarily a matter of relative population size, but rather of political power. Hays (2008) pointed out that Blacks in South Africa during apartheid were a numerical majority but had minority status in relation to the dominant White group. Based on relative political power in the United States, the term minority may apply not only to ethnic, religious, national, and sexual numerical minorities but also to elderly people, people who are poor, those less formally educated, those of rural or Indigenous heritage, those who are disabled, and women and children (Hays, 2008). Minority status may carry positive connotations, including shared cultural meanings, expanded sources of support, and a sense of community (Newman &

Newman, 1999). The meaning of minority status may therefore be multi-faceted in case formulation, with both positive and negative connotations; further, its associations with political empowerment may affect the therapist–client relationship.

CULTURAL UNIVERSALISM AND CULTURAL RELATIVISM

Virtually all discussion of culture in psychology can be organized along a continuum with the universalist perspective at one end and the relativist, or culturalist, at the other (Chentsova-Dutton & Tsai, 2007; Draguns, 1997). The *universalist* perspective holds that fundamental psychopathological processes are shared across all of humanity and that varying expressions of disorders in different cultures are little more than epiphenomena. Adherents of this perspective cite research showing that the core symptoms of depression and schizophrenia, as just two examples, are found in multiple Western and non-Western cultures (Draguns, 1997). At the other end of the continuum, the *cultural relativist* position holds that culture pervades human experience so inextricably that the expression of psychopathology can only be understood in the context of the culture in which it manifests itself and therefore cross-cultural comparisons are futile. The culturalists assert that universalists risk imposing Western mental illness categories on non-Western cultures, producing a misleading appearance of universalism and overlooking unique, culturally constructed meanings of maladaptation. An example would be to apply the Western category "hallucination" to the experience of visions in Native American healing processes (McCabe, 2007). Most scholars find a middle ground between these two extremes.

The universalist–culturalist continuum is relevant to case formulation because it can help the therapist interpret cross-cultural research and thus better understand a client from an unfamiliar culture. It may also help a therapist appreciate his or her limited capacity to understand another's experience, thus increasing motivation to approach individuals from different cultures with greater humility, deference, empathy, patience, and understanding. Understanding these perspectives can also help the case formulator organize and conceptualize cultural issues.

WHY CONSIDER CULTURE IN A CASE FORMULATION?

With these definitions in mind, I suggest five reasons for considering culture in a case formulation. First, failure to do so increases the chance of miscommunication, lack of understanding, and inadequate empathy, which in turn can lead to poorly suited formulations and ineffective treatment (Ridley & Kelly, 2007). Poor understanding of the cultural context from which someone presents can lead to overpathologizing as well as underpathologizing. Pomerantz (2008) cited the example of a White therapist who concluded that an African American client presenting for depression and alcoholism was actually paranoid after the client hesitated to reveal personal details, asked numerous times about confidentiality, and wondered aloud why the therapist asked so many questions. According to Pomerantz, the therapist overpathologized by failing to be aware of African American cultural norms, particularly in regard to seeking psychological services from a White therapist. In these circumstances, it is not unusual for an African American male to exhibit guardedness (Hines & Boyd-Franklin, 2005). Underpathologizing might be illustrated by the woman who inspired Maya Angelou's poem "When I Think About Myself." She was a maid in New York City who rode the bus and laughed a survival laugh. She was proud and poor, a hard and steady worker. One imagines her humiliated and treated as invisible by her employers. In the poem, as she thinks about herself, she laughs until her stomach hurts. As Maya Angelou described her: "If you don't know black features you may think she is smiling. She's not smiling at all. She's exercising that old survival apparatus, that's all" (Angelou, 1977). A therapist who is unfamiliar with "black features," to borrow Angelou's term, might accept her smile, pride, laughter, and work ethic at face value and not explore the possibility that she may be masking depression and a range of painful thoughts and feelings about her life.

A second reason to consider culture in a case formulation is that the language of psychotherapy, and thus of psychotherapy case formulation, is suffused with culture. As Wampold (2001a) wrote, "Psychotherapy is a culturally imbedded healing practice" (p. 69). Culture provides metaphors and meaning systems for the explanatory mechanisms that are offered to clients to help them understand their problems. Following Frank (1961), Wampold (2007) asserted that these explanations are central to psychotherapy. He asserted that clients will only accept explanations of their problems that fall within certain cultural boundaries.

Third, meta-analytic evidence suggests that culturally adapted psychotherapy may be more effective than therapy that is not culturally adapted (Benish, Quintana, & Wampold, 2011; T. B. Smith, Rodriguez, & Bernal, 2011). Therefore, a culturally adapted case formulation may enhance treatment efficacy. It is noteworthy that the sole significant moderator in one meta-analysis was whether or not the client accepted a collaboratively and culturally derived rationale that provided a plausible explanation of the client's problems (Benish et al., 2011).

Fourth, related to the point just made, cultural competence may contribute to improved outcomes. *Cultural competence* refers to "knowledge of those factors that render a particular group distinct from other groups, knowledge of the shared interpersonal and social experiences that characterize a particular cultural group, knowledge of the salience of between-and-within-group experiences for a given group member, and knowledge of the relevance of salient group experiences to the therapeutic process" (Duckworth, 2009, p. 63). Imel and colleagues (2011) found that some therapists had significantly different outcomes when working with White clients than with racial/ethnic minorities. Similarly, Owen, Imel, Adelson, and Rodolfa (2012) studied clients who end therapy without informing the therapist, a form of dropout associated with poor alliance and outcome, and they found greater dropout rates among racial/ethnic minority clients than among White clients. Further, racial/ethnic minority clients were more likely to drop out when treated by some therapists than others. These studies suggest that general competence and cultural competence may be distinct skills, each contributing differentially to psychotherapy outcome.

A fifth reason to consider culture in a case formulation is that cultural factors may directly cause, precipitate, or maintain symptoms and problems. This can occur through mechanisms such as acculturative stress and stereotype threat. *Acculturative stress* refers to psychological problems associated with adapting to a new culture (C. L. Williams & Berry, 1991). These include pressure to alter one's values, attitudes, behavior, and identity; incongruence between cultural practices; language difficulties; and discrimination. Acculturative stress can manifest itself in anxiety, depression, feelings of marginality and alienation, psychosomatic symptoms, and identity confusion. While recent immigrants are particularly vulnerable, acculturative stress can also affect later generations. *Stereotype threat* is a vulnerability to internalize a negative stereotype about one's group (Steele & Aronson, 1995). It has been shown to adversely affect minority academic performance and also may be related to damaged self-esteem, anxiety, loss of motivation, and adverse career choices.

CULTURAL DIFFERENCES IN THE EXPRESSION OF DISORDERS

In this section, I review findings on cultural differences in the expression of three common disorders: major depressive disorder, social anxiety disorder, and alcohol abuse, based on a review by Chentsova-Dutton and Tsai (2007). In reading this section, keep in mind that these are tentative nomothetic findings. The extent to which these generalities apply to your individual client is a matter for exploration and judgment.

Major depressive disorder appears to be present in many or all cultures. In Western cultures, depression tends to be expressed primarily as cognitive and affective symptoms, such as sad mood, worthlessness, or hopelessness. In Asian cultures, depression is often expressed more by somatic symptoms, such as physical pain (literally, "heart ache"), lack of energy, or sleep disturbance. Some have challenged the notion that different cultures express depression differently, observing that clients in Asian cultures may initially present with somatic symptoms but express depression in affective or interpersonal terms once trust is established with the health care provider.

Social anxiety disorder has also been found to be present in many cultures, although lifetime prevalence rates are greater in Western than in Asian countries. Different cross-cultural expressions of social anxiety have also been documented. Westerners with the disorder tend to fear humiliating or embarrassing themselves, whereas Asians worry more about humiliating or embarrassing others, often their family or other close individuals.

Alcohol abuse is also present cross-culturally, with lifetime prevalence rates varying widely across different cultures. Lower rates of alcohol abuse are seen in countries that discourage drinking, such as Egypt, Indonesia, and Iraq. In contrast, alcohol-related problems are more common in countries that culturally value social drinking, such as in France, Germany, Eastern European countries, and Thailand. There is considerable variability within these countries. For example, in the United States, rates of alcohol-related mental health problems are lower among Jewish Americans, Greek Americans, and Italian Americans, but greater in others, such as Irish Americans. Culture also affects the behavioral manifestations of alcohol abuse that are considered problematic. In the United States, for example, physical symptoms such as passing out or slurring of speech are common indicators of alcohol abuse, whereas in Korea disturbing others is a more common indicator.

Again, these are nomothetic findings that can help generate ways to understand clients from different cultures who may be suffering from these three disorders. They do not apply to everyone in these respective cultures. While there is debate about how psychopathology expresses itself in different cultures, it is important to explore these meanings with clients.

RELIGION AND SPIRITUALITY

Religion and spirituality (R/S) may be considered aspects of culture. *Religion* is broadly defined as adherence to a belief system and practice associated with a tradition and community in which there is agreement about what is believed and practiced (Hill et al., 2000; Worthington, Hook, Davis, & McDaniel, 2011). *Spirituality*, on the other hand, has more diverse meanings but generally involves a feeling of closeness and connectedness to the sacred. It can manifest itself through a specific set of religious beliefs, through a sense of closeness and connection to human kind independent of a specific religion, and through a connection to nature or to the cosmos (Hill et al., 2000; Worthington et al., 2011).

Religious belief permeates the United States and the world. A recent large survey showed that about 84% of adults in the United States self-identify with a religion, 78% with a form of Christianity (Pew Research Center's Religion & Public Life Project, 2008). A comprehensive demographic study of more than 230 countries and territories found similar results in terms of the overall proportion of people averring religious belief, although the distribution of adherents to various religions differed significantly. Worldwide, about 32% self-identify as Christian, 23% as Muslim, 15% as Hindu, 7% as Buddhist, 6% with a folk religion, and 0.2% as Jewish (Pew Research Center's Religion & Public Life Project, 2012). Given the pervasiveness of religious identification, psychotherapists are wise to be mindful of religion and spiritual considerations when formulating cases.

A recent set of meta-analyses concluded that R/S focused forms of psychotherapy work are valid alternatives to secular versions of similar therapies; they also concluded that there is no empirical evidence to recommend R/S therapies over established therapies when the primary or exclusive treatment outcome is symptom remission (Worthington et al., 2011). These researchers recommended that the decision to incorporate a client's R/S beliefs or practices into treatment should follow the desires and needs of the client. Therapists should ask about R/S beliefs and commitment as part of the case formulation process and incorporate them into psychotherapy as the therapist feels comfortable, and in line with the preferences of the client. This can be accomplished simply by asking clients about their religious and spiritual beliefs, whether these beliefs influence their view of their problems, and what preferences, if any, they have for incorporating a religious or spiritual component to the treatment. Of course, therapists should always be respectful of a client's religious and spiritual beliefs, whether or not they explicitly enter into the treatment.

MODELS OF CULTURALLY INFORMED CASE FORMULATION

A variety of models have been proposed for developing a culturally informed case formulation (Hays, 2008; Ingram, 2012; Ridley & Kelly, 2007; Sperry & Sperry, 2012). In this section, I present a four-step approach based on features shared by most of these models.

First, assess the client's cultural identity. How is his or her sense of self defined by membership in a cultural or ethnic group? What are the cultural or ethnic reference groups the client feels allegiance to: the country of origin, the adopted country, a subculture within either of these? Note that the client may have multiple and conflicting identities. Consider the degree of acculturation and whether acculturative stress is present.

Second, consider whether or how culture influences the client's explanation of his or her problems. Consider culturally relevant interpretations of social stressors, supports, and levels of functioning. Sperry and Sperry (2012) recommended listening for words, idioms, and explanations that reveal the individual's understanding of their condition. Ingram (2012) recommended that therapists adapt the treatment plan and the therapeutic relationship in view of the client's culturally relevant understanding of his or her problems. This may involve choosing the best balance between a focus on the individual and his or her family, recognizing that an exclusive focus on the individual may be viewed as inappropriate from some cultural perspectives.

Third, integrate cultural data into the rest of the formulation. Consider the extent to which personality factors versus cultural factors are contributing to the individual's problems. According to Sperry and Sperry (2012), for example, when acculturation is high, cultural factors may play a relatively lesser role in the formulation and personality dynamics a larger role. Further, depending on the person's cultural identity and understanding of their problem, the therapist may choose a treatment plan involving relatively directive or less directive interventions.

Fourth, consider how cultural factors affect the therapist–client relationship. The credibility of the therapist and the therapeutic alliance may hinge on the extent to which the therapist can convey respect for the individual's cultural values, attitudes, and behavior. Interaction factors such as eye contact, physical distance, and degree of formality or informality also come into play when conveying respect for the individual's culture. Recognize that cultural differences may lead to mistrust initially. Consider how to frame questions so they are not experienced as intrusive or prying. Consider differences in culture and social status and how these differences may affect treatment.

SUGGESTIONS FOR DEVELOPING A CULTURALLY RESPONSIVE CASE FORMULATION

In this concluding section, I offer six suggestions for preparing culturally responsive case formulations.

First, engage in personal and interpersonal work to understand your cultural influences. Hays (2008) encouraged therapists to engage in reflection about their own cultural experiences and heritage. Questions to consider include those related to your age, how you differ culturally and educationally from the generation of your upbringing, what experiences you may have with disability, and religious influences on your identity. If you are from the dominant culture in a society consider the role of privilege in your life, since privilege can limit your ability to resonate with individuals from nonprivileged cultures. Therapists may inadvertently intimidate others, or be experienced by those from nondominant cultures as condescending, dismissive, or as "not getting it."

Second, aspire to an attitude of humility, charity, and veracity. As Hays (2008) reported, Huston Smith (1991) examined major world religions and identified these three elements as shared by all. *Humility* is the capacity to relate to others as equals, neither superior nor inferior. *Charity* means adopting an attitude of compassion toward others, seeking to understand the experience of others as fully and as generously as possible. *Veracity* goes beyond simple truth-telling to "sublime objectivity, the capacity to see things exactly as they are" (H. Smith, 1991, p. 387). Without these values as foundational attitudes, it is difficult to imagine how any additional training in multicultural competence could succeed.

Third, take time to learn the cultural history of your clients. S. Sue (1998) recommended that therapists learn about the culture of their clients. Learn the social and political history of the environment the individual comes from, so that you can translate your understanding of the client's worldview into effective formulations and then treatment. If the individual is a refugee, what political, economic, religious, or social disputes led to their refugee status? Understanding healing rituals and practices in the individual's home culture can also help shape the formulation and treatment plan. Demonstrating and communicating an effort to understand the larger environment the individual comes from helps to build trust and to put the client at ease.

Fourth, be alert to subtle therapist cultural bias. We are all products of our culture and may not be aware of how culture influences our attitudes and interactions. We are all subject to unconscious bias, a well-documented phenomenon demonstrating how racial attitudes can become automatized in social cognition, influencing us outside of our awareness. D. W. Sue and colleagues (2007) identified *racial microaggressions*, which are "brief everyday exchanges that send denigrating messages to people of color because they belong to a racial minority group" (p. 273). D. W. Sue gave the example of a White therapist asked by an African American client how race might affect therapy and responding, "Race does not affect the way I treat you." This response, although intended to be reassuring, may instead send the message that the client's race is not important or valid, or that the therapist lacks self-awareness.

Fifth, be aware of cultural norms, but do not assume your client shares the norms of his or her culture. Recognize that just because a person comes from a particular culture does not necessarily mean he identifies with the dominant values of that culture. Since psychopathology involves a failure to adapt, one might even expect that some clients will not share these values. However, even if a person does not identify with the norms of the culture in which they live or their culture of origin, they are not necessarily uninfluenced by them. One African American woman informed me early in treatment that she purposely sought out a White psychotherapist such as myself because she did not trust African American men. Conversely, just because you share some aspect of a client's culture, do not assume you know their experience of the culture.

Finally, recognize that identity combines cultural and other influences uniquely in each individual. Culture is just one influence among others that contributes to a client's identity. Every client is unique, and case formulation should neither overemphasize nor underemphasize the contribution of culture to the individual's presentation, in contrast to personality, biology, interpersonal functioning, or any of many other contributors (Hays, 2008; Ridley & Kelly, 2007; Sperry & Sperry, 2012; S. Sue, 1998).

4

Formulation in the Context of Psychotherapy Integration

As stated in the introduction to this book, the case formulation model described in these pages is integrative and evidence based. It is intended to apply to any theoretical approach to psychotherapy. It is integrative because it can be assimilated into different unitheoretical therapy models, and it also allows for different perspectives on therapy to be brought together into a coherent case formulation. There are several reasons to approach case formulation integratively. First, an integrative orientation is widely prevalent among practicing therapists, so much so that it has been described as a "therapeutic mainstay" (Norcross, 2005, p. 3). Surveys show that the majority of therapists in North America identify with more than one orientation, and that cognitive–behavioral therapy (CBT) serves as the dominant approach within an integrative orientation (Cook, Biyanova, Elhai, Schnurr, & Coyne, 2010; Norcross, Karpiak,

http://dx.doi.org/10.1037/14667-005
Psychotherapy Case Formulation, by T. D. Eells

& Santoro, 2005). Very few psychotherapists report practicing entirely within a single orientation; surveys suggest the percentage is between 2% and 10% (Cook et al., 2010; Norcross et al., 2005). International surveys also show a strong commitment to psychotherapy integration. In a survey of more than 3,000 therapists in more than 20 countries, 54% indicated they drew from multiple perspectives rather than a single orientation (Orlinsky & Rønnestad, 2005). Thus, an integrative approach to case formulation is responsive to the theoretical orientation of the majority of practicing therapists.

Another reason to base the general case formulation model on an integrative approach to therapy is that a case-formulation-guided approach allows the therapist to tailor the therapy to the specific combination of problems a client brings in ways that unitheoretical approaches do not. An integrative perspective allows the therapist to draw from multiple theoretical perspectives and intervention strategies as well as on psychological knowledge developed outside of psychotherapy; the latter include findings from cognitive science, developmental psychology, or social psychology that have relevance to psychotherapy. A joint task force of the American Psychological Association's Society of Clinical Psychology and the Society for Psychotherapy Research's North American chapter summarized several empirically supported and cross-theoretical principles of therapeutic change that are beneficial for a range of disorders (Castonguay & Beutler, 2006). For example, extraverted people who are depressed tend to benefit from more action-oriented interventions, whereas introverted depressed individuals benefit more from a reflective approach to treatment.

Persons (2008) articulated several reasons for supporting a tailored approach to CBT that is facilitated by a case formulation. She noted that empirically supported treatments have not been developed for many of the problems people bring to psychotherapy. A case formulation approach allows the therapist to adapt an empirically supported treatment to those problems. By not limiting the formulation to the cognitive–behavioral school, a broader range of explanations and treatment plans may be considered. Unlike treatment manuals, a case formulation guided approach can take into account the roles of multiple concurrent treatments, such as medication management, church-based support groups, and participation in Alcoholics Anonymous, all in addition to individual psychotherapy.

A third reason to take an integrative perspective is that most meta-analyses of psychotherapy outcome studies show that no individual theoretical approach consistently outperforms others, particularly when bonafide treatments are compared and when investigator allegiance to a particular approach is statistically controlled (Lambert, 2013a; Wampold, 2001b). These results suggest that much of what explains outcome is not specific interventions or techniques drawn from individual brands of therapy, but qualities shared by all forms of treatment. These include client and therapist characteristics, change processes, treatment structures, and relationship elements (Grencavage & Norcross, 1990). Based on an extensive review of the research literature, Lambert (2013a) estimated that 40% of improvement in psychotherapy is explained by characteristics of the client and his or her environment; 15% is explained by the client's expectations for improvement, 30% by other common factors, and only 15% by specific therapy techniques. Lambert was careful to point out that techniques are an essential part of psychotherapy, but that their effectiveness should be kept in perspective. He went on to organize common factors into three categories: support, learning, and action. Common support factors include catharsis; mitigation of isolation; provision of a safe environment; recognition of the therapist's expertness; and the therapist's expression of warmth, respect, empathy, acceptance, and genuineness. Common learning factors include affective re-experiencing, assimilation of problematic experiences, cognitive learning, corrective emotional experience, feedback, insight, and exploration of one's internal frame of reference and changing expectations of personal effectiveness. Common action factors include cognitive mastery; encouragement to experiment with new behaviors; facing one's fears; modeling; practicing behavioral and emotional regulation; reality testing; and taking risks.

The role of common factors was first proposed by Rosenzweig (1936) and most expansively developed by Frank (1961; Frank & Frank, 1991; see also Duncan, Miller, Wampold, & Hubble, 2010). Frank conducted a comparative study of psychotherapy and concluded that all therapies share four characteristics that together account for much of the effectiveness of these practices. First, an emotionally charged and confiding relationship is developed between a client and a therapist. The impact of the therapeutic relationship has been extensively studied. The strength of the alliance is estimated to correlate on average .22 with outcome (Martin, Garske, & Davis, 2000). However, controversy exists as to whether a positive relationship is a cause of treatment outcome or an effect of other processes that contribute to outcome (Barber, Khalsa, & Sharpless, 2010).

Frank's second shared characteristic is that the therapeutic relationship exists in a circumscribed, culturally sanctioned context in which well-delineated roles are played: the client presents to a professional who the client believes can provide help and who is trusted to work on behalf of the client. Further, psychotherapy usually takes place for a predetermined session length in an office setting attended only by the client and therapist, for a set fee, and often for a preset number of sessions. Since the original publication of Frank's book in 1961, the power of the social context of psychotherapy has arguably increased as the discipline has aligned itself increasingly with the medical model approach, thus benefiting from a "halo effect" through its association with medical practice. These developments add to the acceptance of psychotherapy within the culture and have supported stable utilization rates for decades (Olfson & Marcus, 2010).

Frank's third characteristic is that a credible and persuasive account of the reasons for the client's symptoms and problems is collaboratively accepted by the client and therapist. The account includes a pathway or set of procedures for resolving the problems. The pathway flows from the explanation and must be accepted by both client and therapist. The explanation must be consistent with the worldview, attitudes, and values of the client; alternatively, the therapist assists the client to come into accord with the rationale. Psychotherapy case formulation is particularly relevant to Frank's third condition. From the perspective of the cognitive model, a client's problems and symptoms are explained by thought patterns that leave the person vulnerable to symptoms and problems. Healing comes through identifying and changing or coping with these thought patterns, often through a sequence of specific action steps. From the psychoanalytic perspective, problems are explained by unconscious and conflicting wishes and fears that lead to symptoms that may be remediated through exploration and insight into the nature of the wishes and fears. From the behavioral standpoint, problems may be explained by maladaptive contingencies of reinforcement and stimulus control environments that can be addressed behaviorally by changing the environment. Each of these approaches has in common the criterion proposed by Frank of offering a persuasive, credible explanation and a treatment plan that flows from the proposed explanation. Frank's claim is controversial because the truth of any of these accounts of the client's problems is not critical; what is critical is whether the client and therapist believe them to be so.

The fourth common characteristic Frank identified is that the prescribed treatment ensues with the active participation of both client and therapist. Unlike most medical treatments, the psychotherapy client is not a passive recipient of care, but rather is an active agent in his or her own change. The client's activity in and of itself is considered to be a curative component of change.

In sum, the integrative case formulation model presented in this book is well suited to an integrative perspective on psychotherapy as well as a unitheoretical approach to therapy. It addresses the approach to therapy followed by a large percentage of practicing therapists. A general case formulation approach allows the therapist to tailor the treatment plan to the specific problems a person has and to plan treatment using the full range of interventions that psychotherapy researchers and writers have offered. Finally, it is consistent with meta-analytic research showing that no single approach to therapy consistently outperforms others, and that common factors appear to account for most change in psychotherapy rather than specific, unitheoretical interventions or techniques. With this background, I now move to a description of an integrative, evidence-based case-formulation-guided model of psychotherapy.

INTEGRATIVE, EVIDENCE-BASED, CASE-FORMULATION-GUIDED PSYCHOTHERAPY

Figure 4.1 shows the case formulation approach described in this book embedded in a model of psychotherapy. The figure incorporates elements from Persons (2008), Fishman (2001), and Peterson (1991) and can be contrasted with other integrative case formulation approaches (e.g., Jose & Goldfried, 2008; Sperry & Sperry, 2012). As can be seen, information is initially gathered, which is used as a basis for formulation. The Formulate component consists of four sequential subcomponents: Create Problem List, Diagnose, Develop Explanatory Hypothesis, and Plan Treatment. Treatment then ensues, as Progress Monitoring also occurs and ultimately treatment terminates. Although Figure 4.1 shows these steps sequentially, the steps do not unfold in a rigid order. For example, information gather-

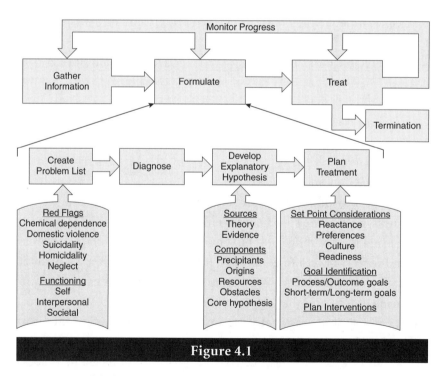

Figure 4.1

Integrative model of case formulation and therapy.

ing and formulation can also be considered aspects of treatment. In this chapter, I briefly discuss each of these components, deferring a full consideration of the Formulate step until Part II.

Gather Information

The first step in any form of psychotherapy is to gather information from the client. This is usually done primarily in the form of an interview. However, therapists may also use symptoms measures, psychometric testing, record reviews, and interviews with others in the client's life, including other current or past treatment providers. The information is used as inputs into the case formulation. This is not an entirely sequential process because information is, of course, elicited throughout the course of psychotherapy. As the process unfolds in actual interactions with clients, the gathering information, formulating, and treating components of treatment are closely intertwined.

Much advice has been offered on how to gather information for case formulation and treatment (e.g., Benjamin, 1996b; Morrison, 2008). Usually, specific categories of information are needed. These include the individual's presenting complaint, history of mental problems and treatment for self and family, medical history of self and family, developmental and social history, education and work history, history of legal problems (if any), and information about the client's mental status. This information is useful but in a limited way for case formulation. In addition, for case formulation one needs process and narrative information.

Process information concerns how the individual presents him- or herself. It is covered to some extent in a mental status examination, but what is needed for case formulation is different from what is reported in a standard mental status examination (e.g., the individual mood and affect, memory, ability to express thought coherently and articulately, whether or not impaired reality testing is present), even though this information is useful. It is helpful in case formulation to reflect on how, as a therapist, you experience the client. Are you able to feel connected to the client? Is the client able to relate coherent narratives of events in his or her life? Do the descriptions of others in the client's life come alive or seem stereotypical or vague? Information of this type can inform the therapist about the quality of a client's mental representations of self and others.

Narrative information is helpful in developing a case formulation, particularly descriptions of specific stories or episodes in the client's life. I ask students to explore the transactional "he-said, she-said" level of detail with clients to more thoroughly understand the nature of interactions with others, self-concept, and sequences of events that lead to problems. This approach is consistent with Luborsky's (Luborsky & Barrett, 2007) emphasis on basing case formulations on narratives of relationship episodes. Similarly, writing from the standpoint of dialectical behavior therapy, Koerner (2007) recommended *chain analysis*, that is, examining the moment-to-moment sequence of events, thought patterns and affect that lead to a culminating problematic event, such as a suicide attempt, an anger outburst, a panic attack, or the onset of a distressing state of mind. Greenberg and Goldman (2007) recommended a similar approach from the emotion-focused approach to psychotherapy. In terms of the process of gathering information for formulation, Benjamin (1993a) advised that therapists employ a "free form" approach instead of mechanically and sequentially gathering information on all the content areas described above. By "free form," she meant following the client's stream of thought; that is, take one's lead from the feeling state of the client or one's sense of the client's unconscious mental processes. In doing so, one still gathers the needed content but also gains critical information about how the client thinks and feels about this content. The result is rich and detailed information on which to base a case formulation.

Formulate

As noted above, this portion of the evidence-based, integrative case-formulation-guided model of psychotherapy is the topic of Part II of this book. For now, I will briefly describe the four basic action steps of the model: (a) Create a Problem List, (b) Diagnose, (c) Develop an Explanatory Hypothesis, and (d) Plan Treatment.

As noted in the Introduction, students often struggle with knowing where to start formulating a case. In the integrative case-formulation-guided model, one always begins by developing a comprehensive problem list. It will be trimmed to a shorter list as the therapist decides how best to focus treatment.

Step 2, Diagnose, is essential for practical reasons, but also has major limitations that are discussed in Chapter 6.

Step 3, Develop an Explanatory Hypothesis, is the most challenging part of case formulation. It involves taking the information gathered and using available empirical resources, theory, and clinical expertise, including cultural competency, to offer the therapist's best account of what is causing, maintaining, and precipitating the problems selected for focus. As shown in Figure 4.1, two broad and intertwined sources of information inform this step: theory and evidence. Theory refers to any empirically supported hypothesis that helps explain the problems. It can include basic research about behavioral and cognitive processes, results from randomized clinical trials, and findings from psychopathology research. Evidence refers to other sources of reliable information that can help account for problems. These sources may include epidemiological studies, results from psychometric testing, and narrative or other autobiographical information provided by the client. In addition, four categories of consideration should be developed for all formulations, regardless of orientation: precipitating stressors, origins, resources, and obstacles. Precipitating stressors are those events that trigger episodes of distress. They are the events that often lead one into therapy to begin with. Origins is an account of the key experiences, traumas, and learning events that not only are presumed to contribute to the current presentation, but that also are presumed to have led to the client's world view, or the broad, axiomatic assumptions the client has about the world, whether articulated or not, that can be captured in statements such as, "Don't trust others," "The world is a harsh place," or "If you work hard and try your best, it will work out in the end." Resources are strengths a client brings to therapy. Obstacles are factors that may interfere with treatment success.

Plan Treatment is the final basic case formulation step. As described in Chapter 8, the goal of this step is to operationalize the explanatory hypothesis into a sequence of steps designed to guide treatment and to help the client resolve the problems that are the focus of therapy. It may include an explicit statement of both short-term and long-term goals, as well as process and ultimate goals, and the steps to be followed to achieve them.

Treat

A tremendous amount has been written about psychotherapy treatment. For current purposes, since treatment is not the focus of this book, I will note three points about the relationship between formulation and treatment. First, a treatment plan is only a plan, and it will inevitably change as treatment progresses. A therapist should always be ready to revise the treatment plan, adjusting treatment depending on the client's response to the implementation of the plan. Further, new and unanticipated problems will arise, and the therapist will need to reformulate for that reason. When considering the relationship between the treatment plan and the treatment implementation phases of therapy, it is wise to keep in mind the words of Dwight D. Eisenhower (1957): "Plans are nothing, planning is everything." The mechanism through which this is accomplished is the "Monitor Progress" step, which is described in the next section.

Second, case formulation skills are distinct from those involved in conducting treatment. One might have a cogent understanding of a client but lack skill in applying that understanding to treatment. In this regard, Binder (1993) called attention to the problem of "inert knowledge" in the context of psychotherapy training. This is information stored as declarative knowledge without the additional procedural step of spontaneously knowing how and when to apply the knowledge when circumstances warrant. I encounter the problem of inert knowledge as a therapy supervisor. Beginning therapists ordinarily have excellent knowledge of the theories of psychotherapy, but struggle with how and when to apply that knowledge in the give-and-take of an unfolding therapy session.

Third, psychotherapy treatment always involves an intermingling of theory and method, on the one hand, and on the other hand, the personness of the therapist encountering the personness of the client in the context of a specific place and time. For this reason, each therapy dyad will be unique, and one cannot closely predict the course of therapy because each participant has the capability of surprising the other.

Monitor Progress

Monitoring progress is a component of evidence-based practice in psychology (APA Presidential Task Force on Evidence-Based Practice, 2006). Its main purpose is to provide objective feedback so the therapist will know whether treatment is proceeding as planned or whether changes are needed. Research shows that progress monitoring improves positive outcomes and reduces treatment failure (Lambert, 2010). Lambert and colleagues (2004) conducted a series of studies and found that deterioration in treatment can be predicted on the basis of a client's initial level of disturbance and response to treatment after just a few sessions as measured by the Outcome Questionnaire-45. When therapists are provided feedback that a client is not on track to succeed, they are able to take action to improve outcomes. Response curves for clients with similar problems and levels of distress have been well established (Howard, Kopta, Krause, & Orlinsky, 1986; Kopta, Howard, Lowry, & Beutler, 1994). For example, Lambert (2007) conducted multiple studies to investigate the relationship between length of treatment and outcome. His results showed that half of clients recover after 11 to 21 sessions, whereas 75% recover after 25 to 45 sessions. Predicted responses varied depending on the initial functioning of the client: The worse the initial functioning, the more treatment that was needed. These results provide useful guidelines for therapists managing progress of their own clients.

Lambert (2007) also found that different aspects of client functioning tend to improve at different rates. First, symptoms improve, then social role functioning, and finally, improvements come in interpersonal functioning. Howard, Lueger, Maling, and Martinovich (1993) described an alternative but similar model that is also useful to monitor client progress. The first phase involves remoralization. In this phase, hope is instilled and clients begin to feel they can master their problems. The second phase is symptom improvement, and in the third phase, well-being improves. These general models provide empirical benchmarks for therapists to mark the progress of their clients in different areas of functioning.

Monitoring provides a means of testing the explanatory hypothesis. Silberschatz (2005a) described a series of studies in which clients' depth of experiencing was measured after the therapist made interventions that were either compatible or incompatible with the formulation. They found that depth of experiencing increased after formulation-consistent interventions and that outcome improved as a function of formulation-compatible interventions. Wilder (2009, p. 112) showed how a formulation was tested to determine which of two hypotheses of problematic behavior of a client with psychosis provided a better explanation.

Research suggests that the use of objective measures maximizes the potential of progress monitoring. Lambert (2007) found that accuracy in predicting clients at risk of treatment failure was much greater when based on objective progress monitoring than when based on therapist judgments alone. Cognitive biases on the part of therapists, as discussed in Chapter 2, may stand in the way of predictive accuracy, particularly the overconfidence bias. Progress monitoring helps counter these biases. Without regular empirical problem and symptom monitoring, therapists appear to be hard pressed to determine objectively whether treatment is succeeding as expected or not.

Another benefit of progress monitoring is that it enables the therapist to test his or her outcomes against those in randomized clinical trials of psychotherapy. Persons, Roberts, Zalecki, and Brechwald (2006), for example, provided case formulation guided CBT to depressed and anxious clients, and monitored progress weekly using the same measures used in randomized clinical trials of CBT for depression and anxiety. They found that their clients improved and recovered at rates comparable to those in the comparison randomized clinical trials.

Monitoring may reveal important information that otherwise might not be revealed, since it provides an additional conduit of communication between the therapist and client. One client came to therapy on a relatively warm day wearing a long-sleeve sweater. As we began, I read her symptom measure and saw that she had endorsed an item about thoughts of harming or mutilating oneself. When I asked about this item, she pulled up her sleeve and showed me where she had cut herself earlier that week. She said she had not planned to say anything about it unless I asked and that she could not lie on the questionnaire.

What, how, and how often should one monitor? At minimum, symptoms and "red flag" issues such as risk of self-harm and harm to others should be monitored on a session-by-session basis. In addition, consider monitoring social role functioning, interpersonal functioning, the therapeutic alliance, and well-being. I suggest using objective, quantifiable measures with known psychometric properties when available. When no readily accessible normed measure is available, one can fashion an idiographic measure to monitor a specific problem. It is preferable for clients to complete them just prior to the session so that the first step in a session can be to review the results. Measures can be made available in the waiting room. I usually explain at the beginning of treatment that these measures will help us to assess how the client has felt in the past week and to ensure that we are on track as we work together.

Several progress-monitoring systems have been developed. These include the Outcome Questionnaire-45 (Lambert et al., 2004), the Clinical Outcomes in Routine Evaluation system (Barkham et al., 2001), the Partners for Change Outcome Management System (Miller, Duncan, Sorrell, & Brown, 2005), and the Shorter Psychotherapy and Counselling Evaluation (Halstead, Leach, & Rust, 2008). In addition, one can use measures such as the Beck Depression Inventory (A. T. Beck, Ward, Mendelson, Mack, & Erbaugh, 1961), Beck Anxiety Inventory (A. T. Beck, Epstein, Brown, & Steer, 1988), or extremely short measures such as the GAD-7 (Spitzer, Kroenke, Williams, & Löwe, 2006), and the Patient Health Questionnaire–9 (Kroenke, Spitzer, & Williams, 2001). These are quick and easy measures that usually take no more than 5 minutes to complete.

While the results of monitoring have clinical application for the immediate session, they must be taken with a grain of salt. For example, one client described himself as relatively asymptomatic on a symptom rating scale administered each session, despite saying during the session that he was depressed and worried. When asked about the inconsistency between his two self-reports, he explained that he did not want "the record to show" that he was symptomatic. We resolved his concerns by agreeing that he could keep his completed form each session if he filled it out more accurately. Another client overstated her symptoms; she explained that she wanted to ensure that I did not terminate treatment before she was ready to end. She added that years earlier she had been "rejected" from a psychotherapy outcome study after being told she was not depressed enough. Thus, therapists should be alert to client response sets that express needs and conflicts beyond what a progress monitoring instrument ostensibly measures.

CONCLUSION

In this chapter, I introduced the integrative, evidence-based case-formulation-guided model within the context of a case-formulation-guided approach to psychotherapy. The model is integrative in that it can be assimilated into unitheoretical approaches to therapy and is also amenable to providing a framework for a therapist to generate a coherent, high-quality formulation that draws from multiple theories, and empirically demonstrated interventions and techniques to develop the formulation. The integrative approach is well justified empirically, as evidenced by Lambert (2013a) in his recent review of the efficacy and effectiveness of psychotherapy:

> Given the growing evidence that there are probably some specific technique effects as well as large common effects across treatments, the vast majority of therapists have become eclectic in orientation. This appears to reflect a healthy response to empirical evidence and a rejection of previous trends toward rigid allegiances to schools of treatment. (p. 206)

With this chapter, Part I draws to a close. I continue in Part II with a detailed, step-by-step look at the general case formulation approach. I also return to Rochelle, the client introduced in Chapter 1, to illustrate how to apply the case formulation steps.

TWO

AN INTEGRATIVE EVIDENCE-BASED CASE FORMULATION MODEL

Step 1: Create a Problem List

A student I supervised years ago described a client she had just seen
for the first time. The client, an unemployed and poorly educated
man in his mid-30s, complained that he had panic disorder and needed
medication. My student asked whether he experienced palpitations, fear
of imminent death, sudden escalation of anxiety that lasted several minutes and then abated, and so on through the criteria for panic disorder. To
each question, the man gave vague and difficult-to-decipher answers. He
reiterated that he had panic, his nerves were shot, and he needed medication and a note from the doctor explaining his problem. My student
persisted, striving to rule in or rule out the diagnosis of panic disorder.
Finally, exasperated, the man blurted out, "My daddy was right! He said I'd
never amount to anything, and now I can't even get disability!" In retro-
spect, both the student and I realized that the "problem" was not what it
appeared to be. This man did not have panic disorder; he had financial

http://dx.doi.org/10.1037/14667-006
Psychotherapy Case Formulation, by T. D. Eells

problems and an internalized injunction from his father that he would "never amount to anything." This incident served as a valuable reminder that things, in this case problems clients report in therapy, are not always what they appear to be. In this chapter, I discuss how to identify problems and to ensure that those identified are the important ones. This is the first step in the generalized case formulation model: Create a problem list.

WHY CREATE A PROBLEM LIST?

Generating a problem list is important for three primary reasons. First, it tells the therapist what to formulate. Problems are what the explanatory hypothesis seeks to explain and what the treatment plan seeks to treat. The problem list helps identify goals for treatment and provides a focus and direction for the therapy. This is important because agreement between the therapist and client on the problems, and the goals, is central to establishing a productive working alliance and also predicts outcome (Orlinsky, Rønnestad, & Willutzki, 2004; Tryon & Winograd, 2011). Second, a problem list ensures that the therapist has a broad understanding of the current state of the client's life and can put the problems that become the focus of treatment into context with the rest of the person's life. As Persons (2008) wrote, a review of the problem list may reveal common elements or themes. A treatment plan may then be developed that focuses on these elements or themes, enabling resolution of multiple problems efficiently. Further, review of the problem list may suggest that focusing on one problem might address others at the same time. For example, encouraging an unemployed depressed person to seek employment can simultaneously address other problems such as behavioral inactivity, hopelessness, social isolation, strained relationships at home, and financial stress. A third reason to generate a problem list is that doing so can contribute directly to a successful outcome. The process of generating a problem list in itself can help clarify what may otherwise appear to be an unsolvable, unarticulated, state of distress for the client. It can help the client begin to find meaning and order in an experience that has previously felt random and out of control, and in this way reduce anxiety and provide a common language in which discussion of key issues may take place (Markowitz & Swartz, 2007).

WHAT IS A PROBLEM?

At first glance, problem identification may appear to be a straightforward process of simply asking clients what brings them to treatment. As the case of the man reporting panic disorder shows, however, problem identification is not always simple. One way to think about problems broadly was suggested by Henry (1997), who observed that "a problem is a discrepancy between a perceived and a desired state of affairs" (p. 239). From this standpoint, I will discuss two basic types of problems: signs and symptoms and problems in living.

Signs and symptoms are types of behavior exhibited by the client. Symptoms are complaints of distress the client reports. They include many of the criteria appearing in the clinical syndrome descriptions of the *DSM–5* and *ICD–10.* The statement "I am sad. I cry every day. I force myself to get out of bed each morning. Every day is a strain," is a report of depression symptoms. A person with schizophrenia who reports hearing voices or the experience of bugs crawling on his or her body is reporting symptoms. Signs, on the other hand, are disturbances that are observable to the therapist and others, but that the client may not report, acknowledge, or even be aware of. If the above symptoms of depression are accompanied by sighs, a slumped posture, a mask-like face, or psychomotor retardation, then these would be signs of depression. Clients with schizophrenia may exhibit looseness of associations, but ordinarily they will not complain of loose associations as a symptom. Horowitz (2005) described "behavioral leakage" as a type of psychiatric sign. These are indications of emotion or unarticulated meaning that are physicalized, are often subtle, and usually appear briefly and then vanish. For example, when a sensitive topic is raised, a client may blush, tear up, clench his or her jaw, display a flash of anger, or stiffen and pull away from the therapist. These signs may indicate "hot topics" that deserve exploration and may belong on the problem list.

Signs and symptoms may result from other problems and may also *cause* a broader array of problems. Thus, a comprehensive problem list goes well beyond a list of psychiatric signs and symptoms, bringing us to the second broad problem type: *problems in living* (H. S. Sullivan, 1954). This term includes an array of life situations; for example, red flags such as chemical dependency, domestic violence, suicidality, homicidality, and neglect; as well as problems related to physical/medical functioning, school, work, housing, legal issues, finances, sexuality, leisure activity, self-concept, and identity. Also included are interpersonal problems such as conflict with others at home or outside the home, inability to connect with others, loneliness, lack of intimacy, deficits in interpersonal skills, and instability in relationships. In addition, problems in living include conflicts related to "existential givens" (Yalom, 1980) such as one's essential aloneness, the inevitability of death, freedom and responsibility, and fundamental meaninglessness. To illustrate using the example of the depressed individual above, the statement "I want to spend time with friends, but I just sit there all day and do nothing" reflects a problem in living. Interpersonal isolation, poor self-care, and inability to maintain gainful employment are problems in living faced by many individuals with schizophrenia.

A FRAMEWORK FOR ORGANIZING PROBLEMS

Several comprehensive classification schemes for organizing signs, symptoms, and problems in living have been proposed (e.g., Gordon & Mooney, 1950; Heppner et al., 1994; Ingram, 2012; Nezu, Nezu, & Lombardo, 2004; Woody, Detweiler-Bedell, Teachman, & O'Hearn, 2003). In this section, I present a framework that draws particularly from that of Nezu, Nezu, and Lombardo (2004). The framework has the advantages of being hierarchically organized, amenable to a cross-theoretical perspective, and comprehensive yet parsimonious. As shown in Table 5.1, it organizes a comprehensive problem list into four perspectives: red flags, self-functioning, social/interpersonal functioning, and societal functioning. Each domain can be viewed temporally as reflecting current or distal

	Table 5.1
	Components of a Comprehensive Problem List

Problem type	Subtypes with examples
1. Red flags	Chemical dependence, domestic violence, suicidality/homicidality, neglect
2. Self-functioning	
a. Behavior	<u>Excesses</u>: intrusiveness; extended, intensive, and unremitting grief; addiction; impulsivity; compulsions; chronic avoidance of anxiety-provoking activity; disinhibition
	<u>Deficits</u>: lack of assertiveness, withdrawal/inhibition, poor study habits, poor self-monitoring, poor self-control skills
b. Cognition	<u>Absences of awareness</u>: failure to appreciate consequences of one's actions, failure to recognize social cues, empathic failures, undervaluing one's thoughts, failures of self-regard
	<u>Distortions</u>: misattributions or errors in interpreting behavior of others, ignoring relevant evidence, jumping to conclusions, over-generalizing, magnifying, minimizing, personalizing, all-or-none thinking, fundamental attribution error
	<u>Identity</u>: cultural identity, identity development, sexual orientation ambivalence
c. Affect and mood	<u>Excesses</u>: anger outbursts, excessive or chronic fear or anxiety, chronic shame and disgust
	<u>Deficits</u>: flatness, blunting, lack of full affect repertoire, empathic failure, numbing
	<u>Dysregulation</u>: unstable extremes and fluctuations, "shimmering," lability
d. Biological	Medical illness; any problem significantly rooted in physical/biological functioning whether genetic, constitutional, or acquired; physical factors that can be problems themselves or contribute to other problems
e. Existential	Essential aloneness; inevitability of death, freedom, and responsibility; fundamental meaninglessness
3. Social/interpersonal functioning	Spouse/intimate other, family, teachers/school, work, mental health providers, lack of intimacy, deficits in interpersonal skills, instability in relationships, inability to connect with others, loneliness, alienation of others, leisure/recreational activities
4. Societal functioning	Legal, war, crime, inadequate housing, crowds, noise pollution, food deserts, transportation, poverty, poor school options, acculturative stress

problems. Considering past problems can help understand current problems. Although some problems overlap multiple categories, this is not a concern since the primary goal is to ensure a comprehensive review of all major areas of the client's functioning.

Red Flags

Red flags are problems that require immediate attention because they reflect potential danger to the client or others. They include suicidality, homicidality, domestic violence, neglect, and chemical abuse/dependence. It is important to ask about these issues even when they do not appear to be problems. Clients often find it difficult to bring up these problems, and may not do so unless asked. But even when they are brought up, the client may not recognize them as problems or may minimize them, particularly domestic violence and substance abuse. When they are present, however, red flags should rise to the top of the priority list of problems to address. It can be helpful to clarify from whose perspective the issue is a problem. Alcohol abuse and chronic anger may not be problems from the client's perspective, for example, but family members may view them as major problems. One task of the therapist may be to help the client recognize the impact of these problems so that there is agreement about the treatment plan.

Problems in Self-Functioning

Problems in self-functioning are those that inhere primarily within the individual. They include problems related to behavior, cognition, affect and mood, biology, and existential issues. Behavior problems can be categorized as either excesses or deficits. Examples of behavioral excesses include interpersonal intrusiveness; extended, intensive, and unremitting grief; addiction; impulsivity; compulsive behavior; chronic avoidance of anxiety-provoking activity; and various forms of disinhibition. Examples of behavioral deficits are lack of assertiveness, interpersonal withdrawal or inhibition, poor study habits, and poor self-monitoring and self-control skills.

Cognitive problems tend to be deficiencies, distortions, or related to identity. Deficiencies are absences of awareness in thinking. Examples include a failure to appreciate the consequences of one's actions, a failure to pick up on interpersonal cues, empathic failures, not appropriately valuing one's thoughts, and failures of self-regard. A cognitive distortion is a misinterpretation or error in cognitive processing. Examples are misattributions or errors in predicting the behavior of others, such as interpreting a neutral or preoccupied facial gesture as rejection or aggression. Beck's (1963, 1964; A. T. Beck et al., 1979) list of cognitive errors contains good examples of cognitive distortions. These include ignoring relevant evidence, jumping to conclusions, overgeneralizing, magnifying or minimizing, personalizing, and all-or-none thinking. Another example is committing the *fundamental attribution error* (L. Ross, 1977), which refers to misattributing causes to either situations or persons. For example, depressed persons tend to blame themselves for negative events even when situational factors provide a better explanation (Abramson et al., 1978; Raps, Peterson, Reinhard, Abramson, & Seligman, 1982). Identity problems are often profound and reflect the absence of a coherent and temporally continuous sense of "selfsameness" (Erikson, 1980), including one's selfsameness for others. Insights into identity problems are often found by exploring the client's psychosocial development.

Problematic affect and mood encompasses a wide range of signs and symptoms related to emotion and emotional control. These include mood and emotion states that cause distress, emotional extremes and fluctuations, and specific problematic emotions such as excessive fear, anxiety, anger, hostility, shame, disgust, guilt, and sadness.

Biological problems include a wide range of physiological, medical, and physical factors that can be problems in themselves or that may contribute to a client's psychosocial problems. Similarly, psychological problems may mask medical disorders. For example, multiple medical conditions can cause or precipitate depression; these include AIDS, cancer, congestive heart failure, diabetes mellitus, fibromyalgia, hypothyroidism, lupus, migraines, and sleep apnea (Morrison, in press). Sometimes the link to depression is direct and physiological, as in the case of hypothyroidism;

sometimes it is indirect, as in the case of eczema that can adversely affect body image and concept, leading to a depressed mood.

A final area of self-functioning problems relates to existential questions. These include one's essential aloneness; the inevitability of death; feelings of meaninglessness and purposelessness; and questions related to freedom and responsibility (Yalom, 1980). Some clients present with otherwise successful and well-functioning lives but experience a profound sense of pointlessness in their daily routines.

Problems in Social/Interpersonal Functioning

Problems in social functioning include relationships with friends and family, one's spouse or significant other, and others in one's social and work communities. These may include associating with individuals who are poor role models; for example, those who abuse substances or commit crimes, exhibit maladaptive interpersonal relationship patterns, are quick to anger, or are abusive. This category also includes interpersonal problems with previous mental health providers. Understanding these relationships is helpful in predicting obstacles to success in the current treatment. Problems in the social sphere may also incorporate aspects of the individual's socioethnic/cultural background. The problem focus may be on the responses of others within the individual's self-identified culture as well as responses from those outside that culture. Problems in the socioethnic/cultural area may be problems in themselves (e.g., language problems), or they may contribute to other psychosocial problems. For example, a transgender individual may be comfortable with his or her gender identity but lonely and isolated due to problems finding intimacy. Similarly, acculturative stress may interfere with finding intimacy.

Problems in Societal Functioning

This category refers to the many ways an individual functions in and relates to society at large. The category includes problems in the legal, financial, and employment domains. Problems related to societal functioning may also include lack of or inadequate housing, living in a crime-ridden neighborhood, poor schools that limit development, lack of adequate transportation that prevents attendance at therapy sessions, living in a "food desert," and lack of easily accessible recreational options. Acculturative stress is also included.

ROCHELLE'S PROBLEM LIST

Rochelle has problems from all four perspectives. One red flag is possible suicidality based on her history of suicide attempts and current stressors. Domestic violence is also a red flag, based on her apparently overcontrolling husband and her own anger episode vandalizing his car. In terms of self-functioning, she is depressed, anxious, exhibits mood instability, has poor anger management, poor sleep, and headaches. Her mood instability may be exacerbated by uncontrolled diabetes. Viewed distally, additional problems may be grief due to the death of her son and the past rape. Social/interpersonal functioning problems include social isolation, possible interpersonal dependency, possible spousal infidelity, and a chemically dependent husband. Problems in societal functioning include financial strain, possible limited motivation or ability to come to treatment, impending housing problems, and underemployment.

SUGGESTIONS FOR PROBLEM FORMULATION

I close this chapter with some tips on problem formulation. Following these tips and developing a comprehensive problem list in a systematic and deliberate fashion is the foundation of case formulation.

First, collaborate with the client when identifying problems, and aim to achieve consensus before proceeding with a treatment plan. Without agreement on what one is working on and why, the relationship with the client will suffer, progress will be more difficult, and you may end up working at cross-purposes with the client. The combination of explicitly identifying the problems, checking with the client about them, regularly monitoring progress, and explicitly seeking agreement is the best way to achieve a collaborative approach.

Second, select and prioritize which problems will receive attention during therapy. All of the client's problems likely cannot be addressed and some will not be amenable to psychotherapeutic treatment at all even though they may affect treatment. For example, one cannot directly address physical illness or housing-related problems, but they can nevertheless influence stress, mood, and the ability to come for treatment.

Third, some problems may not initially seem to be psychotherapy problems, but directly addressing them can help with psychological symptoms. One example is a highly anxious client with panic attacks who exhibited catastrophic thinking. Despite years of positive performance reviews, he was convinced he would lose his job. If he lost his job, the chain of thought went, he would no doubt lose his home and no longer be able to support his young children, causing his wife to divorce him, confirming his core belief that he was a failure. He had practically no savings and had accrued some credit card debt, which added to his anxiety. As part of the treatment, we developed a plan for him to pay off his debt and build up savings of 3 to 6 months of living expenses as a financial cushion. He took initial steps in this direction, consequently felt much more in control of his finances, and his anxiety decreased markedly. Eventually he worked up his courage to find a new job, which led to further gains and sustained reduction in his anxiety and panic symptoms. Thus, identifying, prioritizing, and then addressing a financial problem helped solve a psychological one.

Fourth, frame problems specifically, concretely, and contextually. It is better to describe a problem as "inability to assert self in face of demands from family" than as "passive and unassertive." It is also preferable to think atheoretically and descriptively about problems. For example, it is preferable to label a relationship problem as "inability to form intimate relationships" than as "unresolved oedipal conflict" since the latter is heavily theory-laden. As a test of whether one is describing a problem in an atheoretical manner, strive to describe it in a manner that any therapist, regardless of theoretical orientation, would likely agree with. It is also helpful to use the client's own words in describing problems.

Fifth, be a keen observer, be curious, and avoid unwarranted assumptions. Practice what Zen master Shunryu Suzuki (2008) described as "beginner's mind." This is a state of mind in which one suspends judgment and assumptions. Even if you think you know the answer, be willing to ask questions. By not making assumptions, you are more likely to elicit a full range of problems as viewed from the client's perspective.

Sixth, be alert to "wrong problem syndrome." This term is coined to allude to occasions when the client focuses on one problem in order to avoid a more central and more difficult-to-discuss problem. Wrong problem syndrome may be identified by emotionality or a quick change of topic when the more central problem is broached, by defensiveness, and by the conspicuous absence of a topic. One client, a young man in his early 20s with an obsessive style, presented with painful and prolonged grief after his girlfriend left him. The problem of unresolved grief was identified, and we set out to work on it. He spoke intensely across several sessions about how much he longed for his ex-girlfriend, how much she meant to him, and how he hoped to win her back. He wondered what he did to drive her away and alternatively, how undeserving she was of him and what he had to offer her. After several weeks, little progress had been made, and it became clear that we had misidentified the problem. All the talk about the ex-girlfriend served the goal of avoiding talking about what he was going to do next in his life, a very painful topic for him that he had assiduously avoided. Once the problem was reframed, the therapy took a more productive turn.

CONCLUSION

In summary, the problem list informs the therapist and the client about what is to be formulated. To ensure that a comprehensive problem list is developed, cast a wide net and consider specific domains of information such as those suggested in this chapter. Following a systematic approach ensures that a full problem list is generated and an appropriate diagnosis, explanatory mechanism, and treatment plan can then be developed.

6

Step 2: Diagnose

The goal of this chapter is to discuss the application and use of diagnosis in case formulation. To accomplish this goal, it is important to
understand what a mental disorder diagnosis is, how diagnoses are identified, what role they play in the practice and science of psychotherapy as
well as in society at large, and what diagnosis uniquely contributes to a
case formulation.

Ideally, a system for diagnosing mental and behavioral disorders would
reliably and validly identify the client's disorder in all its cardinal features,
elucidate the underlying etiology and the likely course and outcome, prescribe the most effective treatment, and serve as a basis for research to
advance knowledge about the disorder. Further, it would facilitate communication among mental health providers and with clients, families,
and others in the community who are entitled to diagnostic information.
Finally, a system of diagnoses of mental disorders would ideally catalog the

http://dx.doi.org/10.1037/14667-007
Psychotherapy Case Formulation, by T. D. Eells

range of abnormal conditions, distinguish them from the normal ones, and organize these conditions into a coherent whole. In short, psychiatric diagnosis would, in the words of Plato, "carve nature at its joints."

Diagnosis in mental health care falls far short of the ideal. This is one reason case formulation is important. The current diagnostic nosology in the United States, the fifth edition of the *Diagnostic and Statistical Manual of Mental Disorders* (*DSM–5*), like its forebears dating to the publication of *DSM–III* in 1980 and like the *International Classification of Diseases* (*ICD–10*), which is widely used outside of the United States, makes no pretense of identifying the underlying causes of conditions, although there are a few exceptions, such as posttraumatic stress disorder and adjustment disorders, that hinge on antecedent events leading to the condition; nor do these systems link diagnosis to treatment or identify the likely course or outcomes of disorders.

The *DSM–III* marked a major change from earlier versions and was heralded as a major breakthrough. Unlike its predecessors, it listed explicit criteria for each diagnosis; it greatly expanded the number of diagnoses; and most important, it was promoted as grounded in science and as producing reliable diagnoses (Hyler, Williams, & Spitzer, 1982; Spitzer, Forman, & Nee, 1979). With its introduction, improvement in reliability was touted as a milestone advance. As Allen Frances, who was instrumental in developing the *DSM–III* and led the development of the *DSM–IV*, put it, "Without reliability the system is completely random, and the diagnoses mean almost nothing—maybe worse than nothing, because they're falsely labeling. You're better off not having a diagnostic system" (quoted in Spiegel, 2005, p. 58).

Unfortunately, an empirical review of the reliability of the *DSM–III* and later revisions is disappointing (Kirk & Kutchins, 1992). One particularly extensive study illustrates this point. J. B. W. Williams and colleagues (1992) gave specialized diagnostic training to a group of mental health professionals at six sites in the United States and one in Germany. The mental health professionals then paired off and interviewed nearly 400 patients and 200 nonpatients. The researchers investigated whether the mental health professionals could agree on a *DSM–III–R* diagnosis, if any, when the participants were independently interviewed between 1 day and 2 weeks apart. Results showed moderate agreement when interviewing the patients ($\kappa = .61$) and poor agreement when interviewing the non-patients ($\kappa = .37$). The authors concluded that the results supported the reliability of the *DSM–III–R*, but acknowledged they "had expected higher reliability values" (J. B. W. Williams et al., 1992, p. 635). Kutchins and Kirk (1997) described these results as "not that different from those statistics achieved in the 1950s and 1960s" (p. 52). Although agreement improves when diagnoses are based on reviews of the same clinical material, such as a taped interview, this is a much less stringent test of reliability.

Results from reliability field trials on the *DSM–5* provide no greater comfort (Regier et al., 2013). Test–retest reliability assessments of 23 targeted diagnoses were conducted at 11 academic centers in the United States and Canada. Kappa coefficients for nine of these 23 (39%) were in a range conventionally interpreted as "poor" (Fleiss, 1986); these included major depressive disorder ($\kappa = .28$) and generalized anxiety disorder ($\kappa = .20$). The results have been described as "deplorable" (Frances, 2013a). Even the developers of the *DSM* recognize that reliability is a problem. Robert Spitzer, who led the development of the *DSM–III*, recently observed, "To say that we've solved the reliability problem is just not true. It's been improved. But if you're in a situation with a general clinician it's certainly not very good. There's still a real problem, and it's not clear how to solve the problem" (quoted in Spiegel, 2005, p. 63). Spitzer's point regarding the general clinician is worth noting. The research on reliability was carried out under conditions that should maximize diagnostic reliability. Diagnostic reliability in routine clinical settings is undoubtedly worse. Unfortunately, the alternative of using the *ICD–10* is unlikely to produce improvements since it is mapped closely to the *DSM*.

The *DSM* has also been criticized on grounds that its proponents exaggerated the extent to which diagnostic categories are based on research findings. In contrast to assertions when *DSM–III* was originally published, an insider recently noted, "The vast majority of *DSM–III* definitions . . . were entirely a product of expert consensus" (First, 2014, p. 263).

The *DSM–5* may reflect little improvement. According to Kendler (2013), some of the work groups involved in developing the *DSM–5* produced literature reviews that were central to their proposals for changes; however, others "functioned more within an expert consensus model" (p. 1797). As many as 42% of the proposals for diagnostic changes in the *DSM–5* were judged to have limited or insufficient empirical support (Kendler, 2013). Because the deliberations of the American Psychiatric Association Board of Trustees are not public, it is unknown how many of these questionable changes appear in the final document (First, 2014). The *DSM*, and particularly *DSM–IV*, has also been criticized for high rates of diagnostic comorbidity, which suggests lack of separation of the syndromes; lack of treatment specificity of disorders; considerable diagnostic heterogeneity within individual disorders; and high usage rates of "not otherwise specified" diagnoses in specialty mental health settings (Regier, Narrow, Kuhl, & Kupfer, 2009).

Finally, critics claim *DSM* categories have been included or excluded from the manual on the basis of political, social, and economic factors, and are more the outcome of jockeying among members of committees representing the rising and falling fortunes of various political factions within the American Psychiatric Association than on underlying science (Caplan, 1995; Cosgrove & Krimsky, 2012; Johnson, Barrett, & Sisti, 2013; Kutchins & Kirk, 1997; Sadler, 2005; Schacht, 1985). Events surrounding whether or not to include disorders such as masochistic personality disorder and premenstrual dysphoric disorder, the latter of which has just been added as a formal diagnosis to the *DSM–5*, provide examples of how nonscientific processes influenced the inclusion or exclusion of diagnoses (Caplan, 1995). Critics have further asserted that diagnosis does little more than label and stigmatize individuals by casting them into the realm of the abnormal, sometimes harming them more than helping, and that the system was oversold by inappropriately associating it with diagnosis in general medicine. The *DSM–5* has been singled out as particularly at risk of pathologizing normal human behavior (Frances, 2013b).

What does the future bode for addressing these shortcomings in the diagnosis of mental and behavioral disorders? The *ICD–11*, due in 2017, promises a major reorganization of how mental and behavioral disorders will be classified, which may lead to improvements in reliability and may also address other problem areas. Advantages of the *ICD* system are that it is the world's classification system, it is available at no cost, it is free of commercial influence, it is based on multinational data, and it is the official Health Insurance Portability and Accountability Act–approved United States system for all third-party billing (Goodheart, 2014).

Another promising development in diagnosis is that of the U.S. National Institute of Mental Health to establish the Research Domain Criteria Project. According to the project website (http://www.nimh. nih.gov/research-priorities/rdoc/nimh-research-domain-criteria-rdoc. shtml#toc_background), it will incorporate genetics, imaging, cognitive science, learning theory, and other information to lay the foundation for a new nosology that is not based primarily on symptom presentation. As some experts have noted (Goodheart, 2014; Krueger, Hopwood, Wright, & Markon, 2014), the goal is laudable, but the outcome should link back to clinical manifestations of disorders and meet criteria of clinical utility.

REASONS TO DIAGNOSE

The above criticisms notwithstanding, diagnosis plays a crucial and distinctive role in case formulation. Diagnosis marks a dividing line between what society considers normal and abnormal behavior, and the diagnostic decision can be enormously consequential. It can affect the client's self-concept, both in potentially freeing and constraining ways. To be told one is depressed and that depression is common and treatable can be a great relief to a suffering individual. On the other hand, to be told one is "borderline" can fill a person with hopelessness and despair and lead to or exacerbate feelings of being defective.

Diagnosis has many practical benefits. It facilitates communication among clinical colleagues. As Blashfield and Burgess (2007) observed, diagnosis provides a nomenclature or "a set of nouns that a wide variety of mental health professionals can use to describe . . . individuals who . . . share certain similarities" (p. 101). Diagnostic terms such as bipolar or generalized anxiety disorder provide a shorthand way of exchanging shared ideas. The *DSM* system provides a comprehensive and systematic set of such terms, each with specific criteria, that aims to fulfill this descriptive and communicative role (Millon & Klerman, 1986).

Beyond the narrow confines of the *DSM*, diagnosis helps the therapist organize and retrieve information about psychopathology. As noted in Chapter 2 of the present volume, possession of this knowledge base is characteristic of expertise; it is an invaluable resource in case formulation. A well-trained therapist who diagnoses a client with a disorder will immediately associate a range of empirical knowledge about that disorder, including possible origins, precipitants, maintaining factors, mechanisms of actions, and treatment options. Diagnosis helps with treatment selection since an enormous amount of treatment research has been conducted on the basis of selecting individuals according to diagnostic categories. Diagnosis also provides guidance for decisions related to selection of pharmaceuticals or referral to a psychiatrist. However, diagnosis provides only limited guidance for treatment since multiple treatments are available for the same diagnostic condition, and since multiple combinations of symptoms can lead to the same diagnosis. Diagnosis does not provide guidance on which of multiple treatment options to choose.

More broadly, diagnosis is used by the courts, schools, prisons, and many social agencies to determine who is labeled as having a mental disorder and is therefore eligible for societal services (Kutchins & Kirk, 1997). Another practical function of diagnosis is that it determines whether a psychological condition is eligible for insurance reimbursement. Finally, one must recognize that, despite its limitations, the *DSM* system of diagnosis is the current socially and culturally sanctioned system of organizing information about mental illness in the United States, and the *ICD–10* plays a similar role in other countries; each has widespread acceptance.

Several points have been made so far about problems and benefits associated with psychiatric diagnosis, without yet describing what a mental disorder is. With this balance of views in mind, I now turn to address this question.

WHAT IS A MENTAL DISORDER?

Defining a mental disorder is a complex task. As pointed out in Chapter 1, debate persists about whether to conceptualize mental distress in dimensional or categorical terms, whether psychopathology should be viewed through a medical model lens or in other ways (Beutler & Malik, 2002), and what role biological versus environmental factors play in the development of psychopathology (Lynn, Matthews, Williams, Hallquist, & Lilienfeld, 2007). In addition, there are multiple ways to construe abnormality, such as statistical deviation from a norm of behavior, deviation from an ideal of behavior, the presence of suffering, and poor adaptation to stress (Kendell, 1975). As evidence of the definitional difficulty, Kutchins and Kirk (1997) pointed out that it was not until the *DSM–III* in 1980 that the American Psychiatric Association formally defined a mental disorder. The current definition is as follows (American Psychiatric Association, 2013a):

> A mental disorder is a syndrome characterized by clinically significant disturbance in an individual's cognition, emotional regulation, or behavior that reflects a dysfunction in the psychological, biological, or developmental processes underlying mental functioning. Mental disorders are usually associated with significant distress or disability in social, occupational, or other important activities. An expectable or culturally approved response to a common stress or loss, such as the death of a loved one, is not a mental disorder. Socially deviant behavior (e.g., political, religious, or sexual) and conflicts that are primarily between the individual and society are not mental disorders unless the deviance or conflict results from a dysfunction in the individual, as described above. (pp. 4–5)

Three points may be made about this definition. First, it locates mental disorder in the individual. In doing so, it deemphasizes phenomena that may reside in or be derived primarily from transactions between individuals, such as within a group or a dyad such as a family or couple, except in so far as these transactional phenomena affect an individual's cognition, emotional regulation, or behavior. Consider, for example, a 50-year-old divorced woman client who met criteria for major depression, but whose depression appeared to arise from the role she played in the family constellation. It was suggested to her that her depression appeared to flow from others in the family treating her as the person they could always go to for money, for a favor, or, for that matter, for anything they needed. It was suggested to the client that until she stopped playing the role of "family savior" she was likely to remain depressed. The treatment plan included assertiveness training, which she assiduously exercised, and her depression shortly resolved, while a sibling took on the role of the person anyone in the family could go to for help. Under the definition of mental disorder, her depression is viewed as residing in her, although it was actually a function of her family constellation. Case formulation is well suited to capturing these added dimensions.

A second point about the definition is that it is broad, vague, and circular. Mental disorder is defined as a "clinically significant disturbance" that is associated with "significant distress or disability." The term "disturbance" is not defined, and certainly one can think of "disturbances" that one might not want to describe as abnormal. For example, a soldier's response to combat or an individual's response to physical assault or to a long history of physical, mental, and sexual abuse may reflect a "disturbance" in cognition, emotional regulation, or behavior that might appear understandable, even if not "expectable" or "culturally approved." Further, the modifier "clinically significant" seems to suggest that if a "disturbance" is seen in the context of a clinic visit, it may be a mental disorder simply by virtue of satisfying this condition. Yet the intent of the definition of mental disorder presumably is to identify conditions that warrant clinical attention, not to use the fact of a clinic visit as a criterion indicating a need for clinical attention. In sum, the definition casts an overly broad net that seems to err on the side of inclusion of experiences as disordered rather than exclusion.

A final point about the definition of a mental disorder, and thus a psychiatric diagnosis, is that what is being defined is a construct. It is a socially constructed and consensually agreed upon abstract category that may have varying degrees and types of empirical support and that may be more or less useful in understanding an individual and the world.

As represented in the current manuals, a psychiatric diagnosis exists only in the sense that others have agreed to recognize it as a meaningful category by which to understand mental disturbance. It does not "exist" in the sense that some general medical conditions exist, such as diabetes, lung cancer, congestive heart failure, or a bacterial infection. Independent of social opinion, the latter conditions are rooted in malfunctioning biological structures and processes, have known pathophysiological origins, courses, and outcomes, and the confirmation of diagnosis can commonly be determined upon postmortem examination. The same cannot be said of conditions such as adjustment disorders, posttraumatic stress disorder, anxiety, major depression, bipolar disorder, and schizophrenia. This is not to deny that biological correlates have been identified for some of these conditions, just as psychological correlates have been identified for some general medical conditions. Nor does the definition of a construct preclude scientists from hypothesizing that a particular construct has a determinable psychobiological structure or genetic influences, such as some trait theorists have posited (Harkness, 2007). Examples of other constructs are intelligence; personality traits such as introversion/extraversion and agreeableness; and also democracy, religiosity, and patriotism. The essential point is that psychiatric diagnoses are not discovered but are invented or created.

ROCHELLE'S DIAGNOSIS

Rochelle's diagnosis was based on a diagnostic interview conducted by a 4th-year psychiatry resident. In addition to information gathered from the interview, the resident reviewed a note from the referring physician that presented the reasons for the referral and summarized current and past medical concerns. Hospital records were requested, but were not available at the time a diagnosis needed to be assigned. Although not done, it may also have been helpful to administer a brief symptom measure, to speak with the referring physician, or to speak with family members. Based on the available sources, Rochelle was diagnosed with major depressive disorder, recurrent, moderate (MDD; 296.32) and generalized anxiety disorder (GAD; 302.02). Consideration was also given to posttraumatic stress disorder (PTSD; 309.81) and borderline personality disorder (BPD; 301.83). Medically, her diabetes was noted, and she was noted to have significant psychosocial stress centering on finances, marital conflict, and the death of her son.

MDD was supported by sad mood and diminished interest and pleasure in activities that she reported experiencing most days, nearly every day. In addition, she experienced sleep disturbance, intermittent suicidal ideation, fatigue, feelings of worthlessness, and tearfulness. The "recurrent" modifier was used based on past hospitalizations for depression. GAD was supported by her reported chronic worry and anxiety, inability to control the worry, fatigue, irritability, and sleep disturbance. Consideration was given to the role that diabetes may play in her depression and anxiety. Epidemiological studies show that diabetes increases risk for depression (Morrison, in press); more specifically, low blood sugar level may raise Rochelle's autonomic nervous system arousal and excessive urination during the night may contribute to her insomnia. In addition, the psychological stress of this chronic disease may exacerbate her symptoms of depression and anxiety, especially when the diabetes is uncontrolled as it is in the case of Rochelle. PTSD was considered due to her reported rape at the age of 16, her reluctance to discuss it, her relationship disturbances, and persistent symptoms of increased arousal (e.g., insomnia and anger outbursts). However, it was not clear that she re-experienced the event intrusively or persistently avoided stimuli associated with the trauma. BPD was considered based on her unstable relationship patterns, past suicidality, affective instability, and apparent maladaptive efforts to avoid abandonment, as evidenced by scratching her husband's car. It was not assigned as a diagnosis since Rochelle appeared to function well in some spheres, such as with close friends and in some work relationships. In addition, the resident expressed concern about a potentially stigmatizing effect of assigning this diagnosis.

In some respects, this diagnosis was both satisfying and unsatisfying to the resident who interviewed Rochelle and to others in the case formulation class. It was satisfying in that it resulted from a careful diagnostic interview with attention to the criteria of the *DSM*, and because it appeared to capture important elements in her problem list. Several of her symptoms cohere around the named syndromes. It was not satisfying to the class in that the diagnosis did not appear to capture Rochelle's poor judgment or her generally adequate functioning in some areas of life and poor functioning in others. Nor did it address her maladaptive relationship patterns, and the family dynamics and circumstances that were affecting her life. The closest the diagnosis came to capturing these phenomena was by considering BPD as a "rule out" condition. The diagnosis also did not seem to reflect strengths such as her ability to work, to attend college, and to function well in some relationship spheres.

CONSIDERATIONS WHEN DIAGNOSING IN CASE FORMULATION

The intent of the discussion so far is to put diagnosis into context, to neither overvalue nor undervalue its contribution to case formulation and treatment. With this context in mind, several considerations are suggested when working on a diagnosis.

First, just as with generating a problem list, consider multiple sources of information, including a comprehensive interview. These sources may include self-report symptom checklists or psychological test results; review of medical, psychotherapeutic, or other records of prior mental health treatment; discussion with others involved in the care of the individual; and interviews with family members. When conducting an interview with the client, do not look only at the more obvious considerations, but instead cast the diagnostic net widely. It is possible that an individual has problems they do not think to bring up, are too embarrassed to bring up, or want to "test" the therapist first before bringing up. The person may have problems they do not consider as problems but that might nevertheless help them if addressed.

Second, the diagnosis should flow directly and logically from the problem list. The problem list can be used to assess the presence or absence of specific diagnostic criteria. When treatment is not proceeding as expected, it can also be useful to reassess the diagnosis to determine whether criteria are still met and whether additional diagnoses may be playing a stronger role in the individual's life. This is particularly true for individuals with multiple comorbid disorders.

Third, pay attention to the specific criteria of the diagnostic categories. Although the *DSM* explicitly states that the specific diagnostic criteria are to be used as a guide, not as an absolute requirement for assigning a diagnosis, attending carefully to the criteria will nevertheless improve reliability. As Persons (2008) pointed out, "diagnostic error can lead to treatment failure" (p. 225).

Fourth, be mindful of the potentially harmful and beneficial aspects of diagnosis. As noted, receiving a diagnosis can be a great relief to some individuals, since they are able to accept the client role for a period of time and not view themselves as moral failures or as not trying enough. This is a major point made by those practicing interpersonal psychotherapy for depression (Markowitz & Swartz, 2007). However, others may feel damaged or labeled by a psychiatric diagnosis.

Fifth, do not mistake a diagnosis for an explanation. Be cautious when "explaining" a person's problems by means of a diagnosis, since diagnosis itself is not an explanation but merely a category, noun, or label for a set of interrelated experiences, affects, thoughts, and behaviors. For example, it is usually useless to explain to someone that the reason she is having relationship problems is "because you're borderline." This is circular at best and meaningless and damaging at worst.

Once a problem list and diagnosis are determined, the next step in case formulation is to develop an explanatory account of why the individual has the problems and diagnosis. It is to that step that I now turn.

7

Step 3: Develop an Explanatory Hypothesis

The explanatory hypothesis is the heart of the case formulation. It describes why the individual is having problems. Ideally, the explanation contains a cohesive and cogent understanding of the origins of the problems, the conditions that perpetuate them, the obstacles interfering with their solution, and the resources available to address them. An abundance of theories and empirical research is available to explain a client's signs, symptoms, and problems in living. This wealth of knowledge, while an asset, presents problems for therapists since it can be difficult to know which theory or research to draw upon.

I cannot do justice in this chapter to the extensive body of theory and evidence relevant to explanation in psychotherapy case formulation. Instead, the chapter will provide various routes into this work by suggesting tools and a process. It begins by proposing the diathesis–stress model of psychopathology as a powerful, enduring, and overarching

http://dx.doi.org/10.1037/14667-008
Psychotherapy Case Formulation, by T. D. Eells
Copyright © 2015 by the American Psychological Association. All rights reserved.

integrative explanatory framework. It continues with a review of the primary theories of psychotherapy and sources of evidence for formulation, expanding upon the historical and contemporary influences on case formulation presented in Chapter 1. Finally, it discusses steps to follow when developing the explanatory hypothesis, illustrating each with the case of Rochelle.

DIATHESIS–STRESS AS A FUNDAMENTAL INTEGRATIVE FRAMEWORK

The premise underlying the diathesis–stress model is that psychopathology is the product of two influences: first, an individual's inherent vulnerability to disorder and, second, environmental stress. As stress increases, the vulnerability, or diathesis, is more likely to gain expression as signs, symptoms, and problems. The diathesis concept is consistent with the discontinuity model of psychopathology discussed in Chapter 1 in its assumption that the suffering individual is inherently and qualitatively different from nonsuffering individuals by virtue of having the diathesis. The diathesis concept of illness can be traced to the ancient Greeks. As mentioned in Chapter 1, the second century physician, Galen of Pergamon, is credited with revitalizing Hippocratic thought about illness into a naturalistic explanatory framework. Galen posited nine temperaments that were derived from mixtures of four humors present in all persons: yellow and black bile, blood, and phlegm (Kagan, 1998). Personality, including its disagreeable aspects, was viewed as the product of propensities generated by these biological substances. Another early example of a diathesis model of illness, in this case depression, is that of Burton (1621/2001), who like Galen, drew from humoral theory. Diatheses were originally considered to be strongly if not exclusively biological; for example, temperamental (Kagan, 1998), endophenotypic (Gottesman & Gould, 2003), or genetic in nature. More recently, the diathesis concept has been expanded to include influences such as early attachment experiences (Dozier, Stovall-McClough, & Albus, 2008), other early developmental processes (Tully

& Goodman, 2007), cognition (Abramson, Metalsky, & Alloy, 1989), and social factors (Brown & Harris, 1978).

The idea that stress contributes to psychopathology is of more recent origin, but it can still be traced back hundreds of years (Hinkle, 1974; Monroe & Simons, 1991). References to stress as a physical science phenomenon first appeared in the 17th century and as a contributor to illness in the 19th. Cannon (1932) viewed stress as a homeostatic disturbance, and Selye (1976) used the term *stress* in reference to a set of physiological responses marshaled against noxious agents, including psychological ones. He coined the term *general adaptation syndrome* to describe a three-stage response to such a stressor. First, there is an alarm reaction, then adaptation or resistance, and finally exhaustion. Later, the role of cognitive appraisal in interpreting stress was emphasized (Lazarus & Folkman, 1984). There is consensus among researchers that stress affects mood, well-being, behavior, and physical health (Schneiderman, Ironson, & Siegel, 2005). Further, it is not only major life stressors that can affect health, but also daily hassles, which are relatively minor but irritating events such as constant phone calls, interpersonal disagreements, misplacing or losing things, planning meals, insufficient time for family, unchallenging work, long to-do lists, paying bills, and the frequent annoyances associated with cultural marginalization (Lazarus, 2000; Lazarus & DeLongis, 1983). Although some stress may be adaptive, its harmful effects appear related to its persistence, its nature, and the number of stressful events involved.

The idea of stress as a precursor to psychopathology is consistent with the continuous model of psychopathology discussed in Chapter 1, the idea that psychological disorders lie along a continuum from normality to abnormality and are not distinct states. It is the view that adverse life experiences explain psychopathology, that stress causes people to break down. It has been observed, however, that many individuals exhibit resilience such that they are able to tolerate significant stress and still not develop psychopathology (Bonanno, 2004; Masten, 2001); consequently, it is now widely accepted that a diathesis is also needed.

The combining of diathesis and stress into a single model of psychopathology can be traced to the 1960s and 1970s, mainly as explanatory models of schizophrenia (Meehl, 1962; Zubin & Spring, 1977), and later of depression (A. T. Beck, 1964). The model underlies more recent conceptions of a wide range of disorders (Zuckerman, 1999). For this reason, it can be considered a paradigmatic integrative framework for explanation in psychotherapy case formulation (Davison & Neale, 2001). It is not limited to one school of thought such as psychodynamics, behaviorism, or cognitive. Not only can each of these schools of thought be conceptualized in diathesis–stress terms, but the diathesis–stress model can draw differentially from each of them as well as from other sources of evidence, such as the broader social and biological sciences. Davison and Neale (pp. 55–56) wrote, "A diathesis–stress paradigm allows us to draw on concepts from many sources and to make more or less use of them depending on the disorder being considered." I explain one way to apply the diathesis–stress to develop an explanatory hypothesis in the Steps to Develop an Explanatory Hypothesis section of this chapter.

THEORY AS A SOURCE OF EXPLANATION IN FORMULATION

In this section and the next, I review two broad and closely intertwined sources of information for case formulation explanations: theory and evidence. The review is consistent with the recommendations of the APA Presidential Task Force on Evidence-Based Practice (2006) and the scientist–practitioner model of training and practice in clinical psychology (Shakow, 1976). The therapist's challenge is to apply relevant theory and evidence to the individual case under consideration. Here, I provide an overview of four major theories of psychotherapy: psychodynamic, behavioral, cognitive, and humanistic/experiential. I illustrate the application of each to case formulation. In application, some theories are blended when developing an explanation (e.g., Wachtel, 1977). Later in the chapter when I discuss explanatory templates, we will revisit the fundamental propositions of these theories in a condensed format. The goal here is to provide context for these explanatory templates.

Psychodynamic Psychotherapy

Psychodynamic theory originated in the work of Freud and provides a rich source of inference for case formulation. Freud contributed numerous ideas that have shaped our understanding of normal and abnormal psychology. These include the notions of psychic determinism, unconscious motivation, overdetermination of symptoms, the symbolic meaning of symptoms, symptom production as a compromise formation, ego defense mechanisms as stabilizers of the psyche, and the tripartite theory of the mind (i.e., its division into id, ego, and superego). Messer and Wolitzky (2007) succinctly grouped contemporary psychodynamic theory, at least as practiced in North America, into three broad categories: the traditional Freudian drive/structural theory, object relations theory, and self psychology.

The drive/structural theory may be viewed by some as obsolete and lacking in empirical support. Nevertheless, it is presented due to its historical significance and widespread earlier influence, as well as its potential contemporary value in generating explanatory hypotheses. It proposes that human behavior is driven by intrapsychic conflict originating in sexual and aggressive drives that seek pleasure and avoid pain (the "pleasure principle") but become thwarted when they confront obstacles such as fear, anxiety, or guilt. The structural component of the drive model involves the tripartite division of the mind into the id, which is the repository of drives, the superego, which contains both our conscience and who we ideally would become (the "ego ideal"), and the ego, which mediates between the impulses of the id and the strictures of the superego. The ego utilizes defense mechanisms in an attempt to avoid anxiety and maintain psychic equilibrium. When these attempts fail, neurotic symptoms develop. These mental structures and specific defenses arise as the individual navigates through four psychosexual stages—oral, anal, phallic, and genital—each of which is associated with specific conflicts that if not resolved persist into adulthood. The key feature of a case formulation based on the Freudian drive/structural theory is an "emphasis on unconscious fantasy, the conflicts expressed in such fantasy, and the influence of such conflicts and fantasies on the patient's behavior," and further, the assumption that these conflicts originate in childhood

(Messer & Wolitzky, 2007, p. 71). Treatment focuses on helping clients appreciate the nature and pervasiveness of their unconsciously driven motives and the ways that they avoid awareness of them.

The object relations perspective focuses on mental representations of self and other, and on models of affect-laden transactions between the two. The approach tends to dichotomize self and other into "good" and "bad" components that are unintegrated and compartmentalized. Defense mechanisms associated with this perspective include projective identification, splitting, and role reversal. Relationships constitute basic drives rather than instinct. The object relations perspective has expanded in recent decades into multiple forms, some of which are represented in the explanatory templates discussed later. Case formulations based on object relations focus on the inability to integrate mental representations and the disavowal of rage toward attachment figures that are also loved and needed. The individual may identify the self as "good," while project-ing "bad" aspects of the self onto others.

The self-psychology (Kohut, 1971, 1977) perspective emphasizes the development and maintenance of a cohesive sense of self. Using empathic attunement as his primary empirical tool, Kohut identified disturbances in the self-development of his clients. Some reported "empty" depressions in which life appeared colorless, alienating, pointless, and without vitality. Others reported traumatic states that blocked the integration of experi-ence into a coherent sense of identity. Kohut also treated people subject to unexpected, situationally discrepant states of rage, which he explained in terms of caregivers' failure to provide sufficient empathic responsive-ness. Kohut's most distinctive concept is that of the "selfobject," which is an unconscious mental representation of a self–other connection; it is experi-enced as if the other is an extension of oneself rather than a separate entity. Selfobjects are of two types: idealized and mirroring. An *idealized* selfobject is revealed in the experience of aliveness, vitality, and power through one's connection to an admired other person. The client seems to be saying "I admire you, therefore my sense of self and self-worth are enhanced by my vicarious participation in your strength and power" (Messer & Wolitzky, 2007, p. 73). A *mirroring* selfobject vitalizes the self through affirmation from others to whom one feels connected. Here, the client seems to be saying, "You admire me, and therefore I feel affirmed as a person of worth" (Messer & Wolitzky, 2007, p. 73). Formulations from the self-psychology perspective emphasize explanations of disturbances in a cohesive sense of self due to failures of empathic responsiveness from caretakers. The nature of the client's transference to the therapist—as idealizing or mirroring—is an important component to understanding the client.

In limiting our review of psychodynamic theory to the three basic models just described, it is important to note some omissions that may also serve as a basis for explanations in case formulation. These include those of Jung (1972), Adler (1973), Horney (1950), Erikson (1980), Murray (1938), and Sullivan (1953).

Behavior Therapy

Behaviorism offers a rich source of ideas for case formulation. As noted in Chapter 1, behaviorists have shaped psychotherapy through their emphasis on direct modification of symptoms, on the effect of the environment on behavior, and on empirical assessment (Eells, 2007b). Behavioral approaches are based on operant and/or respondent learning. While both forms of learning involve conditions that precede and follow problematic behavior, operant learning attends relatively more to the consequences, or reinforcers, of behavior, whereas respondent learning attends more to the antecedents, or stimuli, of behavior.

Operant conditioning emphasizes the shaping of behavior by the environment. An example is habit reversal, which is a treatment for conditions such as tics, chronic hair pulling, nail biting, and chronic skin picking (Adams, Adams, & Miltenberger, 2009). It involves identifying events in the environment that precede the behavior and its immediate consequences. Once these are identified, techniques are introduced to alter these conditions in order to eliminate the repetitive behavior. The process of identifying the antecedents and consequences of problematic behavior is called *functional analysis* (Skinner, 1953), and it is at the core of most behavioral and cognitive–behavioral case formulations (e.g., Haynes & Williams, 2003; Nezu et al., 2007; Persons, 2008). Functional analysis takes into account several aspects of operant conditioning. These include establishing operations (e.g., satiation or deprivation states), adaptive and maladaptive shaping of behavior, adaptive and maladaptive extinction, modeling, chaining, avoidance and escape activity that may preempt positively reinforced activity, consequences of debilitating naturalistic schedules of reinforcement, punishers, and variability of behavioral repertoires (Ferster, 1973; Sturmey, 2008).

The operant conditioning framework provides a structure for case formulation since operant learning is involved in the acquisition and maintenance of many forms of maladaptive behavior (Sturmey, 2008). A depressed individual, for example, may withdraw interpersonally and miss out on reinforcers that would counter depressive affect. In addition, others may avoid the depressed person, thus maintaining maladaptive avoidance and isolation. A case formulation based on operant conditioning should assess these possibilities and identify the contingencies that maintain the behavior.

In contrast to operant behavior, which is controlled by its consequences, *respondent* behavior is elicited by its antecedents. The classic example is that of Pavlov's dogs who were conditioned to salivate at the sound of a bell. A clinical example is that of a veteran who panics at the sound of a door closing. It is possible that gunfire in war served as an unconditioned stimulus (US) that elicited fear and a startle reflex as an unconditioned response (UR). The UR can then generalize such that a nonthreatening sound such as a door closing becomes a conditioned stimulus (CS) that elicits fear and a startle response, which are now conditioned responses (CR). Respondent behavior is said to be rooted in responses that are naturally occurring as a result of our evolutionary past. Examples of URs are fear in the face of a genuine threat to life, hunger at the smell of food, and jumping in response to a loud sound. These responses share the characteristic of being unlearned. They can all, however, be brought under the control of other stimuli through pairings, such as the door shutting with gunfire. Respondent conditioning has been associated with many psychological disorders, including posttraumatic stress disorder, phobias, and obsessive–compulsive disorder.

Several principles of classical conditioning help explain the development and maintenance of psychological disorders and how they might be treated (Persons, 2008; Sturmey, 2008). These principles can be incorporated into a case formulation. I will give three examples. One is that the greater the number of pairings of a US and a CS, the more likely is the CS to elicit a CR. The more often one experiences a spontaneous panic attack (a US that elicits a UR of fear) in a restaurant (CS), the more likely visiting a restaurant will elicit a panic attack (which is now a CR). A second principle is that when a CS occurs repeatedly in the absence of a US, the CS will eventually exert lesser and lesser control over a CR. This principle underlies the behavioral technique of flooding, which has been used to treat phobias and other anxiety disorders. Flooding involves continuous exposure to a CS (e.g., plastic spiders, heights, public speaking) until exposure no longer elicits a CR (fear; Zoellner, Abramowitz, Moore, & Slagle, 2009). The third principle is that of counterconditioning, which underlies systematic desensitization (Wolpe, 1958; Wolpe & Turkat, 1985), a technique for treating phobias and anxiety. Wolpe held that one cannot simultaneously experience relaxation and fear. In systematic desensitization, the therapist first teaches relaxation exercises to the client. Then, once relaxed, the client is exposed to increasing levels of anxiety-arousing experiences until those experiences no longer elicit anxiety. In stimulus-response terms, counterconditioning involves the elimination of a CR, such as anxiety, when a CS is paired to a US that elicits a new response that is incompatible with the old CR.

Cognitive Therapy

Theories underlying contemporary cognitive therapies can be traced to the "cognitive revolution," which took place in the mid-20th century as a response to what was increasingly perceived as the inadequacies of behavioristic, stimulus–response models of learning that discounted the role of mentation and human agency (Mahoney, 1991). Borrowing terminology and concepts from information theory, computer science, and general systems theory, the interests of cognitive scientists turned toward "understanding and influencing the fundamental processes by which individual humans attend to, learn, remember, forget, transfer, adapt, relearn and otherwise engage with the challenges of life in development" (Mahoney, 1991, p. 75). As Bruner (1990) put it, "that revolution was intended to bring 'mind' back into the human sciences after a long cold winter of objectivism" (p. 1). It was further intended "to establish meaning as the central concept of psychology—not stimuli and responses, not overtly observable behavior, not biological drives and their transformation, but meaning" (p. 2). Influential writings at the time included works such as Bruner, Goodnow, and Austin (1956); Chomsky (1959); Festinger (1957); Kelly (1955a, 1955b); Newell, Shaw, and Simon (1958); and Postman (1951).

As the cognitive revolution filtered into the social sciences and psychiatry, multiple theories of cognitive therapy took shape. More than 20 years ago, Kuehlwein and Rosen (1993) identified 10 different models of cognitive therapy alone. As Nezu, Nezu, and Cos (2007) pointed out, there is no single cognitive therapy, but a collection of therapies that share a common history and perspective. They hold in common not only their heritage within the cognitive revolution but also the assumption that our appraisals of events are more crucial to our mental well-being than are the events themselves. Most of these models also blend elements of behavior theory, which are discussed later in this chapter.

In this section, I emphasize A. T. Beck's model because it is the most influential and researched. However, other cognitive theories of therapy developed since the cognitive revolution include those of Ellis (1994, 2000); Hayes and Strosahl (2004); and Young, Klosko, and Weishaar (2003). A. T. Beck's (1963) cognitive theory originated from observations of persistent thought patterns in depressed clients he interviewed. These individuals expressed views of themselves as inferior in areas of their lives that mattered to them. They viewed the world as depriving and saw the future as bleak. These observations led Beck to develop his now well-known cognitive triad, which is a framework he proposed to describe the automatic and systematically biased negative thinking of depressed clients, particularly about themselves, the world, and the future (A. T. Beck, Rush, Shaw, & Emery, 1979). It was later expanded to describe a wide range of problems and psychological conditions (A. T. Beck, Emery, & Greenberg, 1985; A. T. Beck,

Freeman, & Davis, 2004; J. S. Beck, 1995). *Automatic thoughts* are brief, episodic, and often emotionally laden forms of thinking that occur unbidden and are often at the threshold of awareness. One might think, for example, "This test is too hard. I'll never pass," which could be followed by a feeling of deflation or demoralization. Negative automatic thoughts are often erroneous, illogical, and unrealistic. Beck identified specific characteristic forms of thought distortion. Examples are arbitrary inferences, selective abstraction, overgeneralizations, catastrophizing, and personalization in which one erroneously explains events in terms of one's own perceived shortcomings rather than consider other explanations (A. T. Beck, 1963; J. S. Beck, 1995).

A third major construct of Beck's theory is that of *schemas*, which are tacit, organized cognitive structures that influence perception and appraisal. The schemas give rise to beliefs about the self, world, and future. At the most fundamental level are *core beliefs* (J. S. Beck, 1995), which are assumed to develop in childhood and to be global, rigid, and overgeneralized. In their negative form they tend to focus on beliefs of helplessness or unlovability. Between core beliefs and situationally specific automatic thoughts lie *intermediate beliefs*, which are rules, attitudes, and assumptions that are more subject to revision and change than core beliefs but less so than automatic thoughts.

Cognitive case formulations entail identifying the client's automatic thoughts, intermediate beliefs, and core beliefs (J. S. Beck, 1995). The assumption that characteristic patterns of thinking are specific to diagnostic categories suggests that implicit nomothetic explanatory mechanisms underlie diagnoses and can serve as templates for formulations (Persons, 2008). If the template fits the client, an empirically supported treatment may be suitable for the individual in question.

Humanistic/Experiential Psychotherapy

Humanistic theory emerged in the 1950s as an alternative to the determinism of the psychodynamic and behavioral approaches current at the time. In contrast to the view that humans are the product of their reinforcement history or their unconscious minds, the humanistic/experiential framework saw humans as self-actualizing and goal directed. The task of therapy was to provide a nondirective, empathic, and supportive environment in which the client could recapture the self-actualization tendency that had gone awry. As noted in Chapter 1, the primary contributions of humanistic psychology to formulation include its emphasis on the client as a person instead of a disorder, the focus on the here-and-now aspect of the human encounter rather than an intellectualized "formulation," and its view of the client and therapist as equal collaborators. An additional contribution of the humanistic/experiential approach is its emphasis on humans as capable of self-determination and free choice.

Historically, formulation or "psychological diagnosis" was deemphasized and viewed as potentially detrimental to the therapeutic process (Rogers, 1951). As Rogers (1951) wrote,

> the very process of psychological diagnosis places the locus of evaluation so definitely in the expert that it may increase any dependent tendencies in the client, and cause him to feel that the responsibility for understanding and improving his situation lies in the hands of another. (p. 223)

In addition, to the extent that the client comes to see the therapist as the only person who can really understand him, there is "a degree of loss of personhood" (p. 224). A second objection to formulation from the humanistic point of view was based on social and philosophical grounds: "When the locus of evaluation is seen as residing in the expert, it would appear that the long-range social implications are in the direction of the social control of the many by the few" (p. 224).

These objections notwithstanding, a distinct theory of personality emerged from the humanistic standpoint that is capable of being formulated. Rogers posited that human nature is driven by one master motive: the *self-actualizing tendency*, which is a drive to survive, grow, and improve. Further, we all live in a subjective world through which we assess what is consistent or inconsistent with self-actualization. The self emerges from experience, and develops positively when met with unconditional positive regard from others. When it is not, incongruence develops, as an individual no longer grows in a manner consistent with the self-actualizing tendency. The self as experienced is incongruent with the real or genuine self. The task of therapy, therefore, is to facilitate greater congruence. When collaboratively developed, formulation can potentially facilitate such a process.

Other theories identified within the humanistic tradition have been developed by Maslow (1987), Kelly (1955a, 1955b), Perls, Hefferline, and Goodman (1965) and more recently, by Bohart and Tallman (1999) and Greenberg (2002), among others. Contemporary proponents of the humanistic school are more accepting of formulation as a useful tool in therapy, although the emphasis tends to be on formulating moment-by-moment experiences rather than developing a global, case formulation (e.g., Greenberg & Goldman, 2007).

EVIDENCE AS A SOURCE OF EXPLANATION IN FORMULATION

The APA Presidential Task Force on Evidence-Based Practice (2006) stated that evidence-based formulations apply the best research, knowledge, experience, and expertise. The task force left open a key question: What constitutes appropriate evidence in a case formulation? Various types of evidence may best be viewed in relative terms along a continuum. At the most clearly evidence-based end, one could imagine well-conducted meta-analyses, compelling outcomes from empirically supported treatments, well-demonstrated mechanisms underlying forms of psychopathology, powerfully predictive epidemiological data, or well-documented and replicated findings about basic psychological processes. At the other end of the continuum one might place a therapist's hunches or intuitions. These might offer valuable insights that could be tested, but in themselves could not be described as evidence-based by most observers. Between these two endpoints might be included data such as psychological test findings, rating scale results, a client's narrative of a relationship episode, a dream account, a thought record, a client's account of automatic thinking, or an assertion by the client or therapist that a thought is a core belief. No consensus currently exists on what constitutes appropriate evidence for a case formulation. With that background, this section describes six sources of evidence useful for generating explanatory hypotheses in case formulation.

The Client

Clients play active, agentic roles in psychotherapy, and evidence suggests that how they perceive, construe, and experience psychotherapy affects outcome (Bohart & Wade, 2013). Therefore, the client as a source of evidence in case formulation is critical. Evidence from the client includes (a) the client's view of what or who is responsible for his or her problems, (b) the client's perception of the relationship with the therapist, (c) direct feedback when a formulation is offered by the therapist, (d) narratives the client tells that either confirm or disconfirm an explanatory hypothesis, (e) dreams or fantasies revealed in therapy, (f) changes in the client's symptoms based on interventions consistent with the formulation, and (g) autobiographical information the client discloses. Although the client is a crucial source of information to refine and revise the formulation, the therapist should attempt to understand the material in the context of the scientific evidence base in psychology. Further, a client's account of historical events will be biased by memory-recall effects, mood, suggestion, and the passage of time.

Psychometrics

As discussed in Chapter 1, psychometric information can inform case formulation. Structured interviews, personality inventories, and brief self-rated and therapist-rated measures provide incremental validity regarding diagnosis, assessment of psychopathology and personality, and prediction of behavior, although the contribution to case formulation validity itself is largely unexplored (Garb, 2003). Symptom rating scales provide a time-efficient, reliable, and valid way of assessing the range of problems, current level of general distress, red flag issues (e.g., dangerousness), and social and adaptive functioning (A. T. Beck et al., 1961, 1988; Derogatis, 1983; Halstead et al., 2008; Kuyken et al., 2009; Lambert & Finch, 1999; Persons, 2008). Further, comprehensive personality tests such as the Minnesota

Multiphasic Personality Inventory or the Personality Assessment Inventory can provide useful information for case formulation that allows the therapist to compare the client's responses against a standardization sample. Interview-based measures can also be helpful; for example, the Structured Clinical Interview for *DSM* Disorders (SCID; First, Spitzer, Gibbon, & Williams, 1995; Spitzer, Williams, Gibbon, & First, 1992).

Psychotherapy Process and Outcome Research

Psychotherapy is a highly researched practice, with an estimated 30,000 academic papers published in the past 30 years (Lambert, 2013b). Psychotherapy models investigated in efficacy studies contain implicit mechanisms of change and, thus, implicit case formulations. Since these implicit formulations are linked to outcome data, they can be useful starting points for individual formulations. Persons (2008) recommended that these implicit case formulations within empirically supported treatments serve as default nomothetic formulations that may then be tailored for individual clients. One should be cautioned, however, that little is known about these presumed mechanisms. Kazdin (2007) observed that although cognitive–behavioral therapy is effective for depression, evidence suggests that symptom change occurs before a change in cognition, which runs counter to the model's assumption that a change in cognition will lead to a change in symptoms. Improving our understanding of the processes involved in helping individuals with specific problems and diagnoses will be important for case formulation. As Kazdin (2008) wrote, "Evidence-based mechanisms of change could prove to be even more interesting or important than EBTs [evidence-based treatments]. We might be able to use multiple interventions to activate similar mechanisms once we know the mechanisms of change and learn how to optimize their use" (p. 152).

Psychopathology Research

Beyond psychotherapy research itself, findings in the biological, social, and behavioral sciences are also relevant to explaining problems presented in psychotherapy. For example, research on psychopathological processes is relevant to case formulation. The more we understand the predictors of psychopathology and the mechanisms that underlie, precipitate, and maintain these conditions, the better we can plan treatment for them. One example is the role of rumination in depression (Nolen-Hoeksema, Wisco, & Lyubomirsky, 2008). *Rumination* as a thinking process is characterized by a perseverative, passive, and nonproductive fixation on symptoms of distress and the possible causes and consequences of the distress, but without any active attempt at problem solving. Nolen-Hoeksema and colleagues (2008) demonstrated that rumination exacerbates depression, enhances negative thinking, impairs problem solving, erodes social support, and interrupts instrumental behavior. Rumination predicts the onset of depression, may contribute to its course, and may also contribute to disorders such as anxiety, posttraumatic stress disorder, binge-eating, binge-drinking, self-harm, and maladaptive grief reactions. These researchers have also investigated methods to combat rumination, such as distraction and increasing awareness of its nonproductive and negative function. This research can inform case formulation and treatment planning. It helps the therapist recognize the seductive but deceptive nature of rumination as a phenomenon that gives the appearance of solving problems when in reality it is a problem in itself. Other examples include research on anxiety (Mineka & Zinbarg, 2006), on adverse effects of repressive coping on subjective well-being (DeNeve & Cooper, 1998), and on the function of psychotic symptoms (Freeman, Bentall, & Garety, 2008).

Epidemiology

Epidemiology is the study of "how disease is distributed in populations and of the factors that influence or determine its distribution" (Gordis, 1990, p. 3). It includes the study of the causes of disease, including mental disorders, and associated risk factors, the extent of disease in a population, and the natural history and prognosis of disease.

While epidemiology focuses on populations not individuals, it is an underused resource in case formulation and can inform the process in a number of ways. First, it sensitizes the therapist to how psychological conditions are predicted by factors such as socioeconomic status, general disease status, and neighborhood safety. Epidemiology helps the therapist understand what is normative in a community, culture, or subgroup about age of onset, gender, ethnicity, and other characteristics. Such normative information contextualizes a client's clinical presentation and facilitates the development of explanatory mechanisms. Second, epidemiology helps with prognosis. Knowing the natural course of disorders such as depression (Kessler & Wang, 2009; Wells, Burnam, Rogers, Hays, & Camp, 1992) or alcoholism (Vaillant, 1995) helps predict risk and shape treatment. Third, epidemiology helps predict comorbidity. Knowing that alcohol abuse commonly co-occurs with social anxiety (Randall, Book, Carrigan, & Thomas, 2008), for example, can lead the therapist to thoroughly assess substance abuse in a socially anxious individual. Fourth, information about prevalence and incidence helps predict sources of problems. As discussed in Chapter 2, evaluating a client who believes she is a victim of ritualistic abuse is helped by knowing, even imperfectly, that the prevalence of such activity is extremely low (Frankfurter, 2006). Tarrier and Calam (2002) noted that causal inferences in case formulation are more credible when based on epidemiological data relevant to base rates associated with the development of a disorder rather than the client's retrospective recall of life events. The latter form of inference risks tautology and is subject to error in retrospective recall. Fifth, epidemiological data can help the therapist assess risk factors a client faces. For example, knowledge of the relative risk factors for suicide attempts and suicide gestures can inform a case formulation and treatment plan (Nock & Kessler, 2006). Explaining the risk of heart disease and diet, for example, can be part of treatment for obesity. Similarly, knowledge of the benefits of exercise, derived from epidemiology research, combined with a therapist's skill in developing behavioral plans, can combine to treat obesity.

Behavioral Genetics

Behavioral genetics research has been cited as among the major contributions of psychology to our understanding of psychopathology. Behavior genetics seeks to understand the etiology of traits and psychological disorders by disentangling the influence of genetic and environmental causes (Waldman, 2007). Behavioral genetics researchers study families, adoptees, and twins, the latter being the strongest methodologically. Twin study designs typically compare identical (monozygotic) twins with fraternal (dizygotic) twins. Since both are raised in substantially similar environments, but the former share identical genetics and the latter share half their genetics, differences between the two groups of twins are attributed to environmental causes. Heritability is a particularly useful concept to consider. It refers to the proportion of variance in a condition that is due to genetic differences among individuals in the population. For example, twin studies have revealed significant heritability in multiple disorders, including schizophrenia (.48), major depression (.43), bipolar disorder (.55), generalized anxiety disorder (.00–.20), antisocial personality disorder (.50–.60), and attention-deficit/hyperactivity disorder (.70–.76; Plomin, DeFries, Knopik, & Neiderhiser, 2013). While heritability says little about the malleability of a trait through behavioral intervention, it is nevertheless useful in case formulation to know that genetics may be playing a strong role in a client's clinical presentation. It is useful for the explanatory hypothesis and for treatment planning.

Genetics research also helps understand comorbidity. It suggests, for example, that several common disorders may be better understood in two broad categories of disorder, internalizing and externalizing, than in terms of their current symptom-based diagnostic classifications (Kendler, Prescott, Myers, & Neale, 2003). *Internalizing* disorders include major depression, generalized anxiety, panic disorder, and phobias. *Externalizing* disorders include antisocial disorder, conduct disorder in children, and substance abuse and dependence disorders. Environmental influences may affect which disorders within each broad cluster are most at risk of developing. This finding is relevant to case formulation because it informs the therapist of disorders a client might be vulnerable to developing.

A study of monozygotic twins suggests that while symptoms of anxiety and depression are stable in populations over time, the role of genetics in maintaining that stability appears strongest in childhood and adolescence, less so in early and mid-adulthood, and then stronger again in late adulthood (Kendler et al., 2011). Environmental vulnerability to anxiety and depression may therefore change over time. For example, early environmental adversity could lead individuals to make poor relationship choices that lead in turn to increased vulnerability to psychopathology in midlife that stabilizes later. The finding also suggests that interventions that lead to cumulatively more positive environmental conditions could reduce vulnerability to depression or anxiety. This has clear impact on case formulation since it can influence both the explanatory hypothesis and choice of interventions.

The six sources of evidence and the four basic theories of psychotherapy just reviewed comprise a broad base of knowledge and theory to draw upon when developing an explanatory hypothesis. The following section presents five steps to help the therapist complete this key portion of the formulation.

STEPS TO DEVELOP AN EXPLANATORY HYPOTHESIS

The five steps discussed in this section are based on a review of the literature on case formulation and represent common threads through many of these approaches. The steps are as follows: (a) identify precipitants, (b) identify origins, (c) identify resources, (d) identify obstacles, and (e) state core hypothesis. As each step is described, it is illustrated using the case of Rochelle.

Identify Precipitants

Precipitants are the triggers of symptoms and problems. There are two classes of precipitants to consider. First, are those that trigger the onset of the episode for which the client is seeking treatment. It could be a life event or stressor, such as a move to a new environment, a relationship change, a change in work status, an injury or illness, or stopping medications against medical advice. These are the stressors in the diathesis–stress paradigm discussed earlier. Stressors of this type often precipitate a decision to enter psychotherapy. It is always a good idea to ask early in therapy what occurred in the client's life that led to the decision to seek therapy.

A second type of precipitant is an event that marks a state shift, either in a therapy session or out. Shifts in state of mind may predict the emergence of emotion-laden topics of discussion (Horowitz, Ewert, & Milbrath, 1996; Horowitz, Milbrath, Ewert, Sonneborn, & Stinson, 1994; Horowitz, Milbrath, Jordan, Stinson, et al., 1994). Luborsky (1996) found that symptom onset in therapy can sometimes be explained by the emergence of the client's previously identified core conflictual relationship theme. Precipitants to problematic states and events that occur outside of therapy are also useful in case formulation. When a client reports a problem, it is helpful to ask about a specific episode or example of the problem and consider what triggered the upset.

An examination of precipitants contributes to case formulation in several ways. It informs the therapist about vulnerabilities and coping resources. It reveals problems, suggests goals and motivators, and also hints at mechanisms that explain the problems. In sum, it is helpful both to identify the events that triggered the onset of problems leading to therapy, and the more episodic events that trigger problematic behavior and cognitive-emotional states during the course of psychotherapy and elsewhere in clients' lives.

Rochelle's Precipitants

Two precipitants appear to have triggered Rochelle's problems. These are learning about her husband's suspected infidelity, and stress caused by anticipating adverse financial consequences of her sister-in-law moving out. Her tears and expressions of anger about her husband suggest possible affect regulation problems. Further, her poorly controlled diabetes and apparent lack of a strong interpersonal support system may have damaged her ability to cope with these precipitating events.

Identify Origins

As Tully and Goodman (2007) wrote, "Psychopathology does not typically appear suddenly but, rather, emerges gradually through the course of development" (p. 313). For this reason, it is important to consider the origins of clients' problems. *Origins* are the predisposing experiences, events, traumas, stressors, and risk factors that are inferred as causally related to the development of current problems. Causality can be direct or contributory. Examples of directly causal events might include divorce, death of a loved one, heart surgery leading to depression, self-neglect, and absence of positive reinforcement from others. Contributory causality refers to events that have established conditions that increase vulnerability to the development of the problem. These may include poor relationship choices leading to a lack of social support, lack of education, underemployment, poor early life role modeling, and lack of social skill development. It is well established that the greater the number of risk factors and stressors that an individual has faced, including maladaptive attachment relationships, the more likely the individual is to develop problems later (Dozier et al., 2008; Garmezy, Masten, & Tellegen, 1984). When considering origins, it is useful to look both proximally and distally. Proximal origins are events occurring relatively recently, say within the previous year or two, that have led directly or contributed to onset of the problems. Distal origins are earlier life events or traumas that may be influencing current problems. Attending to different theoretical orientations can also influence identification of origins. From the cognitive–behavioral standpoint, one might look for invalidating environments, and origins of views of self, others, and the world. From the behavioral standpoint, one might look for stimulus control in experienced environments and contingencies of reinforcement that shaped behavior. From the dynamic standpoint, one might look for traumas, frustrated wishes, abandonment, lack of empathy in caregivers, and the meaning ascribed to these events. From the humanistic/experiential point of view, one might look for lack of unconditional positive regard in early life and other events disrupting the self-actualizing tendency.

Consideration of origins has clear implications for case formulation. It reveals developmental pathways that may have led to current problems, as well as produced protective factors that can be marshaled to help treatment succeed. Knowledge of early relationship with parents or peers, criticism or social rejection, may help uncover core beliefs of being unlovable or unworthy, which can then form the foundation for interventions (Tully

& Goodman, 2007). Benjamin (1996a, 2003; Henry, 1997) proposed social-learning processes by which maladaptive early life relationships are "copied" to the present. One is *identification*, which involves acting like another through imitation. If in childhood one observed Dad withdrawing from Mom when she chronically complained about his behavior, doing the same in current life reflects identification with Dad. In a variation of identification, the client may identify with Mom and become a chronic complainer to others, potentially inducing them to withdraw just as Dad did. A second copy process is *introjection*, which is the process by which a child comes to act toward him or herself as he or she has been treated by others. If a parent is harshly critical, belittling, and invalidating toward the client as a child, the client as an adult may treat him or herself similarly. Interventions could then be developed to address these maladaptive concepts of self and other. Wordsworth captured the idea that early life experiences provide a model for later experiences in his poem "My Heart Leaps Up": "The Child is father of the Man" (Wordsworth, 1807).

Origins of Rochelle's Problems

From the behavioral standpoint, Rochelle's depressed mood may have been established by the absence of positive reinforcers that led to the extinction of healthy behavior sequences. She may have acquired her anxiety and panic through classical conditioning mechanisms and maintains them through operant conditioning. The rape could have functioned as an unconditioned stimulus that elicited fear that has now generalized. The anxiety is maintained though avoidance of potentially anxiety arousing experiences and escape, either through acting out or interpersonal withdrawal.

Alternatively, one could view the origins of Rochelle's problems as follows: Rochelle was born with a biological propensity toward emotional reactivity and raised in an invalidating environment. The rape exacerbated views of the world as harsh, punishing, and unforgiving. Rochelle learned to invalidate her own experiences, and thus chooses inappropriate partners, makes destructive and self-neglecting choices, feels hopeless and powerless, and is subject to bouts of depression, anxiety, panic, and multiple psychosomatic symptoms.

Identify Resources

Resources are the strengths a client brings to therapy that facilitate recovery. Resources may be of two general types: internal and external. *Internal* resources are qualities, skills, and abilities the client possesses. These can be quite broad. For example, Kuyken, Padesky, and Dudley (2009) described a depressed client who enjoyed gardening and used this pastime to distract himself from unpleasant automatic thoughts and a sad mood. Another client had a talent for working with aggressive dogs, which the therapist used to help the client extend that ability to problem areas. Beside hobbies and work skills, resources may include intelligence; ability to initiate (if not sustain) relationships; adaptive defenses and coping mechanisms, such as humor, empathy, forbearance, and toleration of ambiguity; and good education, psychological mindedness, good premorbid functioning, and motivation to improve. *External* resources are all the circumstances in the client's life that facilitate recovery. Examples include a strong family and friend support network, ability to transport oneself to treatment, strong network of health care providers, financial resources, and availability of community services. Kuyken and colleagues noted that strengths may not be apparent to clients and advise that therapists ask about areas of life that are going well in order to identify these strengths.

Rochelle's Resources

Despite Rochelle's significant problems in multiple spheres of life, several resources were identified. She has 2 years of college education, which increases her employability. Also, she has some financial resources in that she co-owns a home. She forms relationships easily and appears to have the capacity to be close to her friends. She also expressed motivation for treatment.

Identify Obstacles

Obstacles are those aspects of the client's life that may interfere with treatment success. It is important to anticipate these and plan how to counter them should they arise. As with resources, they may be categorized as residing within the client and as external to the client. Regarding internal obstacles, the major consideration is maladaptive coping and defense mechanisms. Defense mechanisms are unconscious mental processes that enable us to cope with distressing information by distorting it in some way. Horowitz (Horowitz & Eells, 2007) expanded the list of Freudian defense mechanisms to what he calls control processes of ideas and affect, which have both adaptive and maladaptive components. If maladaptive control processes are not managed skillfully, therapy progress may be limited. Some involve control of mental set, which means the readiness of the individual to do the cognitive and affective processing needed for therapy. Examples are intentional "forgetting," continual focus on crises, numbing, somnolence, and distractibility (in the absence of attention-deficit disorder). One client, a well-educated man in his mid-40s whose wife had just left him, was devastated by and furious at her decision. He had considerable difficulty managing his mental set in therapy. He continually threatened suicide, which prevented us from discussing how he would manage without his wife. Further, whenever we broached the topic of his rage toward his wife he suddenly became sleepy. The threats of suicide were successfully addressed by suggesting to him that he was metaphorically waving a stick of dynamite in therapy each week, threatening to blow himself up, and by doing so, we could not make progress. The somnolence was addressed over time by pointing out the connection between the topic of discussion and his sudden onset of somnolence. Horowitz et al. (1993) conducted an intensive examination of a man with adjustment disorder related to grief and generalized anxiety disorder and measured both heightened level of defensiveness and emotionality when critical therapy topics related to the client's core relationship conflicts were discussed. For further discussion of control processes, see Horowitz (2005) or Horowitz and Eells (2007).

Other theoretical perspectives offer alternative ways of identifying defensive and coping mechanisms. These include cognitive distortions (A. T. Beck, 1963; J. S. Beck, 1995) and safety behaviors (Behar & Borkovec, 2006; Ehlers & Clark, 2000; Salkovskis, 1996). The latter serve only short-term, palliative functions of minimizing anxiety but at the cost of preventing disconfirmation of feared beliefs or exposure to experiences that may lead to extinction of anxiety symptoms. Another example of obstacles are therapy-interfering events, which are behaviors that undermine therapy, such as not coming for sessions, coming late, or always coming with an urgent crisis that precludes exploration of patterns leading to symptoms.

External obstacles may be the inability to attend therapy due to financial constraints, poor transportation, or family members who do not want the client to seek psychotherapy. In addition, the therapist may inadvertently become an obstacle due to inadequate training in a particular form of therapy, empathic failure, nonresponsiveness, countertransference, subtle hostility and rejection, and similar maladaptive responses.

Rochelle's Obstacles

The following were identified as the major obstacles in the case of Rochelle: She missed a session; she is sanctioned by a controlling husband for leaving home, which may prevent her from coming to treatment; financial dependency; and possible intolerance of affect in therapy.

State the Core Hypothesis

The *core hypothesis* is a brief statement of the central mechanism that is generating problems. In what follows, I present a series of explanatory templates to aid in developing the core hypothesis. The advantage of a template is that it provides a succinct distillation of many rich ideas. An explanatory template is useful in rapidly considering several perspectives through which to understand the client's problems. The templates described in this chapter are drawn from well-established theories of psychotherapy. They are not intended to be exhaustive or comprehensive, or to be entirely independent of each other, but rather to represent the range of empirically supported theories of psychotherapy. The assumption throughout this chapter is that expert development of an explanatory hypothesis requires the acquisition of a broad and deep understanding of research and theory related to psychotherapy process and outcome, psychopathology, human development, and cognitive science. The intent in presenting the templates is a pragmatic one: to distill the essential explanatory propositions of these approaches in order to facilitate hypothesis generation in psychotherapy case formulation. Of necessity, the templates are extractions from their more fully developed theoretical contexts. The templates are: (a) diathesis–stress; (b) wish–fear–compromise; (c) representations of self, others, and relationships; (d) cognitive appraisals; (e) functional analysis of behavior; and (f) deficits of emotional awareness. Variations of some of these will be described. In considering these explanatory templates, keep in mind evidence that both supports and fails to support each one. It may be helpful to develop alternative explanations of your clients' problems using multiple templates, then choose which one is the most cogent, compelling, and likely to lead to a successful outcome.

Template 1: Diathesis–Stress

As described earlier in this chapter, the diathesis–stress model of psychopathology is enduring, overarching, and quintessentially integrative. For this reason, it is a good initial explanatory template to use. The template involves listing the client's diatheses and stressors, noting those that seem most critical, and noting the client's appraisal of the stressors. The exercise gives the therapist an initial explanation, which is that the combination of stress and diathesis/es were sufficient to produce the symptoms and problems. Treatment would then focus on relieving stress and/or increasing resilience to stress. In the longer term, treatment would focus on addressing diatheses that are amenable to change. This template can also be viewed as an initial identification of explanatory themes that may be further elaborated through the lens of other templates.

Diatheses to have in mind are genetic, biological, constitutional, or temperamental risk factors of psychopathology. Consider whether biological relatives have mental illness and if so, how genetically close those individuals are to the client. Consider traumatic early life experiences and problematic attachment relationships. Also consider dysfunctional axiomatic beliefs about the self, others, the future, and the world. These might include core beliefs about unlovability, hopelessness, the world being fundamentally threatening and unsafe, or a view of life as existentially pointless. Other considerations are developmental/learning deficits and whether the individual was raised in a developmentally and educationally deprived environment.

In terms of current stressors, look for recent major life-changing events, whether positive or negative, as well as a large number of daily hassles. Domains in life to examine are those discussed in the chapter on problem identification. These include school/work, family and social life, medical problems in self or loved ones, and acculturative stress. In particular, look for divorce or other changes in marital status, recent deaths, significant changes in life circumstances, moves either of self or significant others, changes in employment status, recent life threatening events or potentially life threatening events toward the self or others, and similar major life events. Consider as well the cumulative effect of multiple daily hassles. Common daily hassles were listed earlier in the chapter. Consult the Daily Hassles Scale for a longer list and consider having the client complete it (Holm & Holroyd, 1992).

Diathesis–Stress Explanation of Rochelle's Problems. The following potential diatheses were identified for Rochelle: high emotionally reactive temperament, a view of the world and men as dangerous and threatening stemming from her rape as a teenager, a view of the world as unstable and unpredictable stemming from her lack of stable caretaking as a child and the death of her firstborn son, and vulnerability to depression and anxiety due to diabetes. It was also noted that Rochelle was plagued by appraisals of her life circumstance as hopeless. Stressors identified were as follows: controlling, potentially unfaithful husband with chemical dependence; financial uncertainty; crowded housing conditions; single parenthood; and marginal social support.

Template 2: Wish–Fear–Compromise

The wish–fear–compromise template is based on the assumption that the mind comprises multiple and largely unconscious and conflicting forces. The idea is also based on the commonly accepted assumption that people are motivated to maximize pleasurable experiences and minimize adverse ones. In psychotherapy the idea is rooted most directly in psychodynamic thought (Messer & Wolitzky, 2007), although it can also be traced to multiple philosophical and literary sources (Ellenberger, 1970; Haidt, 2006). The core idea is that symptoms develop as compromise formations when a wish has both desired and undesired consequences. For example, a client may wish to be loved but fear intimacy and thus compromise by settling for nonintimate friendships but consequently become chronically anxious because neither the basic wish nor the fear is mastered. Or a client may wish independence but fear abandonment and then panic upon separation from loved ones; later, a compromise may be to develop counterdependent relationships, perhaps in a hostile-dependent or codependent form.

Variations in this template might also be contemplated. These include wish–wish and fear–fear conflicts. Sometimes wishes conflict with other wishes and fears conflict with other fears, leading to a compromise between these impulses. A client may wish to have an intimate relationship and also wish independence and see these two as in conflict, resulting in psychological symptoms and relationship disturbance. Another client may fear competing with others but also fear failure, which could lead to oscillations between extremes of self-assertion and withdrawal, or immobility in achieving goals. As can be seen, ambivalence is a core feature of the wish-fear-compromise explanatory template and its variations.

Wish–Fear–Compromise Explanation of Rochelle's Problems. Applying the wish-fear-compromise template to Rochelle, the following was developed: Rochelle's major conflict is between a wish to be autonomous, free, and loved, and a fear of abandonment if she allows herself to trust and be genuinely intimate with a loving partner. In addition, an alternate wish was identified, which is to be dependent upon and taken care of by another, abandoning any claim of autonomy. Her compromises for these wish–fear and wish–wish dilemmas are an inability to assert herself with her husband, resentment of her dependence, the onset of an agitated depression, and playing an angry but submissive role in close relationships.

Template 3: Representations of Self, Others, and Relationships

Template 3 shares features of the wish–fear–compromise template but adds the concept of mental representations of self, others, and self-in-relationship-with-other. It has similar origins as Template 1, but with the addition of contributions from object relations theory in psychodynamic psychology (Kernberg, 1975; Kernberg, Selzer, Koenigsberg, Carr, & Appelbaum, 1989; Kohut, 1971, 1977), the self-schema concept from social cognition theory (Baldwin, 1992; Markus & Wurf, 1987; Singer & Salovey, 1991), and the concept of internal working models and other ideas from attachment theory (Bowlby, 1969, 1979; Bretherton & Munholland, 2008). These theories assume that forming and maintaining attachments with others is a fundamental human need to ensure a sense of safety, and that disturbances in early caretaking relationships sow the seeds for disturbed relationships and maladaptive concepts of self and other later in life.

Central to Template 3 is the concept of multiple internal working models, or schemas, of self and others. These mental representations are "organized, feature-linking, enduring, slowly changing, and generalized knowledge structures about people" (Horowitz, Eells, Singer, & Salovey, 1995, p. 626). Schemas include internalized transactional sequences that coordinate perception, thought, emotion, and action. Social psychologist Jonathan Haidt (2006) captured the idea of multiple mental representations of self:

> We assume that there is one person in each body, but in some ways we are each more like a committee whose members have been thrown together to do a job, but who often find themselves working at cross purposes. (pp. 4–5)

The notion is also captured by Shakespeare in *As You Like It:* "All the world's a stage, / And all the men and women merely players; / They have their exits and their entrances, / And one man in his time plays many parts." As in Shakespeare's play, different aspects of self and others take the stage in organizing experience at different points in time, and these parts are not necessarily mutually compatible or internally consistent.

Several structured models of psychotherapy case formulation can be understood in terms of Template 3. These include Luborsky's core conflictual relationship theme (CCRT; Luborsky, 1977; Luborsky & Barrett, 2007), Horowitz's role relationship models configuration (Horowitz & Eells, 2007; Horowitz, Eells, et al., 1995), Silberschatz and Curtis's plan formulation method (Curtis & Silberschatz, 2007; Silberschatz, 2005b), the cognitive analytic therapy case formulation model (Ryle, 1990; Ryle & Bennett, 1997), the cyclical maladaptive patterns approach (Binder, 2004; Levenson & Strupp, 2007; Strupp & Binder, 1984), and structured analysis of social behavior (Benjamin, 2003). Of these, the most researched and perhaps simplest is the CCRT. It involves three components: a wish of the self, a response of the other, and a response of the self. The CCRT is identified by listening to the person's relationship narratives in therapy. From these narratives, the therapist identifies the client's most common interpersonal wishes, the expected responses of others to those wishes, and the responses of the self to the expected responses from others. The CCRT is the most frequent of these wishes and responses.

Early in therapy, Rochelle told three stories about her relationships with others. In the first, she related how she bought her husband his favorite beer, knowing he'd be having friends to the house to watch sports on television, but he made no comment about her gesture. In the second story, she described how, when she was employed, she went out of her way to please her supervisor at work but never got a word of thanks. In the third narrative, she described planning and giving a birthday party for her daughter, with no sign of appreciation afterward. Based on these three narratives, the therapist formulated the following core conflictual relationship theme:

- *Wish of self:* To please others and to be seen and appreciated
- *Response of others*: Ignore
- *Response of self*: Feel dejected, withdraw, become depressed, or become angry

To generate an explanation using Template 3, readers are advised to learn one of the structured case formulation methods cited above, each of which is rich in detail beyond what space here allows for description. Short of that, listen closely to the narratives a client tells and infer schemas and scripts from them. Listen for narratives that lead to distressed states of mind, paying particular attention to the way the client understands self, others, and relationships. Recognize that the client may host a cast of actors who vary in how they view the self and others. To further aid in developing formulations from the perspective of Template 3, three variations are offered.

The first variation of Template 3 is based on Benjamin's (1993b, 2003) construction of psychopathology, which is captured in the phrase "Every psychopathology is a gift of love." This is Benjamin's formulation of the core problem in treatment-resistant clients with major interpersonal relationship problems and persistent symptoms. According to Benjamin, these patterns are driven by dimly understood and destructive primary attachments to early caretakers, characterized by love and loyalty to those figures. She claims that even ostensibly hostile feelings toward the caretaker disguise underlying love. Through a process of social learning mediated by temperament, clients learn to treat themselves and others as they were treated by the primary attachment figure, and may also respond to others as they responded to that caregiver. In effect, the client says to the attachment figure, "My problems are how I show my love and loyalty to you." Psychotherapy that leads to a change in underlying personality structure requires that these patterns be identified and understood, which is where case formulation is essential, and that the client becomes open to learning new patterns.

The second variation of Template 3 is based on Weiss's (1990, 1993; see also Curtis & Silberschatz, 2007; Silberschatz, 2005b) control master theory, which asserts that psychopathology stems from powerful, unconscious, emotion-laden, threatening, and emotionally distressing "pathogenic beliefs" originating in traumatic childhood experiences. These beliefs tend to focus on bearing excessive responsibility for the happiness of others, leading to guilt that is largely or entirely out of awareness and that prevents the client from achieving independence, greater happiness, or greater success than their parents or siblings. Burdened by these pathogenic beliefs, individuals develop an adaptive and usually unconscious "plan" to disconfirm them. In an attempt to disconfirm the pathogenic belief, clients test their therapists. They may miss an appointment, come late, or discuss termination to test whether the therapist feels abandoned as the client imagines the attachment figure would feel. In sum, the core idea is that clients use therapy to disconfirm their pathogenic beliefs.

The third variation of Template 3 is captured by the Kohutian idea of mirroring versus idealizing selfobjects, and the good/bad self/other. Case formulation explanations from the self-psychology perspective emphasize explanations of disturbances in a cohesive sense of self due to failures of empathic responsiveness from caretakers. Look for these relationships in how the client treats you as the therapist as either an idealized or a mirroring selfobject. From the object relations standpoint, look for clients who dichotomize mental representations as "all good" or "all bad," and label others, including you as therapist, as one or the other.

Representations of Self, Others, and Relationships Explanation of Rochelle's Problems. Rochelle's CCRT was described earlier. Expanding beyond it, her problems could be explained as follows based on Template 3: Rochelle's major conflict is between a wish to be, on the one hand, loved, autonomous, and free, and on the other hand, to be loved by and dependent upon another. She has not developed a secure and positive sense of self and consequently looks to others for guidance. She dichotomizes others as loving or as betraying; thus, she resents her dependence while fearing abandonment, which leaves her emotionally deprived. She is plagued by guilt that she has let others down. Her anxiety, depression, and somatization flow from these conflicts.

Template 4: Cognitive Appraisals

Template 4 is drawn from the cognitive school of therapy, which as described earlier, focuses on how clients construe events in their lives rather than on the events themselves. The "cognitive model . . . hypothesizes that people's emotions and behaviors are influenced by their perception of events" (J. S. Beck, 1995, p. 14). From this standpoint, the therapist asks two questions: (a) What dysfunctional thoughts and beliefs are associated with the client's problems and diagnosis? and (b) How does the client respond emotionally, physiologically, and behaviorally to those thoughts and beliefs? The answers to these questions are sought by examining early learnings and experiences, underlying beliefs, coping style, and stressors. The core of the cognitive formulation is called the *working hypothesis* (Persons, 2008; Wright, Basco, & Thase, 2006), which is a brief summary of answers to the above questions that evolves as therapy unfolds. The primary components of the working hypothesis are the client's automatic thoughts, intermediate thoughts, and core beliefs or schemas (J. S. Beck, 1995). Template 4, therefore, involves identifying these components. As described earlier, automatic thoughts are rapid, brief, evaluative thoughts that are situational and occur so effortlessly that one may hardly be aware of them. They are associated with emotional, behavioral, and physiological reactions that may include psychological signs, symptoms, and problems in living. Examples are "Mary hasn't texted me back, so she must be angry at me," "I'll never get through all this work," and "I am surely going to lose it when I give my speech to the class." Core beliefs are fundamental and well-ingrained understandings about oneself, others, and the world. They are often not articulated, but they are the lenses through which the world is viewed and interpreted; they are the most fundamental level of belief, and tend to be global, rigid, and overgeneralized. Examples are "I am unlovable," "Everybody must love me," "I am defective and the future is hopeless," "Nothing will ever change," and "The world is dangerous, threatening, and chaotic." Between automatic thoughts and core beliefs lie "intermediate" beliefs. These are rules, attitudes, and assumptions that are generated by core beliefs and gain expression in automatic thoughts. Examples include "If you're not in a relationship, you are a failure," "If I let myself feel a little emotion, I will completely lose control," "If people don't immediately respond to my requests, I am being disrespected," "I must always be working and trying my best," and "I must end relationships before others end them with me." Intermediate beliefs also include maladaptive coping responses. Examples include "I will avoid all anxiety arousing situations," "Alcohol will help me get through this social event," and "I must always remain in control or something terrible will happen."

In addition to the central cognitive appraisal template just described, several variations have been developed for specific disorders. These include cognitive models of depression (A. T. Beck et al., 1979), anxiety (A. T. Beck et al., 1985; Clark & Wells, 1995; Ehlers & Clark, 2000), personality disorders (A. T. Beck et al., 2004), and substance abuse (A. T. Beck, Wright, Newman, & Liese, 1993), as well as integrative models that include a strong cognitive component (e.g., Young, 1990; Young et al., 2003). One specific example is Ehlers and Clark's (2000) cognitive model of post-traumatic stress disorder (PTSD). These authors proposed that PTSD becomes persistent when cognitive processing leads to a sense of serious, current threat. The feeling of threat is a consequence of two factors. The first is highly negative appraisals of the trauma and events following it (e.g., "I'm disaster prone," "Nowhere is safe," "I'm permanently damaged," "I'm dead inside," "Others think I'm weak"). The second is poor integration and contextualization of the trauma memory into autobiographic memory. The trauma memories are not marked well in time and place, such as before and after other events, and they are poorly elaborated. They are also characterized by the presence of strong associative memory linkages and perceptual priming. For example, the child of a client with PTSD died accidentally of carbon monoxide poisoning when sleeping in the hull of a boat near the client. Later, the client developed a violent reaction to the smell of gasoline, which had come to be associated with traumatic memories of her daughter's death. These two factors—negative appraisals related to the event and poor integration of the event into autobiographical memory—left the individual subject to intrusions and other re-experiencing symptoms, heightened arousal, anxiety, and other emotional responses. The sense of threat also motivates the individual to engage in *safety behaviors*, which are actions taken to prevent or minimize the threat. They may reduce the threat in the short term, but they have the adverse consequence of preventing cognitive change in the long term, and therefore they maintain the disorder. For example, safety behaviors prevent disconfirmation of the belief that the feared event will occur were it not for the safety behavior. For example, one client with PTSD slept every night just inside the front door to her house and kept a knife within reach in case an intruder tried to enter her home. Other safety behaviors cited by Ehlers and Clark are not talking about the event; intentional numbing of emotions; ruminating about how the event might have been avoided; avoiding reminders of the event, including locations such as the site of the event or the cemetery where a person or persons involved in the trauma are buried; carrying a weapon; giving up pleasant activities; avoiding people; not making plans for the future; and staying up late to avoid nightmares.

Cognitive Appraisal Explanation of Rochelle's Problems. Several automatic thoughts of Rochelle's were identified. These include "I can't survive alone," "I must have a partner," "I don't care if I die," "I must show strong emotion to get attention from others," and "No matter what I do it won't make a difference." Core beliefs identified were "I'm unlovable," "I'm helpless," and "The world is cruel and unfair." It is of note that these were balanced by a positive core belief: "I am a good person and able to defend myself and those I love." Intermediate assumptions, attitudes, and rules were "No matter what I do, it won't make a difference," an overgeneralization that "All men are untrustworthy," and a tendency to jump to conclusions by thinking, "If he comes home late, it means he's cheating on me." Finally, safety behaviors are the following: remain dependent on others, avoid friends, and don't get close to others for fear they will hurt or abandon you.

Template 5: Functional Analysis of Behavior

Template 5, or functional analysis, explains problems by analyzing the environment in which the problems occur and by identifying antecedent and consequent conditions that produce or maintain problematic behavior or that fail to produce more adaptive behavior. Principles of respondent conditioning apply primarily to conditions that elicit problematic behavior, whereas principles of operant condition apply more to the reinforcers, or consequences, of behavior. In either case, once target problems are identified, the therapist's role when applying the functional analysis template is to identify these antecedent and consequent events. The treatment plan then focuses on changing them. Note some functional analytic explanations combine respondent and operant principles, whereas others combine both cognitive and behavioral perspectives.

One place to begin a functional analysis is to follow Goldfried and Sprafkin's (1976) SORC model. Here, the task is to identify functional relationships among the antecedent stimuli (S); the biological, behavioral, cognitive, or sociocultural characteristics of the client, or organism (O); the target problem, or response (R); and the consequences (C) that flow from the response. Nezu, Nezu, and Lombardo (2004) suggested starting with the problematic response (R); then assessing what factors and conditions function as antecedents (S); then considering organismic mediators or moderators (O); and finally assessing the consequences (C), such as the intrapersonal, interpersonal, or environmental effects of the response. Similarly, a behavioral chain analysis can be conducted (Koerner, 2007; Linehan, 1993). This involves developing a step-by-step description of the sequence of events leading up to and following the problem behavior.

A second consideration in a functional analysis is the *establishing operation* of problem behavior (Keller & Schoenfeld, 1950; Michael, 2000). This term refers to variables that alter the effectiveness of reinforcement; for example, the client's habitual state of deprivation or satiation when engaging in the target behavior. A client may be "starved" for love, affection, and validation, and thus the attention, empathy, and availability of the therapist may serve as powerful reinforcers that can serve the purposes of therapy. Alternatively, a client with panic disorder, posttraumatic disorder, or generalized anxiety may present in such a physiologically aroused and overstimulated state, so "satiated" with stimuli, that ordinary reinforcers are overwhelming.

A third consideration in a functional analysis is to assess whether the problem behavior is under stimulus control. *Stimulus control* refers to conditions in the environment that by their mere presence shape behavior (operant conditioning) or evoke a powerful association (respondent conditioning). For example, the smell of cigarette smoke may prompt an individual trying to quit smoking to have a cigarette nevertheless. Similarly, the sights and smells from walking into an all-you-can-eat buffet may overwhelm the best intentioned dieter. Conceptualizations involving stimulus control have been used to treat insomnia (Morin et al., 2006), substance abuse (Antony & Roemer, 2011), inability to relax (Sturmey, 2008), and

STEP 3: DEVELOP AN EXPLANATORY HYPOTHESIS

excessive worry in those with generalized anxiety disorder (Behar & Borkovec, 2006). To illustrate in the case of worry, the conceptualization is that chronic worry has many environmental triggers and thus is under broad stimulus control. Instructing the client to "schedule worry time" each day at a particular time and place helps bring worry under better stimulus control.

A fourth consideration in functional analysis, one based on operant principles, is to analyze contingencies of reinforcement, since reinforcement patterns predict patterns of responding. Sturmey (2008) suggested the therapist consider what schedules of reinforcement are present in the client's life, how often and with what regularity reinforcement occurs, why current contingencies do not support adaptive behavior, and whether contingencies that once supported adaptive behavior are now absent. For example, as discussed in Chapter 1, Lewinsohn (1974; Lewinsohn & Shaffer, 1971; Lewinsohn et al., 1987) found that a low rate of positive reinforcement is an antecedent to depression and that increased positive reinforcement helps relieve depression. In other words, low rates of desired behavior indicated reinforcement schedules that were ineffective or even punishing. A therapist observing high rates of behavior, such as anger outbursts in marital conflict, might infer a variable ratio schedule of reinforcement since that schedule results in high rates of responding. This could describe an interaction pattern in which one partner escalates anger and irritability when experiencing the other as walling them off, only rarely and arbitrarily offering attention and responsiveness. To help the couple break the anger cycle, the therapist might prescribe a change in the couple's interactions to support affectionate and supportive behaviors. Couples therapy research has shown that frequent and mutual positive reinforcement patterns are associated with stronger relationships (Epstein & Baucom, 2002; Gottman & Silver, 1999).

A fifth consideration in functional analysis, one based on respondent conditioning, is to identify events that serve as the US, UR, CS, and the CR. The latter is usually the symptom or problem being targeted. To illustrate, Antony and Roemer (2011) described a client whose social anxiety appeared related to a history of high rates of criticism from her father. After criticizing her, he would turn his attention to other people or walk away, leaving her feeling anxious and uncertain. Later, she felt anxious and uncomfortable around others, expecting them to criticize her. Antony and Roemer's analysis was that the father's criticism served as a US that elicited her UR of fear. Later, the pattern was generalized, such that even innocuous behavior of others served as a CS that elicited a now conditioned response of fear, anxiety, and self-doubt. This example demonstrates that it is sometimes necessary when conducting a functional analysis to look for stimulus–response associations that may have been established years earlier. Further, in considering associations among stimuli and responses, note that ostensible exposure to a CS may not be what it appears to be. Behar and Borkovec (2006) hypothesized, for example, that generalized anxiety (CR) persists despite repeated exposure to anxiety-arousing stimuli (CS) because the client employs compensatory mechanisms that psychologically blunt full exposure to the CS; thus, extinction does not occur. Of further note is Bouton's (2002) literature review suggesting that extinction is context-specific and rarely permanent, an important consideration in treatment planning.

Functional Analysis of Behavior Explanation of Rochelle's Problems. This behavioral explanation of Rochelle's problems focuses on her depressed and anxious mood and her episodes of anger: Her depressed mood was established by the absence of positive reinforcers that led to the extinction of healthy behavior sequences. It is maintained through continued lack of reinforcement, by negative reinforcement (e.g., removal of responsibilities), and exacerbated by aversive consequences when, in a depressed state, she attempts but fails to succeed in reaching out to others. She acquired her anxiety and panic through respondent conditioning mechanisms and maintains them through operant conditioning. The rape functioned as a US that elicited fear that has now generalized. The anxiety is maintained though avoidance of potentially anxiety arousing experiences and escape, either through acting out or interpersonal withdrawal.

Template 6: Deficits of Emotional Awareness

This template explains problems in terms of a lack of emotional self-awareness. It grows from humanistic, gestalt, and emotion-focused approaches to psychotherapy (Perls et al., 1965; Rogers, 1951), currently well represented in the work of Leslie Greenberg (2002; Greenberg & Goldman, 2007; Greenberg & Watson, 2005; Watson, 2010). This is a strongly process-oriented approach to explaining problems; the therapist is constantly attending to the moment-by-moment experience of the client, trying to remain emotionally available and responsive to the client. It is consistent with the view that clients are driven by a self-actualizing tendency that has gone awry, and the task of the therapist is to aid the client in achieving greater emotional self-awareness and thus to actualize self development. In order to do so, the therapist strives to remain authentic, empathic, respectful, and accepting of the client.

The template involves first paying close attention to the client's style of processing emotion. Vocal qualities are noted, particularly whether the client is emotionally focused or external in focus. When focused, emotional energy is turned inward as the individual seeks to symbolize their experience in words. In contrast, an external voice is one that appears premonitored, rehearsed, and lacking in spontaneity, conveying a sense to the therapist of being "talked at." In observing how clients process emotion, particular attention is paid to the areas of greatest emotional pain. The therapist also attends to the client's poignancy, vividness of language, interruptions, and topic deflections.

A second step is to identify *task markers.* These are indications from the client of areas of unresolved cognitive–affective problems for which therapeutic interventions are warranted. Greenberg and Goldman (2007) listed the following task markers: (a) "problematic reactions expressed through puzzlement about emotional or behavioral responses to particular situations"; (b) "conflict splits in which one aspect of the self is critical or coercive toward another"; (c) "self-interruptive splits in which one part of the self interrupts or constricts emotional experience and expression"; (d) "an unclear felt sense in which the person is on the surface of, or feeling confused and unable to get, a clear sense of his or her experience"; (e) "unfinished business involving the statement of a lingering unresolved feeling toward a significant other"; and (f) "vulnerability in which the person feels deeply ashamed or insecure about some aspect of his or her experience" (p. 302). Treatment planning and interventions depend on the marker identified. For example, a two-chair enactment might be suggested for the second or third marker in the list above. Other interventions are systematic evocative unfolding, emotional focusing, and the empty-chair technique.

Third, as task markers are identified and worked on from session to session, intrapersonal and interpersonal themes tend to emerge that contribute to the client's emotional pain. Examples might be feelings of insecurity and worthlessness, unresolved anger, or feelings of neglect and abandonment. These themes tend to center on one of four areas: (a) an inability to symbolize internal experience, (b) conflict with different aspects of the self, (c) interpersonal conflict, or (d) existential concerns (Greenberg & Paivio, 1997). These themes provide continuity from session to session, although they tend to arise from what the client reports as his or her experience, rather than a theme initially suggested by the therapist.

Deficits of Emotional Awareness Explanation of Rochelle. Observations of Rochelle's emotional processing suggested that she had a forced quality to her emotional expression; sometimes she was quiet for prolonged periods of time. Episodes of explosive anger were not observed in sessions. She seemed to distance herself from close emotion and to lack awareness of her emotional needs. In terms of task markers, she was puzzled about why she reacted to some situations with such extreme emotion. It was also observed that she could be extremely self-castigating, but she also asserted her independence and strength in a way that seemed forced and with questionable conviction. She avoided talking about her son who died and about her rape experience. She seemed deeply ashamed of her lack of greater accomplishment in life. A pervasive theme seemed to be feelings of inferiority and being defective, as if she did not deserve more, but she also fought against these feelings.

CONCLUSION

A lot of material was covered in this chapter. In focusing on developing an explanatory hypothesis, I covered two major sources of information: theory and evidence. I centered hypothesis generation on the diathesis–stress model of psychopathology, which was proposed as a powerful and integrative framework from which to begin explaining a client's problems. In presenting steps to develop an explanatory framework, I discussed identifying precipitants, origins, resources, and obstacles as components to always consider. I then presented six core explanatory templates, which can be viewed from within a diathesis–stress framework: (a) a basic diathesis–stress explanation; (b) wish–fear–compromise; (c) representations of self, others, and relationships; (d) cognitive appraisals; (e) functional analysis of behavior; and (f) deficits of emotional awareness. These are not presented as exhaustive of all possible core explanations but as a representative range of current thinking among experts in psychotherapy.

Multiple possible explanations for Rochelle's problems were offered: frustrated wishes to be loved and nurtured, a conflict between independence and dependence, a primary focus on her behavior and how it is shaped by the environment. Another core explanation focused on automatic thoughts related to underlying feelings of unlovability and helplessness. Yet another examined problems in Rochelle's emotional life and her lack of a full repertoire of emotional processing that would allow her to engage more fully and meaningfully in life.

How does the therapist choose among these possible explanations? My recommendation is to take your lead from the client and consider more than one. It is useful to tentatively offer a core explanatory hypothesis and see how it fits with the client's experience and values. Consider each preferred explanation through the lens of the client's cultural identity and values, and consider available empirical evidence for the range of problems that will be addressed. Further, evaluate your own competence in delivering interventions based on your best conceptualization of the client. If you are lacking in needed skills, it would be appropriate to refer to a colleague who has the needed training. Finally, remember that explanatory hypotheses are just your best judgment on how to explain that client's problems. After testing it out in practice, and as you monitor progress, revise it as needed. Chapter 8 covers the last major step in case formulation: using everything you have learned so far to develop a treatment plan.

8

Step 4: Plan Treatment

Treatment planning links problems to interventions by way of the diagnosis and explanatory hypothesis. It involves the selection of strategies and tactics to address the problems chosen by the client and therapist for focus in the therapy. Planning orients the therapist to the action in therapy. It is central to the therapeutic alliance because it guides the tasks of therapy, and collaboration on tasks is a major alliance component (Bordin, 1979).

A good treatment plan contains at least seven characteristics. First, it should be developed collaboratively and be mutually acceptable to both the client and therapist. When possible, the therapist should explain remission and recovery rates for the proposed treatment, as well as the client's and therapist's roles.

A second characteristic is that a treatment plan should have sufficient detail to guide action. "Provide CBT" is too general. Better is "establish

http://dx.doi.org/10.1037/14667-009
Psychotherapy Case Formulation, by T. D. Eells

working alliance; explain treatment options and rationale for CBT; if client chooses CBT, identify and evaluate automatic thoughts, and teach relaxation skills to reduce anxiety." Better yet would be to identify and plan specific interventions to address the client's unique maladaptive thoughts and interpersonal style; for example, establish working alliance in light of client's need to defensively dominate relationships; encourage behavioral activation to reduce depression symptoms and remoralize; explore and examine evidence for client's view of self as unlovable and "not normal" and others as "together"; challenge automatic thoughts of worthlessness and self-blame; help client gain insight into basis for improved self-concept; teach thought stopping and distraction to reduce rumination; engage client in exercises to examine views of self and others.

Third, treatment should be planned within a realistic time frame and within the client's capabilities. If a client is cognitively impaired or possesses a limited capacity for psychological mindedness, then a treatment plan focused on self-reflection and increasing self-awareness is ill-advised.

Fourth, as discussed in more detail later, a treatment plan should articulate outcomes. Goal-setting theory suggests the effectiveness of setting goals that are specific, measurable, achievable, realistic, and timely (Latham & Locke, 2007; Locke & Latham, 1990).

A fifth desirable feature of a treatment plan is that it should prioritize and sequence action steps. Prioritizing means that choices are made between alternative courses of action in the treatment, and some steps are given precedence over others. Ensuring client safety is a higher priority, for example, than evaluating potential cognitive distortions in interpreting a social encounter. Similarly, prioritizing involves working with the client to identify which of a number of problems to work on. Sequencing action steps is important because a therapist is always deciding what to do next, whether it is to listen and reflect, express empathy, offer a suggestion, give feedback, ask a question, employ an in-session exercise, and so forth.

Sixth, the plan ideally should test the explanatory hypothesis and provide contingencies based on the client's responses to interventions.

A plan need not be adhered to rigidly or dogmatically but should allow the therapist to respond to unfolding events.

Seventh, a good plan is efficient and parsimonious. Ideally, it provides the most direct and timely route possible to a good endpoint in the therapy.

With these features in mind, this chapter describes a three-step process for developing a treatment plan: First, assess the set point for treatment; second, identify and sequence goals; and third, select interventions to address the goals. I use the case of Rochelle to illustrate each step.

ASSESSING THE SET POINT FOR TREATMENT

The term *set point* originated in physiology and refers to a state of homeostasis in which the stability of a physiological system is maintained at a relatively constant level. The concept has been used to describe the functional stability of heart rate, body weight, visceral regulation, and the interaction of the autonomic and sympathetic nervous systems. In the psychotherapy context, set point refers to pretreatment client and relationship states that act to preserve balance and constancy. Consequently, the therapeutic set point acts to resist change, and therefore must be taken into account when planning treatment. One feature of a set point in physiology is that it is established as a consequence of opposing and mutually reciprocal forces that balance against each other to achieve stability. Similarly, in psychotherapy one must consider not only the client's readiness to change but the therapist's response to the client's readiness and how the client, in turn, is likely to respond. That is, since psychotherapy usually unfolds in a dyad, one must take into account the client, the therapist, and their developing relationship. It is of note that the concept of homeostasis in physiology is slowly giving way to that of homeodynamic regulation. The latter better describes the multiple and complex regulatory mechanisms, including both negative feedback and feedforward processes, as well as the multiple levels of hierarchically organized control that we now know govern physiological systems (Berntson & Cacioppo, 2007). This shift in understanding is equally applicable to psychotherapy, in which stable psychological states are maintained by similarly complex mechanisms, but changes leading to the establishment of new set points are also possible.

Consideration of the therapeutic set point as a first step in treatment planning recognizes the critical contributions of the client and the therapeutic alliance to treatment outcome. As discussed in Chapter 4, the client is estimated to explain about 40% of the variability in outcome (Lambert, 2013a). Given this significant contribution, it is important to estimate how well your clients are likely to capitalize on their influence on outcome and the extent to which you can facilitate that process (Bohart & Tallman, 2010). Therefore, it is helpful to know in what specific ways a client's own efforts can contribute. Norcross and Wampold (2011) reviewed an extensive list of psychotherapy processes and empirical evidence that supports their effectiveness. For current purposes, I focus on four considerations: (a) the client's reactance; (b) client preferences; (c) values and concerns related to culture, religion, and spirituality; and (d) the client's readiness for change. Norcross and Wampold urged caution in applying these findings clinically since the research is correlational and thus causality cannot be assumed. Nevertheless, the findings are sufficiently robust as to warrant consideration in treatment planning.

Reactance

As conceptualized by Beutler, Harwood, Michelson, Song, and Holman (2011), *reactance* is a state or trait that refers to a general refusal to change or a sensitivity to external demands that reduces the client's choices. It is similar to the psychoanalytic term *resistance*, which refers to a client's defensive rejection of efforts on the part of the therapist to induce positive change in the client. It differs, however, in that the concept is not limited to client behavior but also includes the psychotherapy environment. It reflects the idea that a therapist's failure to fit the treatment to the client contributes to the client's noncompliance. The term *reactance* originated in the work of Brehm and Brehm (1981), who defined it as a "state of mind aroused by a threat to one's perceived legitimate freedom, motivating the individual to restore the thwarted freedom" (p. 4). High-reactant individuals tend to be defensive, quick to take offense, and to have less concern than usual about the impression they make on others. They resist following social norms and rules, and may be careless about fulfilling duties and obligations. They may also be intolerant of other's beliefs and values, and inclined to express strong feelings and emotions. In other words, they "march to their own drummer" (Dowd, Milne, & Wise, 1991; Dowd & Wallbrown, 1993; Dowd, Wallbrown, Sanders, & Yesenosky, 1994).

Reactance significantly and inversely mediates the relationship between therapist activity and outcome. That is, outcome worsens as both client reactance and therapist activity increases. In one meta-analysis, the goodness-of-fit between therapist activity and client reactance predicted outcome with an effect size of 0.81 (Beutler et al., 2011), whereas the effect size was 0.38 for therapist activity when goodness-of-fit was not taken into account. This difference in effect size suggests a 10% increased chance of treatment success based solely on the fit of client reactance to therapist activity.

Reactance can be measured in various ways. One is to use paper-and-pencil tests such as the Minnesota Multiphasic Personality Inventory and observing the K scale, the Negative Treatment Indicators (TRT) scale, and the Dominance (DOM) scale. Another is the Therapeutic Reaction Scale (Dowd, Milne, & Wise, 1991), a 28-item inventory that has two factors: behavioral reactance and verbal reactance. One might also assess reactance in a clinical interview by observing expressions of anger, irritation or resentment focused on the treatment or therapist, and suspiciousness or distrust. In addition, the therapist can inquire about the quality of previous relationships with therapists, compliance with homework or attendance in previous therapies, and resistance to authority in extra-therapeutic relationships.

Beutler et al. (2011) offered advice on how to plan treatment on the basis of a client's reactance. For high-reactance clients, they suggest emphasizing autonomy and choice on the part of the client and de-emphasizing the therapist's role as an expert and guide. In terms of specific interventions, they suggest using tasks that enhance client control and self-direction; for example, by avoiding rigid homework assignments and instead offering the client choices of inter-session activity, such as a self-directed assignment or a choice of reading. In addition, the relative balance of listening versus talking should shift toward the client. With regard to novice therapists they also recommend matching the therapist's directiveness to the client's level of reactance and not making the common beginner's mistake of substituting the therapist's level of reactance for that of the client. They also recommend minimizing interventions that arouse resistance and considering a client's increase in state reactance as a sign that ineffective interventions are being employed, not as a deficit on the part of the client. As such, addressing reactance becomes a problem for the therapist to solve, not the client. In summary, the right balance should be struck between encouraging positive changes and minimizing threats to client autonomy and control, and awareness of a client's reactance can help plan treatment in this regard.

Assessing Rochelle's Reactance

Rochelle's reactance was assessed on the basis of her behavior during and just after the initial interview. She was judged to have high reactance. To a significant degree, this judgment was based on her failure to come for or to cancel her second appointment. Although Rochelle appeared compliant during the initial interview, concern was raised that she may be displaying a pattern of therapist placation, that is, outwardly attempting to please the therapist while inwardly resisting. It was also noted that she did not appear angry at the therapist, nor suspicious. Based on these considerations, intervention ideas were to focus on listening and taking special care to allow Rochelle the opportunity to express her own ideas and to experience the therapist as understanding those ideas. Further, the therapist planned to attend carefully to the potential impact her conflict between dependence and independence may play in the client–therapist relationship. Finally, it was agreed not to push too hard with suggestions, and to emphasize support rather than insight.

Client Preferences

Another demonstrably effective factor to assess in determining the set point for beginning treatment is the client's preferences regarding treatment. *Preferences* refer to the client's desires and values regarding therapist roles (e.g., primarily active and advice giving versus listening and reflecting), therapist characteristics (e.g., age, gender, years of experience, ethnicity), and treatment characteristics (e.g., psychodynamic versus cognitive–behavioral; Swift, Callahan, & Vollmer, 2011). Guidelines from the APA's Presidential Task Force on Evidence-Based Practice (2006) also emphasize assessment of client preferences. They state that treatment decisions should be made in collaboration with the client and that efforts should be made to maximize client preferences.

Meta-analyses have shown that client preferences reliably predict dropout rate; specifically, clients receiving treatments that either match or consider their preferences are one half to one third less likely to drop out of treatment than clients whose preferences are either not matched or are ignored (Swift et al., 2011). Taking into account or at least acknowledging client preferences also predicts outcome, with an estimated effect size of .31, which is small but nevertheless reliable and predicts in itself about 3.5% of variance in outcome (Swift et al., 2011).

On the basis of this research, it is recommended that therapists routinely assess client preferences as part of treatment planning (Swift et al., 2011). Doing so should address preferences for therapy roles, therapist preferences, and treatment types. Assessing preferences can be as simple as explaining treatment options to clients and asking directly what the client prefers; for example, therapy without additional mental health care, therapy with medication, or medication alone. It can also include asking about treatment preferences. In this regard, therapy "brands" such as cognitive–behavioral, psychodynamic, dialectical behavior, and so on, need not be emphasized (unless the client mentions them) as much as what the client might expect as the treatment begins. If appropriate, therapists might also ask directly about preferences regarding gender, race, and ethnicity, especially when the therapist is of a different gender, race, ethnicity, or culture than the client. The therapist may also inquire regularly as to how his or her manner and style are received by the client. Therapists should be prepared to educate clients who lack information about therapy options. Although it is preferable to accommodate client preferences, it is not always possible; fortunately, research suggests that sensitivity to these preferences, expressed by directly asking about them, also has a positive influence on therapy (Swift et al., 2011).

Rochelle's Preferences

Rochelle did return to treatment after the therapist called her to ask about the no-show. In the second session, Rochelle explained that she did not have transportation options the previous week and did not think to call and cancel. Since her no-show raised concern about possible dropout, particular care was taken to address her preferences. She was asked how she felt about meeting with her therapist, an African American woman. Rochelle assured the therapist that race and gender were not concerns of hers, and that she was reassured that her therapist was "a doctor." Rochelle was also asked whether the initial session had been helpful for her and how it might have been more so. She confirmed that the initial session had been helpful and had given her hope and much to think about. The therapist invited her to express any concerns as they arise in therapy in the future. On the basis of her behavioral and mood instability, it was recommended that Rochelle receive both psychotherapy and mood-stabilizing medication, and she agreed to both. Her therapist asked Rochelle about her preferences in regard to frequency of meetings. After goals were agreed upon (discussed later in this chapter), they decided to meet weekly.

Culture, Religion, and Spirituality

I made the case in Chapter 3 that a client's culture, including the client's religious and spiritual orientation, is important to take into account when formulating. In the last chapter, I discussed how these issues play into the explanatory hypothesis. They are also relevant to treatment planning.

Meta-analytic research shows that psychosocial treatments that explicitly accounted for clients' culture, ethnicity, or race predicted outcome with an effect size of 0.46 as compared with control groups (T. B. Smith, Rodriguez, & Bernal, 2011). This means that culturally adapted mental health therapies may be moderately superior to those that do not explicitly incorporate cultural considerations.

But what does it mean to "culturally adapt" a mental health therapy? Bernal, Jiménez-Chafey, and Domenech Rodríguez (2009) defined *cultural adaptation* as "the systematic modification of an evidence-based treatment (EBT) or intervention protocol to consider language, culture, and context in such a way that it is compatible with the client's cultural patterns, meanings and values" (p. 362). In general, one can consider a culturally adapted psychotherapy as one in which treatment is tailored to clients' cultural beliefs and values, is provided in a setting considered "safe" by the client, and is conducted in the client's preferred language (T. B. Smith et al., 2011). Draguns (2008) summarized the work of several international scholars with expertise in cross-cultural psychotherapy and identified common themes defining cultural adaptation. These include (a) practicing with flexibility, (b) remaining open to what clients bring to therapy, (c) providing services that are meaningful within the cultural context in which they are delivered, (d) drawing on traditional treatments if they can benefit the client, (e) experiencing and communicating empathy in a culturally appropriate manner, and (f) proceeding with caution in interpreting cultural differences as deficits.

Rochelle's Cultural, Religious, and Spiritual Considerations

Rochelle grew up in a working class family in which education was not emphasized. She was raised Catholic, but is not practicing and is in fact angry at God for letting bad things happen to her and to others in her life. Her family of origin emphasized conservative, even authoritarian, values that she rebelled against. Alcohol was frequently consumed in her childhood home and was a contributing factor to her sexual abuse and to the death of her son. She is unsure of her ethnic heritage beyond her grandparents' generation. These details led the therapist to consider the following in regard to treatment planning: (a) consistent with Rochelle's lead, use language that is down-to-earth and not overly formal; (b) respect her possible religious and spiritual ambivalence, recognizing the likelihood that her early religious experiences may still influence her, even as she professes anger at God and rejection of those values; (c) respect and acknowledge the work ethic displayed in her family of origin as a positive influence in her life; (d) acknowledge how she has taken steps to define herself apart from the values of her upbringing, including her embrace of education as a path to financial security and independence; and (e) respect and acknowledge her aversion to authoritarianism while also understanding that she may have an internalized authoritarian style, and its inverse, oversubmissiveness.

Readiness for Change

Assessing a client's readiness to change helps the therapist plan suitable interventions. Prochaska and DiClimente (2005) described a transtheoretical approach to psychotherapy that identifies five stages of change: precontemplation, contemplation, preparation, action, and maintenance. *Precontemplation* means there is no intention to change in the foreseeable future. The client is not thinking about it. *Contemplation* is the stage in which clients become aware that a problem exists and have begun to think about what they might do to address it, but they have not yet made a commitment to do so. In the *preparation* stage the individual has developed the intention to change imminently and has planned specific steps; for example, seeing a therapist. They may have already begun to take some of these steps, but are not yet committed to a specific program of change. In the *action* stage, the individual has modified his or her behavior, experiences, and/or environment in order to solve a problem or set of problems. This stage involves considerable commitment, energy, and time. Finally, *maintenance* is the stage in which a person has achieved significant change and begins to take steps to prevent relapse. Most clients entering psychotherapy are likely in the contemplation or preparation stage. Some, for example those referred by courts or compelled by a spouse as a condition of staying married, may be in precontemplation. Others may have already initiated action, for example, by reading a self-help book or talking with supportive friends. Clients may be in one stage of change for some problems and a different stage in regard to other problems. Some may come motivated and prepared to address depression and relationship problems, but be in the precontemplation stage when it comes to alcohol or cannabis use, although the latter may be contributing to the depression and relationship problems. (For an alternative perspective on assessing stages of change, see Benjamin, 1993b.)

Studies show that pretreatment readiness to change predicts outcome with an effect size of about 0.46, which is considered medium and means that the amount of progress a client makes in therapy is a function of their readiness to change at the outset of treatment (Norcross, Krebs, & Prochaska, 2011). Further, it has been estimated that progressing from one stage to the next during the first month of treatment doubles the chance of taking action within six months. Unfortunately, there is insufficient research to draw conclusions about whether matching interventions to the client's readiness to change also predicts outcome.

Nevertheless, knowing a client's readiness to change informs the treatment plan. Prochaska and DiClimente (2005) recommended specific interventions depending on the client's stage of change. They asserted that the correct match of intervention to stage of change facilitates movement from one stage to another. For clients in the precontemplation stage they suggest consciousness-raising interventions such as observations or reading material that increase clients' awareness of the causes, consequences, and potential solutions to their problems. Also recommended is experiencing and expressing feelings about one's problems and solutions, such as through role-playing and discussion of the effects problematic behavior is having on others. Someone in the precontemplation stage with an alcohol problem may reject a suggestion to attend an AA meeting, but be willing to read a brochure describing alcohol dependence and its consequences. For those in the contemplation stage, consideration of personal values and life priorities, as well as corrective emotional experiences, can help move that person to the preparation stage. The process of self-liberation comes to the foreground in the preparation stage. Emphasis is placed on enhancing self-efficacy and hope for a positive outcome, as well as moving beyond willpower as a change process. Interventions appropriate for the preparation stage include giving clients choices about action steps and helping them weigh the pros and cons of acting versus not acting. Once at the action stage, specific interventions might involve giving choices, and giving feedback on how willpower is being exercised. Prochaska and DiClimente (2005) specifically recommend reinforcement for positive steps taken, counter-conditioning, and various forms of assessing and gaining stimulus control. For those in the maintenance phase, awareness of triggers that can lead one back into problematic behavior can be particularly effective.

Although research measures have been developed (Norcross et al., 2011), one can assess a client's stage of change in a clinical setting simply by asking whether the person seriously intends to address their problems in the near future; for example, within the next 6 months. If the answer is no, consider the client a precontemplator. If the response is affirmative, consider the client a contemplator. If action is intended within a month consider the individual in the preparation stage. If the client is currently changing his or her behavior, they may be considered in the action stage.

Rochelle's Readiness to Change

Rochelle was assessed as being in the preparation stage of change. She had considered psychotherapy for some time, and scheduling an appointment was an important step for her. Concerns were raised, however, about her commitment to continued treatment. On the basis of her stage of change, interventions considered were to build self-efficacy by emphasizing choices among treatment options, building hope and remoralization by offering a treatment with known effectiveness, beginning a discussion of short- and long-term goals, expressing empathy, and otherwise building the therapeutic alliance.

To sum up this section, assessing the set point for treatment is the initial step of treatment planning. Four elements have been described: (a) reactance; (b) client preferences; (c) cultural, religious, and spiritual concerns and values; and (d) readiness for change. Each of these elements correlates with outcome, and consideration of them enables the therapist to collaborate productively with the client to develop the next step in treatment planning: identifying treatment goals.

IDENTIFY GOALS

Like problems, goals provide direction, focus, and orientation. In the sometimes rapidly changing context of therapy, goals serve as a "north star" to help assess whether progress is being made. Two broad classes of goals may be identified: outcome goals and process goals (Nezu, Nezu, & Cos, 2007; Persons, 2008). Each of these can be considered within a long-term and a short-term framework. *Outcome goals* are end states. Within the short term, by which I mean the first two to four therapy sessions, outcome goals are milestone achievements. Short-term outcome goals might include collaboratively agreeing to a set of problems to work on, establishing a therapeutic contract that governs the process and plan for therapy, establishing a positive therapeutic working alliance, instilling hope for a successful outcome in the client, and achieving initial symptom reduction. Long-term outcome goals are the ultimate end states for treatment. The problem list is a prime source of potential outcome goals. Common outcome goals are to no longer experience the signs, symptoms, and problems in living that are identified on the problem list.

Process goals are the steps and activities that lead to the outcome goals. Short-term process goals might include listening carefully, empathizing with the client and having the client experience feeling understood, addressing potential obstacles to attending treatment sessions, gathering history, generating a problem list, and generating a case formulation. In the longer term, if an outcome goal is to no longer be depressed, process goals may include behavioral activation; initiating an exercise regimen; practicing relaxation techniques; gaining insight into how incipient thoughts can trigger episodes of depressed affect and thought; becoming more aware of and in control of one's internal "vicious dialogue," as one client described his self-talk; and identifying and minimizing safety behaviors that lead to avoidance of anxiety-arousing situations rather than mastery of them. Treatment manuals for specific disorders serve as useful sources of process goals. Since process goals are closely related to treatment interventions and techniques, we will discuss them further in the next section on planning interventions to address outcome goals.

Goals vary in quality. Usually, a good goal is a SMART goal. This acronym stands for goals that are specific, measurable, achievable, realistic, and timely. Specific goals are those that are discrete enough to be identified and measured. Examples include being able to sit in a meeting without having a panic attack, to initiate a conversation with at least one person each day, to identify when one is becoming angry and maintain composure rather than explode at someone, and so on. Examples of nonspecific goals are to understand oneself better, to feel better, or to get along with others better, to love more, or to be a good parent. These are laudable goals, but they are so broad that it becomes difficult to know when they are achieved and to what degree.

A measurable goal can help the therapist and client track progress and make adjustments if needed. When considering measurable goals, include nonarbitrary measures of goals when possible (Blanton & Jaccard, 2006). These are goals that are objective and observable and thus not entirely reliant on the client's self-report of a cognitive or mood state, and are clearly linked to improved functioning. Examples of nonarbitrary measures are increasing body mass index when treating someone with anorexia nervosa, weight loss when treating obesity, finding a job, initiating a relationship, initiating conversations with an agreed upon number of persons per day, exercising three to five times per week, and practicing good sleep hygiene. Arbitrary goals are useful but less so than nonarbitrary goals. Examples might include bringing the Beck Depression Inventory (A. T. Beck, Ward, Mendelson, Mock, & Erbaugh, 1961) score to 12 or lower, or a self-report of satisfaction with treatment outcome.

An achievable goal is one that is possible to accomplish. One client might be able to start a business or complete a college degree, whereas for another these might be unachievable.

A realistic goal is not only achievable but reasonable and likely to succeed given the current constraints in the client's life. For example, the goal of becoming an artist may be achievable, but it may not be realistic if the person needs to provide an income to their family.

Finally, a goal should be timely. This means it is a goal that can be achieved within a reasonable period of time. If a goal is not timely, it becomes impossible to determine whether one is making progress toward it.

Although one should be mindful of SMART goals, some goals are difficult to frame within the SMART rubric but are nevertheless worthwhile pursuing. Achieving a particular goal may require effort long exceeding the time frame of therapy. Some clients may wish to be able to look back on their life in the future and feel they have made a contribution to society, that they have made the world a better place. Others may wish to have had a good life, however that might be defined. The therapist should be aware that some goals that clients offer are aspirational or "reach" goals that, while not meeting the specific criteria of SMART goals, nevertheless motivate, inspire, and energize the person. The therapist may not want to squelch these goals, no matter whether they fit the SMART criteria. These goals can be addressed by prioritizing and by discussing process goals that could lead to the "big" goals.

Sometimes it is not the client with the big goal; the therapist may present a goal that seems SMART, but the client may view it as beyond reach. These goals may be aligned with what Benjamin (2003) described as "green" motives; that is, those that are oriented toward psychological growth and health, such as affirmation, trust, acceptance, hope, nurturance, love, and compassion for the self. One client had been so abused in childhood that he could not imagine the possibility of meeting someone, falling in love, getting married, and having a happy, conventional family life, despite longing for these things. He tended toward what Benjamin called "red" motives, which are regressive and limit growth in the service of loyalty to a loved but abusive caretaker. Red behaviors include walling others off, sulking, attacking, hating, shutting down, and neglecting the self. For my client, this meant giving up on the possibility of ever finding love, nurturing bitterness, trying to satisfy himself with his career alone, and living a socially marginal life. Part of the work of therapy was to help him choose between his green and his red life goals, and to encourage him to consider seeking what may have seemed inconceivable at the time.

When discussing goals, one can simply ask, "What would you like to accomplish in therapy?" "What are your goals for treatment?" or "What would you like to be different in your life at the end of treatment?" Understand that some clients struggle to identify goals despite the therapist's best attempts at collaboration. Clients with identity problems are among those particularly likely to struggle with goal identification. In these cases, identifying goals can become part of the process of self-identification; the goal may become to identify goals and to encourage the client to think about them.

Rochelle's Outcome Goals

Three primary outcome goals were agreed upon with Rochelle: The first was to improve her mood stability and self-control, the second was to decrease depression and anxiety, and the third was to improve problem-solving and interpersonal skills. Other goals discussed were for her to consider employment or furthering her education in order to gain more financial and interpersonal independence and to appropriately confront and respond to her husband's substance abuse and possible infidelity. These goals would be measured in the following ways: (a) self-report of symptom reduction on a progress monitoring scale, (b) fewer reported episodes of crying outside the therapy session, (c) improved anger management, (d) elimination of damage to property, (e) evidence that she is asserting herself more appropriately in her relationship with her husband, (f) addressing the financial problems precipitated by her sister-in-law's decision to move out, and (g) compliance with mood-stabilizing medications. The therapist was also mindful of possible suicidal ideation and was ready to take appropriate preventive actions if necessary. In the following section, I describe process goals designed to achieve these outcome goals.

PLAN INTERVENTIONS TO ADDRESS OUTCOME GOALS

Process goals may be considered the stepping stones to the achievement of outcome goals. They are desired endpoints of planned interventions that, if achieved, should lead to achievement of outcome goals. Process goals can be listed in rough sequential order, from short-term to intermediate-term focus.

Most treatment plans include short-term process goals that are tailored to the current client. Examples are establishing a strong working alliance; assessing and acting when necessary on red flag issues such as neglect or dangerousness to self or others; agreeing on the frame for treatment (Langs, 1998), such as fee, length of session, frequency of meetings, and respective roles of the client and therapist; and consideration of the set point for treatment and initial discussion and agreement on outcome goals.

When considering the sequence of process goals, it is useful to think about the course successful treatment tends to follow, as discussed in Chapter 4 (Howard, Lueger, Maling, & Martinovich, 1993; Lambert, 2007). That is, begin with goals that encourage remoralization and reestablishment of hope for relief of suffering; then those leading to immediate symptom relief; and finally, those that produce pattern change as reflected in improved social role functioning, improved interpersonal functioning, improved self-concept, and improved overall adaptation and well-being.

Once process goals are listed, plan interventions to achieve them. One way to do this is to take components of the explanatory hypothesis and develop process goals that address them. For example, if the hypothesis is that a client's worry and anxiety about his upcoming wedding reflects fear that his fiancée will act toward him as the client's mother did toward his father, then process goals can be set to address this dynamic. Similarly, if the hypothesis is that the client is an intellectualizer, then steps to encourage more affect would be appropriate. In following this process, you ensure that your treatment plan is consistent with the explanatory hypothesis.

Many sources exist for selecting interventions, and fully describing them falls well outside the scope of this book. Suggested sources are theories of psychotherapy as discussed in Chapter 7, components of treatment manuals, empirically supported treatment interventions, results of psychopathology research, and catalogs of empirically supported techniques (O'Donohue & Fisher, 2009) and relationship processes (Norcross, 2011).

Rochelle's Process Goals and Interventions to Achieve Them

Immediate process goals for Rochelle were to consider set point issues in order to establish a strong working alliance; to discuss suicidality risk, including a plan of action should she become more actively suicidal; to describe the proposed treatment and the respective roles of herself and the therapist; and for her to come for weekly sessions initially. After considering specific components of the explanatory hypothesis, and particularly the wish–fear–compromise explanatory template, the plan was as follows: Address dependency conflict by exploring needs, wishes, and fears regarding current and past husbands and major caretakers; address her splitting defense by naming it, exploring alternatives, examining specific episodes; increase emotional self-regulation through exploration of acting out episodes, examining alternatives; examine guilt and role of forgiveness and compassion for the self; and examine how each of the above components affects anxiety, depression, physical state, and self-concept.

Viewed from the standpoint of the functional analysis explanatory template, the following plan was developed: Increase understanding of depression triggers and anger episodes through functional analysis of anger episodes and develop self-assertiveness tools. Other process goals were to increase social connectivity, increase self-care by improving diabetes management, identify and evaluate maladaptive automatic thoughts, and decrease sensitivity to fear-related stimuli through graduated exposure to feared situations.

Other aspects of the treatment plan were to teach distress tolerance skills from the dialectical behavior therapy manual (Linehan, 1993); identify, assess, and challenge automatic thoughts, schemas of the self as worthless, the world as harsh, and the future as hopeless using cognitive therapy techniques; teach behavioral activation and activity scheduling; and build coping and self-management to address depression, social isolation, behavioral dyscontrol, and lack of interpersonal reinforcement.

SUGGESTIONS FOR TREATMENT PLANNING

First, discuss and collaboratively develop the treatment plan with the client, and regularly review progress toward process and outcome goals, using progress monitoring measures as one basis for discussion.

Second, when developing a treatment plan and particularly goals, be mindful of maximizers and satisficers (Simon, 1956). *Maximizers* wish to optimize their outcomes no matter the odds or the time required. They want the perfect mate, perfect job, or perfect college, and so on. They aim to achieve their highest ideals and are not satisfied until they achieve them. As Schwartz (2004) observed, however, this can be a recipe for an unhappy life when carried to an extreme. *Satisficers* are realistic and take into account constraints and limitations such as bad luck, not having a genius IQ, not having the looks of a model, or the gifts of a professional athlete, singer, musician, or actor; but they can still achieve satisfaction. They are satisfied with a good enough outcome. When encountering a maximizer, honor the values that underlie the client's drives, but also explore when appropriate the motives and needs underlying these drives and the costs and benefits of the client's style of making choices.

Third, do not underestimate the power of goal setting. Goals inspire hope and provide a vision of a future self that may seem inconceivable to the client before treatment.

Fourth, the treatment plan should flow directly and logically from the explanatory hypothesis. If you find yourself developing interventions that do not readily flow from the explanatory hypothesis, then revise either the former or the latter.

CONCLUSION

This chapter on treatment planning covered three basic steps: assessing the set point for treatment, determining treatment goals, and selecting and organizing interventions to address those goals. Treatment planning is the final step in the description of the evidence-based integrative model of case formulation. At this point, you should have a complete case formulation with a comprehensive problem list, a diagnosis, an evidence-based explanatory hypothesis that accounts for the problems and diagnosis, and a treatment plan that is solidly grounded in empirical evidence. Chapter 9 describes steps you can take to ensure that you have constructed a high-quality and useful case formulation.

9

Evaluating Case Formulation Quality

O nce you have formulated a case, it is useful to step back and evaluate it. Developing a formulation, reflecting upon it and then revising often improves the formulation and can help identify categories of information you may have overlooked or which you might interconnect in ways you had not thought of before. This chapter presents a scale for assessing the quality of a case formulation. It is based on a research project aimed at understanding the process of case formulation (Eells, 2008; Eells & Lombart, 2003; Eells et al., 2005, 2011). To set the context for describing the quality-assessment tool, the chapter first describes the research project. After reviewing this research and describing the scale, the chapter closes with a checklist to consider as part of the process of developing a case formulation.

http://dx.doi.org/10.1037/14667-010
Psychotherapy Case Formulation, by T. D. Eells

RESEARCH ON CASE FORMULATION QUALITY

Imagine you are in a case formulation race. For 2 minutes you listen to a case summary describing a client's identity, presenting complaints, past mental health care, developmental history, social history, and mental status. Then you have 5 minutes to formulate the case and 2 minutes to plan treatment. Next, another case is presented, then another, and another, and another, and another until nearly an hour has passed and you have formulated and planned treatment for six cases. This demanding task was performed by expert, experienced, and novice cognitive–behavioral and psychodynamic case formulators (Eells et al., 2005). One seasoned participant described it as "the oral licensing exam from hell." Our purpose was to explore whether the experts would do a better job formulating cases than the others, and if they did, how their formulations differed.

Before reporting the results, I describe an earlier study that asked a more basic question: "What do therapists actually do when they formulate a case?" To answer that question, we examined written intake evaluations of therapists at a university-based psychiatry outpatient clinic (Eells, Kendjelic, & Lucas, 1998). We randomly selected more than 50 intake evaluations prepared by senior psychiatry residents ($n = 9$), licensed clinical social workers ($n = 4$), and a psychiatric nurse. We developed a content-coding manual to categorize what they wrote. The manual included descriptive information, diagnosis, inferential information, and treatment planning. Under descriptive information, we coded for demographics; presenting complaints and symptoms; history of previous mental health and medical problems; and any social or developmental history, or any other biographical information that was mentioned. For inferential information, we coded any explanation of symptoms and problems, including psychodynamic, cognitive, and behavioral explanations, as well as those based on social role or cultural factors. We included codes for precipitating stressors, strengths, therapy-interfering events, and overall level of functioning. Treatment planning codes included modes and theoretical approaches to treatment, recommendations for further assessment, specific techniques recommended, and any mention of topics that treatment should focus on. Finally, we rated how well the therapists developed and articulated the ideas expressed in the formulation. We were able to content code the formulations with a high level of agreement among coders.

What we found surprised us. Rather than generating hypotheses about the problems clients were experiencing, the therapists mainly summarized psychosocial information they had presented earlier in the intake evaluation. Most listed symptoms and problems; fewer than one in four said anything about precipitating stressors or predisposing life events that could have led to the symptoms. Just as few offered a psychological, biological, or sociocultural mechanism explaining the problem or symptoms. When an explanatory mechanism was offered, little was said about how it related to symptoms, problems, precipitating stressors, or other predisposing life events.

Since this was a retrospective chart review study, we assumed the written formulations reflected these therapists' representative work, not their best work. We also understood that our results may not generalize to other therapists because we were looking at charts in just one clinic. However, our findings turned out to be consistent with what others were finding. In an earlier study, Perry, Cooper, and Michels (1987) concluded that psychodynamic formulation is a poorly defined skill and therapists are neither taught the skill consistently nor practice it regularly. Kuyken, Fothergill, Musa, and Chadwick (2005) examined cognitive–behavioral formulations generated by 115 mental health practitioners and concluded that less than half were "at least good enough." Also, a study of psychiatry residents across four institutions found deficits in the ability to generate biopsychosocial formulations (McClain, O'Sullivan, & Clardy, 2004). Our research team concluded from these studies that therapists would value efforts to help them improve their case formulation skills.

Toward this end, we set out to explore whether therapists differ in their case formulation ability when performing at their best (Eells et al., 2005), which led to the study described in the beginning of this section. An immediate challenge was to define case formulation expertise and find experts. We faced a different challenge than encountered when studying an area such as expertise in chess, since a point system based on number of games won clearly identifies chess masters (de Groot, 1965). Obviously, no such system exists for psychotherapy case formulation. Instead, we defined strict criteria for expertise and searched for individuals who met them. First, we looked for highly experienced therapists, which we defined as those having practiced psychotherapy for at least 10 years. We restricted ourselves to clinical psychologists or psychiatrists who practiced either cognitive–behavioral or psychodynamic psychotherapy since these are common treatment modalities. Second, since we sought recognized national experts on case formulation, they had to have (a) developed a specific method of case formulation; (b) led professional workshops on case formulations; and/or (c) published scientific articles, books, or book chapters on case formulation. For comparison, we also sought novices, or beginning therapists, who we defined as those with fewer than 1,500 hours of experience practicing psychotherapy and who self-identified as cognitive–behavioral or psychodynamic in orientation. Most were 3rd-year graduate students in clinical or counseling psychology. Finally, we sought experienced cognitive–behavioral and psychodynamic psychologists or psychiatrists who did not meet the additional expertise criteria. These therapists each had at least 10 years of experience providing psychotherapy.

Since we were interested in case formulation as a general skill and not one specific to a particular psychological disorder, we developed six case vignettes that varied by psychological disorder (anxiety, depression, and personality disorder) and were either highly characteristic of the disorder or were less prototypical, that is, less "textbook," while still containing sufficient information to meet diagnostic criteria. As described in the opening paragraph of this chapter, the experimental task was demanding for the therapists. We tape recorded the therapists' formulations and treatment plans, then transcribed them, segmented them into short meaningful units before rating and coding them according to criteria developed for assessing quality and content. Quality measures were comprehensiveness, elaboration, precision of language, complexity, coherence, formulation plan elaboration, goodness-of-fit of the formulation to the treatment plan, evidence that the therapist followed a consistent and systematic process in developing each vignette, and a summary score. The content measures were similar to those described in the earlier study.

So, what did we find? As predicted, the formulations of the experts were of higher quality than those of the experienced and the novice therapists. They were

- More comprehensive, mentioning more of the following domains: (a) problems in global psychological, social, or occupational functioning; (b) inferred symptoms or problems; (c) predisposing experiences, events, traumas, or stressors inferred as explanatory; (d) precipitating or current stressors and/or events; (e) inferred psychological mechanisms (including problematic aspects or traits of the self, problematic aspects of relatedness to others, dysfunctional thoughts and/or core beliefs, affect regulation or dysregulation, defense mechanisms or problematic coping style, skills, or social learning deficits); (f) inferred biological mechanisms; (g) inferred social or cultural mechanisms (including absence of or poor psychosocial support; demographic or cultural factors as the source of a problem, role conflict, role strain, role transition, role dispute); (h) strengths in global psychological, social, or occupational functioning (including adaptive skills, positive aspects or traits of self; adaptive perceptions of or beliefs about others; positive motivation for treatment; adaptive wishes, hopes or goals; good psychosocial support); and (i) identification of potential therapy interfering events.
- More elaborated; once an explanatory hypothesis was offered, it was developed further as compared to the other formulations.
- More complex in that they integrated several facets of the person's problems into a meaningful presentation.
- Much more likely to follow a systematic process. It was as if these therapists had a predeveloped format for organizing information into a formulation and followed the format with each vignette. One cognitive–behavioral expert began each formulation by considering the client's self-concept, then concept of others, then concept of the world. A psychodynamic expert always began with problems; then discussed

states of mind; moved to concepts of self, others, and relationships and how they may reflect wishes, fears, and compromises; and finally discussed coping mechanisms.

- More elaborated with regard to treatment plans; the experts' treatment plans flowed logically from the explanatory hypothesis by addressing the themes articulated in the explanation.

When examining the content of the experts' formulations (Eells et al., 2011), we found additional differences. Primarily, they were much richer in ideas. Not only did the experts address more of the symptoms present in the vignettes, they also used that information as a springboard to infer additional possible symptoms and problems. So, if a vignette mentioned interpersonal problems at home, the experts tended also to wonder about similar problems at work or school. The experts' formulations also contained more ideas about diagnosis, explanations of problems, and treatment. They were more likely to consider overall adaptive functioning, precipitants of symptoms, biological mechanisms, sociocultural influences, strengths, and potential therapy-interfering events. The experts seemed to be aware of information gaps, as they more often requested additional background or assessment results about the client. The cognitive–behavioral experts in particular were more likely to recommend further evaluation, to focus on the treatment contract and treatment expectations, and to focus treatment on symptoms. In sum, there were quite a few differences in quality and content between the formulations of the experts and the others.

Having shown that expert case formulators developed better formulations, we next asked, "How do expert case formulators reason through cases?" We were particularly interested in whether experts base their explanations on a priori ideas they have about psychological problems and disorders or on case information. The answer was "both." The experts used both inferential and deductive strategies more than the other therapists, and were more likely to balance System 1 processing, as discussed in Chapter 2, with System 2 processing (Eells et al., 2011). To further understand the process of developing a high-quality case formulation, we identified the cognitive–behavioral and psychodynamic formulations that were rated as highest in quality and compared them with the two counterpart formulations rated at the 25th percentile in quality (Eells, 2010). We used the most difficult to formulate vignette, which was that of a client with low prototypical borderline personality disorder. Our analysis identified the following differences:

- The expert formulations were more like each other than they were like their theoretical counterparts that were rated as lesser in quality.
- The therapists producing the better formulations stayed close to the descriptive clinical information; they made low-level inferences and interwove facts given about the case with inferences as they developed the formulation.
- These therapists used both System 1 and System 2 thinking. They tended to offer an inferential insight or suggest a pattern or theme (System 1), then examine evidence for that inference in the descriptive information (System 2).
- They continually reflected on the case material, assessing where more information was needed to draw a conclusion while also making the best use they could of what information they had, seeking to identify patterns, yet adhering to a systematic and disciplined process in considering the case.
- They tended to identify a range of problems, but then centered on a central problematic theme that was subsequently elaborated upon.

In contrast, the comparison formulations drew far fewer inferences and made even less use of the descriptive information. The formulations were less well articulated, thus making it difficult to determine whether System 1 or System 2 thinking was involved. One said very little in the way of an explanatory hypothesis or list of problems, but moved swiftly into treatment considerations.

In conducting the studies just described, we developed a manual to code therapists' formulations and rate them on various quality measures in a statistically reliable manner. Since the manual involves time-consuming, meticulous work and extensive training of raters, it is not ideal for clinical use. An adaptation was therefore developed, called the Case Formulation Quality Scale (CFQS), and it is presented in the following section. Four goals were kept in mind as the CFQS was developed. First was to develop a tool specifically for the evidence-based, integrative case formulation model described in this book. Second, the focus shifted from one of expertise to one of competence. The distinction is that expertise suggests mastery of a skill, whereas competence refers to a level of skill sufficient to perform a task proficiently. The CFQS is aimed at helping therapists achieve competence as a step toward mastery. A third goal was to develop a tool that can be learned and applied with relative ease and speed. Fourth, although designed primarily to help therapists evaluate their own case formulations, the CFQS may also be useful in assessing case formulation competence in clinical training settings, in the context of board and licensing examinations, and in large-scale research studies of case formulation competence.

CASE FORMULATION QUALITY SCALE (CFQS)

Figure 9.1 presents the CFQS. As shown, it is organized around the four major content components of the general case formulation model: creating a problem list, diagnosing, generating an explanatory hypothesis, and planning treatment. Primary emphasis is placed on the explanatory hypothesis. The range is from 0 to 19 points. An interpretive guide is provided at the end of Figure 9.1 to give an overall qualitative assessment of the formulation. Since Figure 9.1 is largely self-explanatory, each section of the CFQS is only briefly discussed below.

Problem List

When evaluating the problem list, primary attention should be given to the comprehensiveness of the list. Particular focus should be on potential red flag issues since these involve situations that potentially endanger your client or others. Another major focus when evaluating the problem list is to select and prioritize the problems that therapy will address.

1. Problem List: Rate how well the problem list is developed, taking into account the following:
- Addresses red flag issues such as chemical dependency, domestic violence, neglect, suicidality, or homicidality, if present.
- Addresses problems related to self-functioning including behavior, cognition, affect, mood, biology, and/or existential conflicts.
- Addresses social/interpersonal functioning (e.g., problems with spouse/intimate other, family, teachers/schoolmates, coworkers, mental health providers); excesses or deficits in interpersonal skills; leisure/recreational activities.
- Addresses societal functioning (e.g., legal, financial, underemployment, housing, noise pollution, transportation, poverty, acculturative stress), when relevant.
- Prioritizes and gives rationale for problems that will be the focus of treatment.
- Does not overlook problems suggested by the case material.

Problem List Scoring:

0 = Absent or insufficient development of problem list

1 = Problem list present but with little development

2 = Problem list moderately developed

3 = Problem list well developed   Score: _____

2. Diagnosis: Rate how well the client was diagnosed, taking into account the following:
- Does the diagnosis fit the problems?
- Are required criteria met?
- Are all potential diagnoses considered?
- Are all diagnoses supported by appropriate evidence?

Diagnosis Scoring:

0 = Absent or insufficient diagnosis

1 = Diagnosis present but with little development

2 = Diagnosis moderately or well developed   Score: _____

3. Explanatory Hypothesis: Rate how well each component of the explanatory hypothesis below was developed.
> **3.1 Precipitants:** Consider the following:
> - Are events that led to seeking treatment or to the onset of the episode or disorder described?
> - Are phenomena related to symptom onset or shifts in state of mind noted?

Precipitants Scoring:

0 = Absent or insufficient identification of precipitants

1 = Precipitants present but with little development

2 = Precipitants moderately or well developed   Score: _____

Figure 9.1

Case Formulation Quality Scale.

3.2 Origins: Consider the following:
- Are both proximal and distal origins considered?
- Are links between stated origins and problems evidence-based, theoretically sound, plausible, and well supported?

Origins Scoring:

0 = Absent or insufficient identification of origins

1 = Origins identified but with little or no development

2 = Origins moderately or well developed   *Score:* _____

3.3 Resources:
- Are both internal and external resources identified and developed?
- Are the resources listed sound, plausible, and well supported?

Resources Scoring:

0 = Absent or insufficient identification of resources

1 = Resources identified but with little or no development

2 = Resources moderately or well developed   *Score:* _____

3.4 Obstacles:
- Are both internal and external obstacles identified and developed?
- Are the obstacles listed sound, plausible, and well supported?

Obstacles Scoring:

0 = Absent or insufficient identification of obstacles

1 = Obstacles present but with little or no development

2 = Obstacles are moderately or well developed   *Score:* _____

3.5 Explanatory Template/Hypothesis:
- Considering both the explanatory template and hypothesis as a whole, how many of the following are noted, developed, and integrated into a coherent whole: diagnosis; problems in global psychological, social, or occupational functioning; symptoms/problems; predisposing experiences, events, traumas, stressors; precipitating or current stressors; psychological, biological, and/or sociocultural factors; strengths in psychological, social, or occupational functioning; potential therapy-interfering events?
- Is the hypothesis adequately complex, elaborated, coherent, and supported by theory or evidence?

Figure 9.1 (*Continued*)

Case Formulation Quality Scale.

4. Treatment Planning:
Rate how well the treatment plan was developed, taking into account the following:
- Was the plan developed collaboratively and does it take into account the client's capabilities?
- Is the client's set point for treatment considered (i.e., reactance; client preferences; issues related to culture, religion, and spirituality; readiness for change)?
- Are process/outcome and short-term/long-term goals identified with appropriate milestones identified, and are the goals SMART (specific, measurable, achievable, realistic, and timely)?
- Are interventions planned and sequenced to address goals?
- Does the plan have sufficient detail to guide action?
- Is the plan well elaborated and explained? Does it cover the full range of problems that treatment will address and flow logically and coherently from the preceding components of the formulation?

CFQS SUMMARY:	
Problem List Score (0–3):	
Diagnosis Score (0–2):	
Explanatory Hypothesis Score (0–11):	
Treatment Plan Score (0–3):	
OVERALL SCORE:	

Interpretive Guide (range: 0–19):
0–16: formulation needs more work
17–19: competent formulation

Figure 9.1 (*Continued*)

Case Formulation Quality Scale.

Diagnosis

The diagnosis section is straightforward. Despite the lack of adequate reliability of psychiatric diagnoses, not attending to the criteria before diagnosing only exacerbates the problem. Be careful to consider a full range of potential diagnoses while also being parsimonious in diagnosing, and take care that the client's problems are captured by a diagnosis, when possible.

Explanatory Hypothesis

As discussed in Chapter 7, the explanatory hypothesis is the heart of the formulation. That is why this section of the CFQS earns more than half the points of the entire scale. The CFQS breaks down the task of generating a explanatory hypothesis into its separate components, as discussed in Chapter 7.

Treatment Planning

When evaluating treatment planning, several points should be kept in mind, and these are bulleted in Figure 9.1. As with all aspects of case formulation, primary consideration should be given to collaborating with the client. Collaboration is particularly important in planning treatment since without collaboration, client compliance with treatment recommendations will certainly suffer as will outcome.

CHECKLIST FOR EVALUATING THE PROCESS OF CASE FORMULATION

To conclude this chapter, I offer a 25-point checklist to consider when reviewing your process of case formulation development. It is offered as a shorthand way of ensuring that you have covered the major points emphasized in this book.

Did You Consider . . .

1. Cognitive heuristics that may have biased your inferences, specifically, the availability, affect, and representative heuristics?
2. Base rate effects and the risk of overconfidence?
3. How well are you monitoring System 1 thinking with System 2 thinking?
4. The client's cultural and religious/spiritual values and identity?
5. How the client's presentation of problems may be influenced by cultural and religious/spiritual values?
6. How to integrate cultural data into the rest of the formulation?
7. How cultural factors affect the therapist–client relationship?

When Creating a Problem List, Did You Consider . . .

8. A comprehensive range of problems, including those that may not be the focus of treatment?
9. How to narrow the problems to those you can work on in therapy?

When Diagnosing, Did You Consider . . .

10. A full range of diagnoses, even those that might not appear to be most salient, while also exercising parsimony in diagnosing?

When Developing an Explanatory Hypothesis, Did You Consider . . .

11. Precipitants, origins, resources, and obstacles?
12. Diatheses and stressors?
13. Empirically supported theories of psychotherapy and relevant evidence from the broader research literature?
14. How to stay close to the client's reported history, experience, and narratives when making explanatory inferences?
15. Alternative explanatory templates to the one you chose? Why the template you chose is preferable to others?

16. Whether the explanatory hypothesis cogently accounts for the problems that therapy will focus on?

When Planning Treatment, Did You Consider ...

17. Collaborating with the client in developing a treatment plan?
18. The client's reactance, preferences for treatment, readiness for change?
19. How treatment might be adapted to the client's cultural, religious, and spiritual values and identity?
20. SMART goals as well as short-term and long-term goals?
21. A plan to establish and maintain a positive therapeutic alliance?
22. Empirically supported treatments that might be used or adapted to address the problems that will be treated?
23. Specific techniques to address specific problems?
24. How to sequence interventions to efficiently and effectively carry out treatment?
25. How well the treatment plan flows logically from the explanatory hypothesis to address the client's problems?

Coda

As a final word, I wish to make three brief points. First, while the book champions "evidence-based" approaches to clinical practice, it is important to realize that the current state of empirical knowledge takes us only so far in answering the question that opened Chapter 1: How do you know what to do in psychotherapy? In fact, it is hard to imagine that our scientific knowledge could ever reach a point at which we can rely solely upon scientific evidence to guide us. As Zeldow (2009) persuasively argued, some decisions about what to do next in therapy must rely on our best judgment at the time. Clinical activity is inherently and fundamentally narrative, interpretive, subjective, and in the words of the poet William Blake, consists of "minute particulars." Science can guide some behavior in this domain, but not all. As I hope is made clear in the clinical vignettes in the book, in some situations sound clinical judgment, coupled with empathic listening and the practice of common sense and caring, is the best guide the therapist has.

The second point has to do with the integrative focus of this book. As with evidence, the book championed an integrative approach to case formulation and clinical practice. Yet, as Messer (1986) and Messer and

http://dx.doi.org/10.1037/14667-011
Psychotherapy Case Formulation, by T. D. Eells

Winokur (1980) have asserted, there are limits to the extent to which theories of psychotherapy can be integrated. In important ways, the psychodynamic and cognitive–behavioral schools of therapy embody irreconcilably alternate axiomatic assumptions and visions about reality and life. They asserted that the psychodynamic worldview is of life as a quest; the view is comfortable with contradiction and ambiguity, and it recognizes the inevitability of pain and suffering. In contrast, the worldview underlying the cognitive–behavioral perspective is pragmatic, economic, champions unambiguous outcomes, and is more optimistic. Whether one accepts this distinction or not, there is little question that these two views differ dramatically. Recent developments suggest that a greater degree of integration may be possible, but not without trade-offs that may not be worth the cost.

Finally, I hope this book will be a useful resource for you. Of necessity and by intent, I did not cover every possible aspect of case formulation or every possible explanation of a client's problems. Psychotherapy is a constantly changing field, research in psychotherapy and psychology is vibrant, and new findings and treatment approaches emerge regularly. I hope this book provides a framework for you to organize and stay up-to-date with current information in the field, while also adhering to findings that have passed the test of time.

References

ABC News. (1993). Devilish deeds. *Primetime Live.* New York, NY: ABC News.

Abramson, L. Y., Metalsky, G. I., & Alloy, L. B. (1989). Hopelessness depression: A theory-based subtype of depression. *Psychological Review, 96,* 358–372. http://dx.doi.org/10.1037/0033-295X.96.2.358

Abramson, L. Y., Seligman, M. E., & Teasdale, J. D. (1978). Learned helplessness in humans: Critique and reformulation. *Journal of Abnormal Psychology, 87,* 49–74. http://dx.doi.org/10.1037/0021-843X.87.1.49

Achenbach, J. (1995, September 22). Pleased to meet all of you. *The Washington Post,* p. D5.

Adams, A. N., Adams, M. A., & Miltenberger, R. G. (2009). Habit reversal training. In W. T. O'Donohue & J. E. Fisher (Eds.), *General principles and empirically supported techniques of cognitive behavior therapy* (2nd ed., pp. 343–350). Hoboken, NJ: Wiley.

Adler, A. (1973). *The practice and theory of individual psychology.* Totowa, NJ: Littlefield, Adams.

American Board of Psychiatry & Neurology. (2009). *Psychiatry and neurology core competencies: Version 4.1* Retrieved from http://www.abpn.com/downloads/core_comp_outlines/core_psych_neuro_v4.1.pdf

American Psychiatric Association. (1980). *Diagnostic and statistical manual of mental disorders* (3rd ed.). Washington, DC: Author.

American Psychiatric Association. (2013a). *Desk reference to the diagnostic criteria from DSM–5.* Arlington, VA: Author.

American Psychiatric Association. (2013b). *Diagnostic and statistical manual of mental disorders* (5th ed.). Arlington, VA: Author.

Angelou, M. (1977). *Commencement address.* Retrieved from http://newsroom. ucr.edu/announcements/2009-10-24maya-angelou.html

Angst, J. (2009). Psychiatry NOS (not otherwise specified). [Editorial]. *Salud Mental, 32*(1), 1–2.

Antony, M. M., & Roemer, L. (2011). *Behavior therapy.* Washington, DC: American Psychological Association.

APA Presidential Task Force on Evidence-Based Practice. (2006). Evidence-based practice in psychology. *American Psychologist, 61,* 271–285. http://dx.doi. org/10.1037/0003-066X.61.4.271

Arkes, H. R., Faust, D., Guilmette, T. J., & Hart, K. (1988). Eliminating the hindsight bias. *Journal of Applied Psychology, 73,* 305–307. http://dx.doi. org/10.1037/0021-9010.73.2.305

Baldwin, M. W. (1992). Relational schemas and the processing of social information. *Psychological Bulletin, 112,* 461–484. http://dx.doi.org/10.1037/ 0033-2909.112.3.461

Barber, J. P., Khalsa, S.-R., & Sharpless, B. A. (2010). The validity of the alliance as a predictor of psychotherapy outcome. In J. C. Muran & J. P. Barber (Eds.), *The therapeutic alliance: An evidence-based guide to practice* (pp. 29–43). New York, NY: Guilford Press.

Barkham, M., Margison, F., Leach, C., Lucock, M., Mellor-Clark, J., Evans, C., . . . McGrath, G. (2001). Service profiling and outcomes benchmarking using the CORE-OM: Toward practice-based evidence in the psychological therapies. *Journal of Consulting and Clinical Psychology, 69,* 184–196. http:// dx.doi.org/10.1037/0022-006X.69.2.184

Beck, A. T. (1963). Thinking and depression: I. Idiosyncratic content and cognitive distortions. *Archives of General Psychiatry, 9,* 324–333. http://dx.doi. org/10.1001/archpsyc.1963.01720160014002

Beck, A. T. (1964). Thinking and depression: II. Theory and therapy. *Archives of General Psychiatry, 10,* 561–571. http://dx.doi.org/10.1001/archpsyc.1964. 01720240015003

Beck, A. T., Emery, G., & Greenberg, R. (1985). *Anxiety disorders and phobias: A cognitive perspective.* New York, NY: Basic Books.

Beck, A. T., Epstein, N., Brown, G., & Steer, R. A. (1988). An inventory for measuring clinical anxiety: Psychometric properties. *Journal of Consulting and Clinical Psychology, 56,* 893–897. http://dx.doi.org/10.1037/0022-006X.56.6.893

Beck, A. T., Freeman, A., & Davis, D. D. (2004). *Cognitive therapy of personality disorders* (2nd ed.). New York, NY: Guilford Press.

Beck, A. T., Rush, A. J., Shaw, B. F., & Emery, G. (1979). *Cognitive therapy of depression.* New York, NY: Guilford Press.

Beck, A. T., Ward, C. H., Mendelson, M., Mock, J., & Erbaugh, J. (1961). An inventory for measuring depression. *Archives of General Psychiatry, 4*, 561–571. http://dx.doi.org/10.1001/archpsyc.1961.01710120031004

Beck, A. T., Wright, F. D., Newman, C. F., & Liese, B. S. (1993). *Cognitive therapy of substance abuse.* New York, NY: Guilford Press.

Beck, J. S. (1995). *Cognitive therapy: Basics and beyond.* New York, NY: Guilford Press.

Behar, E., & Borkovec, T. D. (2006). The nature and treatment of generalized anxiety disorder. In B. O. Rothbaum (Ed.), *Pathological anxiety: Emotional processing in etiology and treatment* (pp. 181–196). New York, NY: Guilford Press.

Benish, S. G., Quintana, S., & Wampold, B. E. (2011). Culturally adapted psychotherapy and the legitimacy of myth: A direct-comparison meta-analysis. *Journal of Counseling Psychology, 58*, 279–289. http://dx.doi.org/10.1037/a0023626

Benjamin, L. S. (1993a). Every psychopathology is a gift of love. *Psychotherapy Research, 3*, 1–24. http://dx.doi.org/10.1080/10503309312331333629

Benjamin, L. S. (1993b). *Interpersonal diagnosis and treatment of personality disorders.* New York, NY: Guilford Press.

Benjamin, L. S. (1996a). *Interpersonal diagnosis and treatment of personality disorders* (2nd ed.). New York, NY: Guilford Press.

Benjamin, L. S. (1996b). The interviewing and treatment methods *Interpersonal diagnosis and treatment of personality disorders* (2nd ed., pp. 69–111). New York, NY: Guilford Press.

Benjamin, L. S. (2003). *Interpersonal reconstructive therapy: Promoting change in nonresponders.* New York, NY: Guilford Press.

Bennett, D., & Parry, G. (1998). The accuracy of reformulation in cognitive analytic therapy: A validation study. *Psychotherapy Research, 8*, 84–103. http://dx.doi.org/10.1080/10503309812331332217

Bergner, R. M. (1998). Characteristics of optimal clinical case formulations. The linchpin concept. *American Journal of Psychotherapy, 52*, 287–300.

Bernal, G., Jiménez-Chafey, M. I., & Domenech Rodríguez, M. M. (2009). Cultural adaptation of treatments: A resource for considering culture in evidence-based practice. *Professional Psychology: Research and Practice, 40*, 361–368. http://dx.doi.org/10.1037/a0016401

Berntson, G., & Cacioppo, J. T. (2007). Integrative physiology: Homeostasis, allostasis, and the orchestration of systemic physiology. In J. T. Cacioppo, L. G. Tassinary, & G. Berntson (Eds.), *Handbook of psychophysiology* (pp. 433–452). New York, NY: Cambridge University Press. http://dx.doi.org/10.1017/CBO9780511546396.019

Betancourt, H., & López, S. R. (1993). The study of culture, ethnicity, and race in American psychology. *American Psychologist, 48,* 629–637. http://dx.doi.org/10.1037/0003-066X.48.6.629

Beutler, L. E., Harwood, T. M., Michelson, A., Song, X., & Holman, J. (2011). Reactance/resistance level. In J. C. Norcross (Ed.), *Psychotherapy relationships that work: Evidence-based responsiveness* (2nd ed., pp. 261–278). New York, NY: Oxford University Press. http://dx.doi.org/10.1093/acprof:oso/9780199737208.003.0013

Beutler, L. E., & Malik, M. L. (Eds.). (2002). *Rethinking the* DSM: *A psychological perspective.* Washington, DC: American Psychological Association.

Bieling, P. J., & Kuyken, W. (2003). Is cognitive case formulation science or science fiction? *Clinical Psychology: Science and Practice, 10,* 52–69. http://dx.doi.org/10.1093/clipsy.10.1.52

Binder, J. L. (1993). Is it time to improve psychotherapy training? *Clinical Psychology Review, 13,* 301–318. http://dx.doi.org/10.1016/0272-7358(93)90015-E

Binder, J. L. (2004). *Key competencies in brief dynamic psychotherapy: Clinical practice beyond the manual.* New York, NY: Guilford Press.

Blanton, H., & Jaccard, J. (2006). Arbitrary metrics in psychology. *American Psychologist, 61,* 27–41. http://dx.doi.org/10.1037/0003-066X.61.1.27

Blashfield, R. K., & Burgess, D. R. (2007). Classification provides an essential basis for organizing mental disorders. In S. O. Lilienfeld & W. T. O'Donohue (Eds.), *The great ideas of clinical science: 17 principles that every mental health professional should understand* (pp. 93–117). New York, NY: Routledge/Taylor & Francis.

Bohart, A. C., & Tallman, K. (1999). *How clients make therapy work: The process of active self-healing.* Washington, DC: American Psychological Association. http://dx.doi.org/10.1037/10323-000

Bohart, A. C., & Tallman, K. (2010). Clients: The neglected common factor in psychotherapy. In B. L. Duncan, S. D. Miller, B. E. Wampold, & M. A. Hubble (Eds.), *The heart and soul of change: Delivering what works in therapy* (2nd ed., pp. 83–111). Washington, DC: American Psychological Association. http://dx.doi.org/10.1037/12075-003

Bohart, A. C., & Wade, A. G. (2013). The client in psychotherapy. In M. J. Lambert (Ed.), *Bergin and Garfield's Handbook of Psychotherapy and Behavior Change* (6th ed., pp. 219–257). New York, NY: Wiley.

Bonanno, G. A. (2004). Loss, trauma, and human resilience: Have we underestimated the human capacity to thrive after extremely aversive events? *American Psychologist, 59,* 20–28. http://dx.doi.org/10.1037/0003-066X.59.1.20

Bonanno, G. A., & Singer, J. L. (1990). Repressive personality style: Theoretical and methodological implications for health and pathology. In J. L. Singer

(Ed.), *Repression and dissociation: Implications for personality theory, psychopathology, and health* (pp. 435–470). Chicago, IL: University of Chicago Press.

Bordin, E. S. (1979). The generalizability of the psychoanalytic concept of the working alliance. *Psychotherapy: Theory, Research & Practice, 16,* 252–260. http://dx.doi.org/10.1037/h0085885

Bouton, M. E. (2002). Context, ambiguity, and unlearning: Sources of relapse after behavioral extinction. *Biological Psychiatry, 52,* 976–986. http://dx.doi.org/10.1016/S0006-3223(02)01546-9

Bowlby, J. (1969). *Attachment and loss: Vol. 1. Attachment.* New York, NY: Basic Books.

Bowlby, J. (1979). *The making and breaking of affectional bonds.* London, England: Tavistock.

Brehm, S. S., & Brehm, J. W. (1981). *Psychological reactance: A theory of freedom and control.* New York, NY: Wiley.

Bretherton, I., & Munholland, K. A. (2008). Internal working models in attachment relationships: Elaborating a central construct in attachment theory. In J. Cassidy & P. R. Shaver (Eds.), *Handbook of attachment: Theory, research, and clinical applications* (2nd ed., pp. 102–127). New York, NY: Guilford Press.

Brown, G. W., & Harris, T. O. (1978). *Social origins of depression: A study of psychiatric disorder in women.* New York, NY: Free Press.

Bruner, J. S. (1990). *Acts of meaning.* Cambridge, MA: Harvard University Press.

Bruner, J. S., Goodnow, J. J., & Austin, G. A. (1956). *A study of thinking.* Oxford, England: John Wiley & Sons.

Burton, R. (2001). *The anatomy of melancholy.* New York, NY: *New York Review of Books* Classics. (Original work published 1621)

Cannon, W. B. (1932). *The wisdom of the body.* New York, NY: Norton.

Caplan, P. J. (1995). *They say you're crazy: How the world's most powerful psychiatrists decide who's normal.* Cambridge, MA: Da Capo Press.

Caspar, F. (1995). *Plan analysis: Toward optimizing psychotherapy.* Seattle, WA: Hogrefe & Huber.

Caspar, F. (1997). What goes on in a psychotherapist's mind? *Psychotherapy Research, 7,* 105–125. http://dx.doi.org/10.1080/10503309712331331913

Caspar, F. (2007). Plan analysis. In T. D. Eells (Ed.), *Handbook of psychotherapy case formulation* (2nd ed., pp. 251–289). New York, NY: Guilford Press.

Caspar, F., Berger, T., & Hautle, I. (2004). The right view of your patient: A computer-assisted, individualized module for psychotherapy training. *Psychotherapy: Theory, Research & Practice, 41,* 125–135. http://dx.doi.org/10.1037/0033-3204.41.2.125

Caston, J. (1993). Can analysts agree? The problems of consensus and the psycho-analytic mannequin: I. A proposed solution. *Journal of the American Psycho-analytic Association*, *41*, 493–511. http://dx.doi.org/10.1177/000306519304100208

Caston, J., & Martin, E. (1993). Can analysts agree? The problems of consensus and the psychoanalytic mannequin: II. Empirical tests. *Journal of the American Psychoanalytic Association*, *41*, 513–548. http://dx.doi.org/10.1177/000306519304100209

Castonguay, L. G., & Beutler, L. E. (Eds.). (2006). *Principles of therapeutic change that work*. New York, NY: Oxford University Press.

Charman, D. P. (2004). Effective psychotherapy and effective psychotherapists. In D. P. Charman (Ed.), *Core processes in brief psychodynamic psychotherapy* (pp. 3–22). Mahwah, NJ: Erlbaum.

Chentsova-Dutton, Y. E., & Tsai, J. L. (2007). Cultural factors influence the expression of psychopathology. In S. O. Lilienfeld & W. T. O'Donohue (Eds.), *The great ideas of clinical science: 17 principles that every mental health professional should understand* (pp. 375–396). New York, NY: Routledge/Taylor & Francis.

Chi, M. T. H. (2006). Two approaches to the study of experts' characteristics. In K. A. Ericsson, N. Charness, P. J. Feltovich, & R. R. Hoffman (Eds.), *The Cambridge handbook of expertise and expert performance* (pp. 21–30). New York, NY: Cambridge University Press. http://dx.doi.org/10.1017/CBO9780511816796.002

Chi, M. T. H., Glaser, R., & Farr, M. J. (Eds.). (1988). *The nature of expertise*. Hillsdale, NJ: Erlbaum.

Chomsky, N. (1959). A review of B. F. Skinner's Verbal Behavior. *Language*, *35*, 26–58.

Clark, D. M., & Wells, A. (1995). A cognitive model of social phobia. In R. G. Heimberg & M. R. Liebowitz (Eds.), *Social phobia: Diagnosis, assessment, and treatment* (pp. 69–93). New York, NY: Guilford Press.

CNN. (1993). Repressed memories stir difficult controversy. *News*. Washington, DC: Author.

Cook, J. M., Biyanova, T., Elhai, J., Schnurr, P. P., & Coyne, J. C. (2010). What do psychotherapists really do in practice? An Internet study of over 2,000 practitioners. *Psychotherapy: Theory, Research & Practice*, *47*, 260–267. http://dx.doi.org/10.1037/a0019788

Cosgrove, L., & Krimsky, S. (2012). A comparison of *DSM–IV* and *DSM–5* panel members' financial associations with industry: A pernicious problem persists. *PLoS Medicine*, *9*, e1001190. http://dx.doi.org/10.1371/journal.pmed.1001190

Croskerry, P., & Norman, G. (2008). Overconfidence in clinical decision making. *The American Journal of Medicine*, *121*(Suppl. 5), S24–S29. http://dx.doi.org/10.1016/j.amjmed.2008.02.001

Curtis, J. T., & Silberschatz, G. (2007). Plan formulation method. In T. D. Eells (Ed.), *Handbook of psychotherapy case formulation* (2nd ed., pp. 198–220). New York, NY: Guilford Press.

Davison, G. C., & Neale, J. M. (2001). *Abnormal psychology* (8th ed.). New York, NY: Wiley.

de Groot, A. (1965). *Thought and choice in chess.* New York, NY: Norton.

DeNeve, K. M., & Cooper, H. (1998). The happy personality: A meta-analysis of 137 personality traits and subjective well-being. *Psychological Bulletin, 124,* 197–229. http://dx.doi.org/10.1037/0033-2909.124.2.197

Derogatis, L. R. (1983). *SCL-90-R Administration, scoring, and procedures manual II* (2nd ed.). Towson, MD: Clinical Psychometric Research.

Division of Clinical Psychology. (2001). *The core purpose and philosophy of the profession.* Leicester, England: The British Psychological Society.

Dowd, E. T., Milne, C. R., & Wise, S. L. (1991). The Therapeutic Reactance Scale: A measure of psychological reactance. *Journal of Counseling & Development, 69,* 541–545. http://dx.doi.org/10.1002/j.1556-6676.1991.tb02638.x

Dowd, E. T., & Wallbrown, F. (1993). Motivational components of client reactance. *Journal of Counseling & Development, 71,* 533–538. http://dx.doi.org/10.1002/j.1556-6676.1993.tb02237.x

Dowd, E. T., Wallbrown, F., Sanders, D., & Yesenosky, J. M. (1994). Psychological reactance and its relationship to normal personality variables. *Cognitive Therapy and Research, 18,* 601–612. http://dx.doi.org/10.1007/BF02355671

Dozier, M., Stovall-McClough, K. C., & Albus, K. E. (2008). Attachment and psychopathology in adulthood. In J. Cassidy & P. R. Shaver (Eds.), *Handbook of attachment: Theory, research, and clinical applications* (2nd ed., pp. 718–744). New York, NY: Guilford Press.

Draguns, J. G. (1997). Abnormal behavior patterns across cultures: Implications for counseling and psychotherapy. *International Journal of Intercultural Relations, 21,* 213–248. http://dx.doi.org/10.1016/S0147-1767(96)00046-6

Draguns, J. G. (2008). What have we learned about the interplay of culture with counseling and psychotherapy? In U. P. Gielen, J. G. Draguns, & J. M. Fish (Eds.), *Principles of multicultural counseling and therapy* (pp. 393–417). New York, NY: Routledge/Taylor & Francis.

Duckworth, M. P. (2009). Cultural awareness and culturally competent practice. In W. O'Donohue & J. E. Fisher (Eds.), *General principles and empirically supported techniques of cognitive behavior therapy* (pp. 63–76). Hoboken, NJ: Wiley.

Duncan, B. L., Miller, S. D., Wampold, B. E., & Hubble, M. A. (Eds.). (2010). *The heart and soul of change: Delivering what works in therapy* (2nd ed.). Washington, DC: American Psychological Association.

Eells, T. D. (Ed.). (2007a). *Handbook of psychotherapy case formulation* (2nd ed.). New York, NY: Guilford Press.

Eells, T. D. (2007b). Psychotherapy case formulation: History and current status. In T. D. Eells (Ed.), *Handbook of psychotherapy case formulation* (2nd ed., pp. 3–32). New York, NY: Guilford Press.

Eells, T. D. (2008, June). *The unfolding case formulation: Defining quality in development of the core inference.* Paper presented at the 39th Meeting of the Society for Psychotherapy Research, Barcelona, Spain.

Eells, T. D. (2010). The unfolding case formulation: The interplay of description and inference. *Pragmatic Case Studies in Psychotherapy, 6,* 225–254. http://dx.doi.org/10.14713/pcsp.v6i4.1046

Eells, T. D., Kendjelic, E. M., & Lucas, C. P. (1998). What's in a case formulation? Development and use of a content coding manual. *The Journal of Psychotherapy Practice & Research, 7,* 144–153.

Eells, T. D., & Lombart, K. G. (2003). Case formulation and treatment concepts among novice, experienced, and expert cognitive–behavioral and psychodynamic therapists. *Psychotherapy Research, 13*(2), 187–204. http://dx.doi.org/10.1093/ptr/kpg018

Eells, T. D., & Lombart, K. G. (2004). Case formulation: Determining the focus in brief dynamic psychotherapy. In D. P. Charman (Ed.), *Core processes in brief psychodynamic psychotherapy* (pp. 119–144). Mahwah, NJ: Erlbaum.

Eells, T. D., Lombart, K. G., Kendjelic, E. M., Turner, L. C., & Lucas, C. P. (2005). The quality of psychotherapy case formulations: A comparison of expert, experienced, and novice cognitive–behavioral and psychodynamic therapists. *Journal of Consulting and Clinical Psychology, 73,* 579–589. http://dx.doi.org/10.1037/0022-006X.73.4.579

Eells, T. D., Lombart, K. G., Salsman, N., Kendjelic, E. M., Schneiderman, C. T., & Lucas, C. P. (2011). Expert reasoning in psychotherapy case formulation. *Psychotherapy Research, 21,* 385–399. http://dx.doi.org/10.1080/10503307.2010.539284

Ehlers, A., & Clark, D. M. (2000). A cognitive model of posttraumatic stress disorder. *Behaviour Research and Therapy, 38,* 319–345. http://dx.doi.org/10.1016/S0005-7967(99)00123-0

Eisenhower, D. D. (1957, November 14). Remarks at the National Defense Executive Reserve Conference. Retrieved from http://www.presidency.ucsb.edu/ws/?pid=10951

Ellenberger, H. F. (1970). *The discovery of the unconscious: The history and evolution of dynamic psychiatry.* New York, NY: Basic Books.

Elliott, R., Bohart, A. C., Watson, J. C., & Greenberg, L. S. (2011). Empathy. In J. C. Norcross (Ed.), *Psychotherapy relationships that work: Evidence-based responsiveness* (2nd ed., pp. 132–152). New York, NY: Oxford University Press. http://dx.doi.org/10.1093/acprof:oso/9780199737208.003.0006

Ellis, A. (1994). *Reason and emotion in psychotherapy (revised and updated).* Secaucus, NJ: Birch Lane.

Ellis, A. (2000). Rational emotive behavior therapy (REBT). *Encyclopedia of psychology, Vol. 7.* (pp. 7–9). Washington, DC: American Psychological Association; New York, NY: Oxford University Press.

Epstein, N. B., & Baucom, D. H. (2002). *Enhanced cognitive–behavioral therapy for couples: A contextual approach.* Washington, DC: American Psychological Association. http://dx.doi.org/10.1037/10481-000

Ericsson, K. A. (2006). The influence of experience and deliberate practice on the development of superior expert performance. In K. A. Ericsson, N. Charness, P. J. Feltovich, & R. R. Hoffman (Eds.), *The Cambridge handbook of expertise and expert performance* (pp. 683–704). New York, NY: Cambridge University Press. http://dx.doi.org/10.1017/CBO9780511816796.038

Ericsson, K. A., Charness, N., Feltovich, P. J., & Hoffman, R. R. (Eds.). (2006). *The Cambridge handbook of expertise and expert performance.* New York, NY: Cambridge University Press. http://dx.doi.org/10.1017/CBO9780511816796

Erikson, E. (1980). *Identity and the life cycle.* New York, NY: Norton.

Evans, J. S. B. T. (2008). Dual-processing accounts of reasoning, judgment, and social cognition. *Annual Review of Psychology*, *59*, 255–278. http://dx.doi.org/10.1146/annurev.psych.59.103006.093629

Faust, D. (2007). Decision research can increase the accuracy of clinical judgment and thereby improve patient care. In S. O. Lilienfeld & W. T. O'Donohue (Eds.), *The great ideas of clinical science: 17 principles that every mental health professional should understand* (pp. 49–76). New York, NY: Routledge/Taylor & Francis.

Ferster, C. B. (1973). A functional analysis of depression. *American Psychologist*, *28*, 857–870. http://dx.doi.org/10.1037/h0035605

Festinger, L. (1957). *A theory of cognitive dissonance.* Stanford, CA: Stanford University Press.

First, M. B. (2014). Empirical grounding versus innovation in the *DSM–5* revision process: Implications for the future. *Clinical Psychology: Science and Practice*, *21*, 262–268. http://dx.doi.org/10.1111/cpsp.12069

First, M. B., Spitzer, R. L., Gibbon, M., & Williams, J. B. W. (1995). The Structured Clinical Interview for *DSM–III–R* Personality Disorders (SCID-II): I. Description. *Journal of Personality Disorders*, *9*, 83–91. http://dx.doi.org/10.1521/pedi.1995.9.2.83

Fischhoff, B. (1975). Hindsight is not equal to foresight: The effect of outcome knowledge on judgment under uncertainty. *Journal of Experimental*

Psychology: Human Perception and Performance, 1, 288–299. http://dx.doi. org/10.1037/0096-1523.1.3.288

Fischhoff, B. (1982). For those condemned to study the past: Heuristics and biases in hindsight. In D. Kahneman, P. Slovic, & A. Tversky (Eds.), *Judgment under uncertainty: Heuristics and biases* (pp. 335–352). Cambridge, MA: Cambridge University Press. http://dx.doi.org/10.1017/CBO9780511809477.024

Fishman, D. B. (2001). From single case to database: A new method for enhancing psychotherapy, forensic, and other psychological practice. *Applied & Preventive Psychology, 10,* 275–304. http://dx.doi.org/10.1016/S0962-1849(01)80004-4

Fleiss, J. L. (1986). *The design and analysis of clinical experiments.* New York, NY: John Wiley and Sons.

Frances, A. (2013a). Newsflash from APA meeting: *DSM–5* has flunked its reliability tests. *Psychology Today.* Retrieved from http://www.psychologytoday. com/blog/dsm5-in-distress/201205/newsflash-apa-meeting-dsm-5-has-flunked-its-reliability-tests

Frances, A. (2013b). *Saving normal: An insider's revolt against out-of-control psychiatric diagnosis,* DSM–5, *Big Pharma, and the medicalization of ordinary life.* New York, NY: William Morrow.

Frank, J. D. (1961). *Persuasion and healing: A comparative study of psychotherapy.* Baltimore, MD: The Johns Hopkins University Press.

Frank, J. D., & Frank, J. B. (1991). *Persuasion and healing: A comparative study of psychotherapy* (3rd ed.). Baltimore, MD: The Johns Hopkins University Press.

Frankfurter, D. (2006). *Evil incarnate: Rumors of demonic conspiracy and satanic abuse in history.* Princeton, NJ: Princeton University Press.

Freeman, D., Bentall, R., & Garety, P. (Eds.). (2008). *Persecutory delusions: Assessment, theory and treatment.* Oxford, England: Oxford University Press.

Garb, H. N. (2003). Incremental validity and the assessment of psychopathology in adults. *Psychological Assessment, 15,* 508–520. http://dx.doi.org/10.1037/ 1040-3590.15.4.508

Garmezy, N., Masten, A. S., & Tellegen, A. (1984). The study of stress and competence in children: A building block for developmental psychopathology. *Child Development, 55,* 97–111. http://dx.doi.org/10.2307/1129837

Ghaderi, A. (2011). Does case formulation make a difference to treatment outcome? In P. Sturmey & M. McMurran (Eds.), *Forensic case formulation* (pp. 61–79). Chichester, England: Wiley-Blackwell. http://dx.doi.org/10.1002/ 9781119977018.ch3

Gigerenzer, G. (2007). *Gut feelings: The intelligence of the unconscious.* New York, NY: Viking.

Gigerenzer, G., Todd, P. M., & the ABC Research Group. (1999). *Simple heuristics that make us smart.* New York, NY: Oxford University Press.

Goldfried, M. R. (1995). Toward a common language for case formulation. *Journal of Psychotherapy Integration, 5,* 221–244.

Goldfried, M. R., & Sprafkin, J. N. (1976). Behavioral personality assessment. In J. T. Spence, R. C. Carson, & J. W. Thibaut (Eds.), *Behavioral approaches to therapy* (pp. 295–321). Morristown, NJ: General Learning Press.

Goodheart, C. D. (2014). *A primer for* ICD–10–CM *users: Psychological and behavioral conditions.* Washington, DC: American Psychological Association. http://dx.doi.org/10.1037/14379-000

Gordis, L. (1990). *Epidemiology.* Philadelphia, PA: Saunders.

Gordon, L. V., & Mooney, R. L. (1950). *Mooney problem checklist manual: Adult form.* New York, NY: The Psychological Corporation.

Gottesman, I. I., & Gould, T. D. (2003). The endophenotype concept in psychiatry: Etymology and strategic intentions. *The American Journal of Psychiatry, 160,* 636–645. http://dx.doi.org/10.1176/appi.ajp.160.4.636

Gottman, J., & Silver, N. (1999). *Seven principles for making marriage work.* New York, NY: Three Rivers Press.

Greenberg, L. S. (2002). *Emotion-focused therapy: Coaching clients to work through their feelings.* Washington, DC: American Psychological Association.

Greenberg, L. S., & Goldman, R. (2007). Case formulation in emotion-focused therapy. In T. D. Eells (Ed.), *Handbook of psychotherapy case formulation* (2nd ed., pp. 379–411). New York, NY: Guilford Press.

Greenberg, L. S., & Paivio, S. C. (1997). *Working with emotions.* New York, NY: Guilford Press.

Greenberg, L. S., & Watson, J. C. (2005). *Emotion focused therapy for depression.* Washington, DC: American Psychological Association.

Grencavage, L. M., & Norcross, J. C. (1990). Where are the commonalities among the therapeutic common factors? *Professional Psychology: Research and Practice, 21,* 372–378. http://dx.doi.org/10.1037/0735-7028.21.5.372

Groopman, J. (2007). *How doctors think.* Boston, MA: Houghton Mifflin.

Haidt, J. (2006). *The happiness hypothesis: Finding modern truth in ancient wisdom.* New York, NY: Basic Books.

Halstead, J. E., Leach, C., & Rust, J. (2008). The development of a brief distress measure for the evaluation of psychotherapy and counseling (sPaCE) *Psychotherapy Research, 17,* 656–672.

Harkness, A. R. (2007). Personality traits are essential for a complete clinical science. In S. O. Lilienfeld & W. T. O'Donohue (Eds.), *The great ideas of clinical science: 17 principles that every mental health professional should understand* (pp. 263–290). New York, NY: Routledge/Taylor & Francis.

Hayes, S. C., & Strosahl, K. D. (Eds.). (2004). *A practical guide to acceptance and commitment therapy.* New York, NY: Springer. http://dx.doi.org/10. 1007/978-0-387-23369-7

Haynes, S. N., & Williams, A. E. (2003). Case formulation and design of behavioral treatment programs: Matching treatment mechanisms to causal variables for behavior problems. *European Journal of Psychological Assessment, 19,* 164–174. http://dx.doi.org/10.1027//1015-5759.19.3.164

Hays, P. A. (2008). *Addressing cultural complexities in practice: Assessment, diagnosis, and therapy* (2nd ed.). Washington, DC: American Psychological Association.

Henry, W. P. (1997). Interpersonal case formulation: Describing and explaining interpersonal patterns using the Structural Analysis of Social Behavior. In T. D. Eells (Ed.), *Handbook of psychotherapy case formulation* (pp. 223–259). New York, NY: Guilford.

Henry, W. P., Schacht, T. E., & Strupp, H. H. (1990). Patient and therapist introject, interpersonal process, and differential psychotherapy outcome. *Journal of Consulting and Clinical Psychology, 58,* 768–774. http://dx.doi. org/10.1037/0022-006X.58.6.768

Henry, W. P., Schacht, T. E., Strupp, H. H., Butler, S. F., & Binder, J. L. (1993). Effects of training in time-limited dynamic psychotherapy: Mediators of therapists' responses to training. *Journal of Consulting and Clinical Psychology, 61*(3), 441–447. http://dx.doi.org/10.1037/0022-006X.61.3.441

Heppner, P. P., Kivlighan, D. M., Good, G. E., Roehlke, H. J., Hills, H. J., & Ashby, J. S. (1994). Presenting problems of university counseling center clients: A snapshot and multivariate classification scheme. *Journal of Counseling Psychology, 41,* 315–324. http://dx.doi.org/10.1037/0022-0167.41.3.315

Hill, P. C., Pargament, K. I., Hood, R. W., Jr., McCullough, M. E., Swyers, J. P., Larson, B., & Zinnbauer, B. J. (2000). Conceptualizing religious and spirituality: Points of commonality, points of departure. *Journal for the Theory of Social Behaviour, 30,* 51–77. http://dx.doi.org/10.1111/1468-5914.00119

Hines, P. M., & Boyd-Franklin, N. (2005). African American families. In M. McGoldrick, J. Giordano, & N. Garcia-Preto (Eds.), *Ethnicity and family therapy* (3rd ed., pp. 87–100). New York, NY: Guilford Press.

Hinkle, L. E., Jr. (1974). The concept of "stress" in the biological and social sciences. *International Journal of Psychiatry in Medicine, 5,* 335–357. http://dx.doi. org/10.2190/91DK-NKAD-1XP0-Y4RG

Hogarth, R. M. (2001). *Educating intuition.* Chicago, IL: University of Chicago Press.

Holm, J. E., & Holroyd, K. A. (1992). The Daily Hassles Scale (Revised): Does it measure stress or symptoms? *Behavioral Assessment, 14,* 465–482.

Horney, K. (1950). *Neurosis and human growth: The struggle toward self-realization.* New York, NY: Norton.

Horowitz, M. J. (1997). *Formulation as a basis for planning psychotherapy treatment.* Washington, DC: American Psychiatric Press.

Horowitz, M. J. (2005). *Understanding psychotherapy change: A practical guide to configurational analysis.* Washington, DC: American Psychological Association.

Horowitz, M. J., Eells, T., Singer, J., & Salovey, P. (1995). Role-relationship models for case formulation. *Archives of General Psychiatry, 52,* 625–632. http://dx.doi.org/10.1001/archpsyc.1995.03950200015003

Horowitz, M. J., & Eells, T. D. (2007). Configurational analysis: States of mind, person schemas, and the control of ideas and affect. In T. D. Eells (Ed.), *Handbook of psychotherapy case formulation* (2nd ed., pp. 136–163). New York, NY: Guilford Press.

Horowitz, M. J., Ewert, M., & Milbrath, C. (1996). States of emotional control during psychotherapy. *The Journal of Psychotherapy Practice and Research, 5*(1), 20–25.

Horowitz, M. J., Milbrath, C., Ewert, M., Sonneborn, D., & Stinson, C. (1994). Cyclical patterns of states of mind in psychotherapy. *The American Journal of Psychiatry, 151,* 1767–1770.

Horowitz, M. J., Milbrath, C., Jordan, D. S., Stinson, C. H., Ewert, M., Redington, D. J., . . . Hartley, D. (1994). Expressive and defensive behavior during discourse on unresolved topics: A single case study of pathological grief. *Journal of Personality, 62,* 527–563. http://dx.doi.org/10.1111/j.1467-6494.1994.tb00308.x

Horowitz, M. J., Stinson, C., Curtis, D., Ewert, M., Redington, D., Singer, J., . . . Hartley, D. (1993). Topics and signs: Defensive control of emotional expression. *Journal of Consulting and Clinical Psychology, 61,* 421–430. http://dx.doi.org/10.1037/0022-006X.61.3.421

Howard, K. I., Kopta, S. M., Krause, M. S., & Orlinsky, D. E. (1986). The dose-effect relationship in psychotherapy. *American Psychologist, 41,* 159–164. http://dx.doi.org/10.1037/0003-066X.41.2.159

Howard, K. I., Lueger, R. J., Maling, M. S., & Martinovich, Z. (1993). A phase model of psychotherapy outcome: Causal mediation of change. *Journal of Consulting and Clinical Psychology, 61,* 678–685. http://dx.doi.org/10.1037/0022-006X.61.4.678

Hyler, S. E., Williams, J. B. W., & Spitzer, R. L. (1982). Reliability in the *DSM–III* field trials: Interview v case summary. *Archives of General Psychiatry, 39,* 1275–1278. http://dx.doi.org/10.1001/archpsyc.1982.04290110035006

Imel, Z. E., Baldwin, S., Atkins, D. C., Owen, J., Baardseth, T., & Wampold, B. E. (2011). Racial/ethnic disparities in therapist effectiveness: A conceptualization and initial study of cultural competence. *Journal of Counseling Psychology, 58,* 290–298. http://dx.doi.org/10.1037/a0023284

Ingram, B. L. (2012). *Clinical case formulations: Matching the integrative treatment plan to the client* (2nd ed.). Hoboken, NJ: Wiley

Johnson, R. A., Barrett, M. S., & Sisti, D. A. (2013). The ethical boundaries of patient and advocate influence on *DSM–5. Harvard Review of Psychiatry, 21,* 334–344.

Jose, A., & Goldfried, M. (2008). A transtheoretical approach to case formulation. *Cognitive and Behavioral Practice, 15,* 212–222. http://dx.doi.org/10.1016/j.cbpra.2007.02.009

Jung, C. G. (1972). *Two essays on analytical psychology.* Princeton, NJ: Princeton University Press.

Kagan, J. (1998). *Galen's prophecy: Temperament in human nature.* New York, NY: Basic Books.

Kahneman, D. (2011). *Thinking, fast and slow.* New York, NY: Farrar, Straus and Giroux.

Kahneman, D., & Frederick, S. (2002). A model of heuristic judgment. In T. Gilovich, D. Griffin, & D. Kahneman (Eds.), *Heuristics and biases: The psychology of intuitive judgment* (pp. 49–81). New York, NY: Cambridge University Press. http://dx.doi.org/10.1017/CBO9780511808098.004

Kahneman, D., & Klein, G. (2009). Conditions for intuitive expertise: A failure to disagree. *American Psychologist, 64,* 515–526. http://dx.doi.org/10.1037/a0016755

Kahneman, D., Slovic, P., & Tversky, A. (Eds.). (1982). *Judgment under uncertainty: Heuristics and biases.* Cambridge, MA: Cambridge University Press. http://dx.doi.org/10.1017/CBO9780511809477

Kazdin, A. E. (2007). Mediators and mechanisms of change in psychotherapy research. *Annual Review of Clinical Psychology, 3,* 1–27. http://dx.doi.org/10.1146/annurev.clinpsy.3.022806.091432

Kazdin, A. E. (2008). Evidence-based treatment and practice: New opportunities to bridge clinical research and practice, enhance the knowledge base, and improve patient care. *American Psychologist, 63,* 146–159. http://dx.doi.org/10.1037/0003-066X.63.3.146

Keller, F. S., & Schoenfeld, W. N. (1950). *Principles of psychology: A systematic text in the science of behavior.* New York, NY: Appleton, Century Crofts.

Kelly, G. A. (1955a). *The psychology of personal constructs. Vol. 1. A theory of personality.* Oxford, England: Norton.

Kelly, G. A. (1955b). *The psychology of personal constructs. Vol. 2. Clinical diagnosis and psychotherapy.* Oxford, England: Norton.

Kendell, R. E. (1975). *The role of diagnosis in psychiatry.* Philadelphia, PA: Blackwell Scientific.

Kendler, K. S. (2013). A history of the *DSM–5* scientific review committee. *Psychological Medicine, 43,* 1793–1800. http://dx.doi.org/10.1017/S0033291713001578

Kendler, K. S., Eaves, L. J., Loken, E. K., Pedersen, N. L., Middeldorp, C. M., Reynolds, C., . . . Gardner, C. O. (2011). The impact of environmental experiences on symptoms of anxiety and depression across the life span. *Psychological Science, 22,* 1343–1352. http://dx.doi.org/10.1177/0956797611417255

Kendler, K. S., Prescott, C. A., Myers, J., & Neale, M. C. (2003). The structure of genetic and environmental risk factors for common psychiatric and substance use disorders in men and women. *Archives of General Psychiatry, 60,* 929–937. http://dx.doi.org/10.1001/archpsyc.60.9.929

Kernberg, O. F. (1975). *Borderline conditions and pathological narcissism.* New York, NY: Jason Aronson.

Kernberg, O. F., Selzer, M. A., Koenigsberg, H. W., Carr, A. C., & Appelbaum, A. H. (1989). *Psychodynamic psychotherapy of borderline patients.* New York, NY: Basic Books.

Kessler, R. C., Chiu, W. T., Demler, O., Merikangas, K. R., & Walters, E. E. (2005). Prevalence, severity, and comorbidity of twelve-month *DSM–IV* disorders in the National Comorbidity Survey Replication (NCS-R). *Archives of General Psychiatry, 62,* 617–627.

Kessler, R. C., & Wang, P. S. (2009). Epidemiology of depression. In I. H. Gotlib & C. L. Hammen (Eds.), *Handbook of depression* (2nd ed., pp. 5–22). New York, NY: Guilford Press.

Kirk, S. A., & Kutchins, H. (1992). *The selling of* DSM: *The rhetoric of science in psychiatry.* New York, NY: Aldine.

Klein, G. (1998). *Sources of power: How people make decisions.* Cambridge, MA: MIT Press.

Koerner, K. (2007). Case formulation in dialectical behavior therapy for borderline personality disorder. In T. D. Eells (Ed.), *Handbook of psychotherapy case formulation* (2nd ed., pp. 317–348). New York, NY: Guilford Press.

Kohut, H. (1971). *Analysis of the self.* New York, NY: International Universities Press.

Kohut, H. (1977). *Restoration of the self.* New York, NY: International Universities Press.

Kopta, S. M., Howard, K. I., Lowry, J. L., & Beutler, L. E. (1994). Patterns of symptomatic recovery in psychotherapy. *Journal of Consulting and Clinical Psychology, 62,* 1009–1016. http://dx.doi.org/10.1037/0022-006X.62.5.1009

Krass, J., Kinoshita, S., & McConkey, K. M. (1989). Hypnotic memory and confident reporting. *Applied Cognitive Psychology*, *3*, 35–51. http://dx.doi.org/10.1002/acp.2350030105

Kroeber, A. L., & Kluckhohn, C. (1952). *Culture: A critical review of concepts and definitions.* Cambridge, MA: The Museum.

Kroenke, K., Spitzer, R. L., & Williams, J. B. (2001). The PHQ-9: Validity of a brief depression severity measure. *Journal of General Internal Medicine*, *16*, 606–613. http://dx.doi.org/10.1046/j.1525-1497.2001.016009606.x

Krueger, R. F., Hopwood, C. J., Wright, A. G. C., & Markon, K. E. (2014). *DSM–5* and the path toward empirically based and clinically useful conceptualization of personality and psychopathology. *Clinical Psychology: Science and Practice*, *21*, 245–261. http://dx.doi.org/10.1111/cpsp.12073

Kuehlwein, K. T., & Rosen, H. (1993). *Cognitive therapies in action: Evolving innovative practice.* San Francisco, CA: Jossey-Bass.

Kutchins, H., & Kirk, S. A. (1997). *Making us crazy: DSM: The psychiatric bible and the creation of mental disorders.* New York, NY: The Free Press.

Kuyken, W., Fothergill, C. D., Musa, M., & Chadwick, P. (2005). The reliability and quality of cognitive case formulation. *Behaviour Research and Therapy*, *43*, 1187–1201. http://dx.doi.org/10.1016/j.brat.2004.08.007

Kuyken, W., Padesky, C. A., & Dudley, R. (2009). *Collaborative case conceptualization: Working effectively with clients in cognitive–behavioral therapy.* New York, NY: Guilford Press.

Lambert, M. J. (2007). Presidential address: What we have learned from a decade of research aimed at improving psychotherapy outcome in routine care. *Psychotherapy Research*, *17*(1), 1–14. http://dx.doi.org/10.1080/10503300601032506

Lambert, M. J. (2010). Yes, it is time for clinicians to routinely monitor treatment outcome. In B. L. Duncan, S. D. Miller, B. E. Wampold, & M. A. Hubble (Eds.), *The heart and soul of change: Delivering what works in therapy* (2nd ed., pp. 239–266). Washington, DC: American Psychological Association. http://dx.doi.org/10.1037/12075-008

Lambert, M. J. (2013a). The efficacy and effectiveness of psychotherapy. In M. J. Lambert (Ed.), *Bergin and Garfield's handbook of psychotherapy and behavior change* (6th ed., pp. 169–218). New York, NY: Wiley.

Lambert, M. J. (2013b). Introduction and historical overview. In M. J. Lambert (Ed.), *Bergin and Garfield's handbook of psychotherapy and behavior change* (6th ed., pp. 3–20). New York, NY: Wiley.

Lambert, M. J., & Finch, A. E. (1999). The Outcome Questionnaire. In M. E. Maruish (Ed.), *The use of psychological testing for treatment planning and outcomes assessment* (2nd ed., pp. 831–869). Mahwah, NJ: Erlbaum.

Lambert, M. J., Morton, J. J., Hatfield, D., Harmon, C., Hamilton, S., Reid, R. C., & Burlingame, G. M. (2004). *Administration and scoring manual for the Outcome Questionnaire-45.* Orem, UT: American Professional Credentialing Services.

Langs, R. (1998). *Ground rules in psychotherapy and counselling.* London, England: Karnac Books.

Latham, G. P., & Locke, E. A. (2007). New developments in and directions for goal-setting research. *European Psychologist, 12,* 290–300. http://dx.doi.org/10.1027/1016-9040.12.4.290

Lazarus, R. S. (2000). Toward better research on stress and coping. *American Psychologist, 55,* 665–673. http://dx.doi.org/10.1037/0003-066X.55.6.665

Lazarus, R. S., & DeLongis, A. (1983). Psychological stress and coping in aging. *American Psychologist, 38,* 245–254. http://dx.doi.org/10.1037/0003-066X.38.3.245

Lazarus, R. S., & Folkman, S. (1984). *Stress, appraisal, and coping.* New York, NY: Springer.

Levenson, H. (1995). *Time-limited dynamic psychotherapy: A guide to clinical practice.* New York, NY: Basic Books.

Levenson, H., & Strupp, H. H. (2007). Cyclical maladaptive patterns: Case formulation in time-limited dynamic psychotherapy. In T. D. Eells (Ed.), *Handbook of psychotherapy case formulation* (2nd ed., pp. 164–197). New York, NY: Guilford Press.

Lewinsohn, P. M. (1974). A behavioural approach to depression. In R. M. Friedman & M. M. Katz (Eds.), *The psychology of depression: Contemporary theory and research* (pp. 157–178). New York, NY: Wiley.

Lewinsohn, P. M., Antonuccio, D. O., Breckenridge, J., & Teri, L. (1987). *The coping with depression course: A psychoeducational intervention for unipolar depression.* Eugene, OR: Castaglia.

Lewinsohn, P. M., & Shaffer, M. (1971). Use of home observations as an integral part of the treatment of depression; preliminary report and case studies. *Journal of Consulting and Clinical Psychology, 37,* 87–94. http://dx.doi.org/10.1037/h0031297

Linehan, M. M. (1993). *Cognitive–behavioral treatment of borderline personality disorder.* New York, NY: Guilford Press.

Locke, E. A., & Latham, G. P. (1990). *A theory of goal setting and task performance.* Englewood Cliffs, NJ: Prentice-Hall.

Luborsky, L. (1977). Measuring a pervasive psychic structure in psychotherapy: The core conflictual relationship theme. In N. Freedman & S. Grand (Eds.), *Communicative structures and psychic structures* (pp. 367–395). New York, NY: Plenum Press. http://dx.doi.org/10.1007/978-1-4757-0492-1_16

Luborsky, L. (1996). *The symptom-context method: Symptoms as opportunities in psychotherapy.* Washington, DC: American Psychological Association.

Luborsky, L., & Barrett, M. S. (2007). The core conflictual relationship theme: A basic case formulation method. In T. D. Eells (Ed.), *Handbook of psychotherapy case formulation* (2nd ed., pp. 105–135). New York, NY: Guilford Press.

Lynn, S. J., Matthews, A., Williams, J. C., Hallquist, M. N., & Lilienfeld, S. O. (2007). Some forms of psychopathology are partly socially constructed. In S. O. Lilienfeld & W. T. O'Donohue (Eds.), *The great ideas of clinical science: 17 principles that every mental health professional should understand* (pp. 347–373). New York, NY: Routledge.

Mack, A. H., Forman, L., Brown, R., & Frances, A. (1994). A brief history of psychiatric classification: From the ancients to *DSM–IV. Psychiatric Clinics of North America, 17,* 515–523.

Mahoney, M. J. (1991). *Human change processes: The scientific foundations of psychotherapy.* New York, NY: Basic Books.

Markowitz, J. C., & Swartz, H. A. (2007). Case formulation in interpersonal psychotherapy of depression. In T. D. Eells (Ed.), *Handbook of psychotherapy case formulation* (2nd ed., pp. 221–250). New York, NY: Guilford Press.

Markus, H., & Wurf, E. (1987). The dynamic self-concept: A social psychological perspective. *Annual Review of Psychology, 38,* 299–337. http://dx.doi.org/10.1146/annurev.ps.38.020187.001503

Martin, D. J., Garske, J. P., & Davis, M. K. (2000). Relation of the therapeutic alliance with outcome and other variables: A meta-analytic review. *Journal of Consulting and Clinical Psychology, 68,* 438–450. http://dx.doi.org/10.1037/0022-006X.68.3.438

Maslow, A. H. (1987). *Motivation and personality* (3rd ed.). New York, NY: Harper & Row.

Masten, A. S. (2001). Ordinary magic. Resilience processes in development. *American Psychologist, 56,* 227–238. http://dx.doi.org/10.1037/0003-066X.56.3.227

McCabe, G. H. (2007). The healing path: A culture and community-derived indigenous therapy model. *Psychotherapy: Theory, Research, Practice, Training, 44,* 148–160. http://dx.doi.org/10.1037/0033-3204.44.2.148

McClain, T., O'Sullivan, P. S., & Clardy, J. A. (2004). Biopsychosocial formulation: Recognizing educational shortcomings. *Academic Psychiatry, 28,* 88–94. http://dx.doi.org/10.1176/appi.ap.28.2.88

McGoldrick, M., Giordano, J., & Garcia-Preto, N. (Eds.). (2005). *Ethnicity and family therapy* (3rd ed.). New York, NY: Guilford Press.

Meehl, P. E. (1954). *Clinical versus statistical prediction: A theoretical analysis and a review of the evidence.* Minneapolis: University of Minnesota Press.

Meehl, P. E. (1962). Schizotaxia, schizotypy, schizophrenia. *American Psychologist*, *17*, 827–838. http://dx.doi.org/10.1037/h0041029

Meehl, P. E. (1973a). *Psychodiagnosis: Selected papers*. New York, NY: Norton.

Meehl, P. E. (1973b). Why I do not attend case conferences. In P. E. Meehl (Ed.), *Psychodiagnosis: Selected papers* (pp. 225–302). New York, NY: Norton.

Messer, S. B. (1986). Behavioral and psychoanalytic perspectives at therapeutic choice points. *American Psychologist*, *41*, 1261–1272. http://dx.doi.org/10.1037/0003-066X.41.11.1261

Messer, S. B., & Winokur, M. (1980). Some limits to the integration of psychoanalytic and behavior therapy. *American Psychologist*, *35*, 818–827. http://dx.doi.org/10.1037/0003-066X.35.9.818

Messer, S. B., & Wolitzky, D. L. (2007). The traditional psychoanalytic approach to case formulation. In T. D. Eells (Ed.), *Handbook of psychotherapy case formulation* (2nd ed., pp. 67–104). New York, NY: Guilford Press.

Michael, J. (2000). Implications and refinements of the establishing operation concept. *Journal of Applied Behavior Analysis*, *33*, 401–410. http://dx.doi.org/10.1901/jaba.2000.33-401

Miller, S. D., Duncan, B. L., Sorrell, R., & Brown, G. S. (2005). The partners for change outcome management system. *Journal of Clinical Psychology*, *61*, 199–208. http://dx.doi.org/10.1002/jclp.20111

Millon, T., & Klerman, G. L. (1986). On the past and future of the *DSM–III*: Personal recollections and projections. In T. Millon & G. L. Klerman (Eds.), *Contemporary directions in psychopathology: Toward the* DSM–IV (pp. 29–70). New York, NY: Guilford Press.

Mineka, S., & Zinbarg, R. (2006). A contemporary learning theory perspective on the etiology of anxiety disorders: It's not what you thought it was. *American Psychologist*, *61*, 10–26. http://dx.doi.org/10.1037/0003-066X.61.1.10

Monroe, S. M., & Simons, A. D. (1991). Diathesis–stress theories in the context of life stress research: Implications for the depressive disorders. *Psychological Bulletin*, *110*, 406–425. http://dx.doi.org/10.1037/0033-2909.110.3.406

Morin, C. M., Bootzin, R. R., Buysse, D. J., Edinger, J. D., Espie, C. A., & Lichstein, K. L. (2006). Psychological and behavioral treatment of insomnia: Update of the recent evidence (1998–2004). *Sleep*, *29*, 1398–1414.

Morrison, J. (in press). *When psychological problems mask medical disorders: A guide for psychotherapists* (2nd ed.). New York, NY: Guilford Press.

Morrison, J. (2008). *The first interview* (3rd ed.). New York, NY: Guilford Press.

Mumma, G. H. (2011). Current issues in case formulation. In P. Sturmey & M. McMurran (Eds.), *Forensic case formulation* (pp. 33–60). Chichester, England: Wiley-Blackwell. http://dx.doi.org/10.1002/9781119977018.ch2

Murray, H. A. (1938). *Explorations in personality: A clinical and experimental study of fifty men of college age.* New York, NY: Oxford University Press.

Myers, D. G. (2002). *Intuition: Its powers and perils.* New Haven, CT: Yale University Press.

Nathan, P. E., & Gorman, J. M. (2007). *A guide to treatments that work* (3rd ed.). Oxford, England: Oxford University Press.

Nelson-Gray, R. O. (2003). Treatment utility of psychological assessment. *Psychological Assessment, 15,* 521–531. http://dx.doi.org/10.1037/1040-3590.15.4.521

Newell, A., Shaw, J. C., & Simon, H. A. (1958). Elements of a theory of human problem solving. *Psychological Review, 65,* 151–166. http://dx.doi.org/10.1037/h0048495

Newman, B. M., & Newman, P. R. (1999). *Development through life: A psychosocial approach.* Belmont, CA: Wadsworth.

Nezu, A. M., Nezu, C. M., & Cos, T. A. (2007). Case formulation for the behavioral and cognitive therapies. In T. D. Eells (Ed.), *Handbook of psychotherapy case formulation* (2nd ed., pp. 349–378). New York, NY: Guilford Press.

Nezu, A. M., Nezu, C. M., & Lombardo, E. R. (2004). *Cognitive–behavioral case formulation and treatment design: A problem-solving approach.* New York, NY: Springer.

Nock, M. K., & Kessler, R. C. (2006). Prevalence of and risk factors for suicide attempts versus suicide gestures: Analysis of the National Comorbidity Survey. *Journal of Abnormal Psychology, 115,* 616–623. http://dx.doi.org/10.1037/0021-843X.115.3.616

Nolen-Hoeksema, S., Wisco, B. E., & Lyubomirsky, S. (2008). Rethinking rumination. *Perspectives on Psychological Science, 3,* 400–424. http://dx.doi.org/10.1111/j.1745-6924.2008.00088.x

Norcross, J. C. (2005). A primer on psychotherapy integration. In J. C. Norcross & M. R. Goldfried (Eds.), *Handbook of psychotherapy integration* (2nd ed., pp. 3–23). New York, NY: Oxford University Press.

Norcross, J. C. (2011). *Psychotherapy relationships that work: Evidence-based responsiveness* (2nd ed.). New York, NY: Oxford University Press. http://dx.doi.org/10.1093/acprof:oso/9780199737208.001.0001

Norcross, J. C., Karpiak, C. P., & Santoro, S. O. (2005). Clinical psychologists across the years: The division of clinical psychology from 1960 to 2003. *Journal of Clinical Psychology, 61,* 1467–1483. http://dx.doi.org/10.1002/jclp.20135

Norcross, J. C., Krebs, P. M., & Prochaska, J. O. (2011). Stages of change. In J. C. Norcross (Ed.), *Psychotherapy relationships that work: Evidence-based responsiveness* (2nd ed., pp. 279–300). New York, NY: Oxford University Press. http://dx.doi.org/10.1093/acprof:oso/9780199737208.003.0014

Norcross, J. C., & Wampold, B. E. (2011). Evidence-based therapy relationships: Research conclusions and clinical practices. In J. C. Norcross (Ed.), *Psychotherapy relationships that work: Evidence-based responsiveness* (2nd ed., pp. 423–430). New York, NY: Oxford University Press. http://dx.doi.org/10.1093/acprof:oso/9780199737208.003.0021

Nuland, S. B. (1995). *Doctors: The biography of medicine.* New York, NY: Vintage Books.

O'Donohue, W. T., & Fisher, J. E. (2009). *General principles and empirically supported techniques of cognitive behavior therapy* (2nd ed.). Hoboken, NJ: Wiley.

Ogden, T. H. (1979). On projective identification. *The International Journal of Psychoanalysis, 60,* 357–373.

Olfson, M., & Marcus, S. C. (2010). National trends in outpatient psychotherapy. *The American Journal of Psychiatry, 167,* 1456–1463. http://dx.doi.org/10.1176/appi.ajp.2010.10040570

Ondersma, S. J., Chaffin, M., Berliner, L., Cordon, I., Goodman, G. S., & Barnett, D. (2001). Sex with children is abuse: Comment on Rind, Tromovitch, and Bauserman (1998). *Psychological Bulletin, 127,* 707–714. http://dx.doi.org/10.1037/0033-2909.127.6.707

Orlinsky, D. E., & Rønnestad, M. H. (2005). *How psychotherapists develop: A study of therapeutic work and professional growth.* Washington, DC: American Psychological Association.

Orlinsky, D. E., Rønnestad, M. H., & Willutzki, U. (2004). Fifty years of psychotherapy process-outcome research: Continuity and change. In M. J. Lambert (Ed.), *Bergin and Garfield's handbook of psychotherapy and behavior change* (pp. 307–389). New York, NY: Wiley.

Owen, J., Imel, Z., Adelson, J., & Rodolfa, E. (2012). "No show": Therapist racial/ethnic disparities in client unilateral termination. *Journal of Counseling Psychology, 59,* 314–320. http://dx.doi.org/10.1037/a0027091

Perls, F., Hefferline, R. F., & Goodman, P. (1965). *Gestalt therapy.* Oxford, England: Dell.

Perry, S., Cooper, A. M., & Michels, R. (1987). The psychodynamic formulation: Its purpose, structure, and clinical application. *The American Journal of Psychiatry, 144,* 543–550.

Persons, J. B. (2008). *The case formulation approach to cognitive–behavior therapy.* New York, NY: Guilford Press.

Persons, J. B., Roberts, N. A., Zalecki, C. A., & Brechwald, W. A. G. (2006). Naturalistic outcome of case formulation-driven cognitive–behavior therapy for anxious depressed outpatients. *Behaviour Research and Therapy, 44,* 1041–1051. http://dx.doi.org/10.1016/j.brat.2005.08.005

Peterson, D. R. (1991). Connection and disconnection of research and practice in the education of professional psychologists. *American Psychologist, 46,* 422–429. http://dx.doi.org/10.1037/0003-066X.46.4.422

Pew Research Center's Religion & Public Life Project. (2008). *U.S. Religious Landscape Survey.* Washington, DC: Author.

Pew Research Center's Religion & Public Life Project. (2012). *The global religious landscape: A report on the size and distribution of the world's major religious groups as of 2010.* Washington, DC: Author.

Plomin, R., DeFries, J. C., Knopik, V. S., & Neiderhiser, J. M. (2013). *Behavioral genetics.* San Francisco, CA: Freeman.

Pomerantz, A. (2008). *Clinical psychology: Science, practice and culture.* Thousand Oaks, CA: Sage.

Postman, L. (1951). Toward a general theory of cognition. In J. H. Rohrer & M. Sherif (Eds.), *Social psychology at the crossroads; the University of Oklahoma lectures in social psychology* (pp. 242–272). Oxford, England: Harper.

Potchen, E. J. (2006). Measuring observer performance in chest radiology: Some experiences. [Review]. *Journal of the American College of Radiology, 3,* 423–432. http://dx.doi.org/10.1016/j.jacr.2006.02.020

Prochaska, J. O., & DiClemente, C. C. (2005). The transtheoretical approach. In J. C. Norcross & M. R. Goldfried (Eds.), *Handbook of psychotherapy integration* (pp. 147–171). New York, NY: Oxford University Press.

Randall, C. L., Book, S. W., Carrigan, M. H., & Thomas, S. E. (2008). Treatment of co-occurring alcoholism and social anxiety disorder. In S. Stewart & P. Conrod (Eds.), *Anxiety and substance use disorders: The vicious cycle of comorbidity.* (pp. 139–155): New York, NY: Springer Science + Business Media.

Raps, C. S., Peterson, C., Reinhard, K. E., Abramson, L. Y., & Seligman, M. E. P. (1982). Attributional style among depressed patients. *Journal of Abnormal Psychology, 91,* 102–108. http://dx.doi.org/10.1037/0021-843X.91.2.102

Regier, D. A., Narrow, W. E., Clarke, D. E., Kraemer, H. C., Kuramoto, S. J., Kuhl, E. A., & Kupfer, D. J. (2013). *DSM-5* field trials in the United States and Canada, Part II: Test–retest reliability of selected categorical diagnoses. *The American Journal of Psychiatry, 170,* 59–70. http://dx.doi.org/10.1176/appi.ajp.2012.12070999

Regier, D. A., Narrow, W. E., Kuhl, E. A., & Kupfer, D. J. (2009). The conceptual development of *DSM-V. The American Journal of Psychiatry, 166,* 645–650. http://dx.doi.org/10.1176/appi.ajp.2009.09020279

Reik, T. (1948). *Listening with the third ear.* New York, NY: Farrar, Straus and Giroux.

Ridley, C. R., & Kelly, S. M. (2007). Multicultural considerations in case formulation. In T. D. Eells (Ed.), *Handbook of psychotherapy case formulation* (2nd ed.). New York, NY: Guilford Press, pp. 33–64.

Rind, B., Tromovitch, P., & Bauserman, R. (1998). A meta-analytic examination of assumed properties of child sexual abuse using college samples. *Psychological Bulletin, 124,* 22–53. http://dx.doi.org/10.1037/0033-2909.124.1.22

Rind, B., Tromovitch, P., & Bauserman, R. (2001). The validity and appropriateness of methods, analyses, and conclusions in Rind et al. (1998): A rebuttal of victimological critique from Ondersma et al. (2001) and Dallam et al. (2001). *Psychological Bulletin, 127,* 734–758. http://dx.doi.org/10.1037/0033-2909.127.6.734

Rogers, C. R. (1951). *Client-centered therapy, its current practice, implications, and theory.* Boston, MA: Houghton Mifflin.

Rosenzweig, P. (2007). *The halo effect . . . and the eight other business delusions that deceive managers.* New York, NY: Free Press.

Rosenzweig, S. (1936). Some implicit common factors in diverse methods of psychotherapy. *American Journal of Orthopsychiatry, 6,* 412–415. http://dx.doi.org/10.1111/j.1939-0025.1936.tb05248.x

Ross, L. (1977). The intuitive psychologist and his shortcomings: Distortions in the attribution process. In L. Berkowitz (Ed.), *Advances in experimental social psychology* (Vol. 10, pp. 173–220). Orlando, FL: Academic Press.

Ross, M., & Sicoly, F. (1979). Egocentric biases in availability and attribution. *Journal of Personality and Social Psychology, 37,* 322–336. http://dx.doi.org/10.1037/0022-3514.37.3.322

Ruscio, J. (2007). The clinician as subject: Practitioners are prone to the same judgment errors as everyone else. In S. O. Lilienfeld & W. T. O'Donohue (Eds.), *The great ideas of clinical science: 17 principles that every mental health professional should understand* (pp. 29–47). New York, NY: Routledge/Taylor & Francis.

Ryle, A. (1990). *Cognitive analytic therapy: Active participation in change.* Chichester, England: Wiley.

Ryle, A., & Bennett, D. (1997). Case formulation in cognitive analytic therapy. In T. D. Eells (Ed.), *Handbook of psychotherapy case formulation* (pp. 289–313). New York, NY: Guilford Press.

Sadler, J. Z. (2005). *Values and psychiatric diagnosis.* Oxford, England: Oxford University Press.

Safran, J. D., Muran, J. C., & Eubanks-Carter, C. (2011). Repairing alliance ruptures. In J. C. Norcross (Ed.), *Psychotherapy relationships that work: Evidence-based responsiveness* (pp. 224–254). New York, NY: Oxford University Press. http://dx.doi.org/10.1093/acprof:oso/9780199737208.003.0011

Salkovskis, P. M. (1996). The cognitive approach to anxiety: threat beliefs, safety-seeking behaviour and the special case of health anxiety and obsessions. In P. M. Salkovskis (Ed.), *Frontiers of cognitive therapy* (pp. 48–74). New York, NY: The Guilford Press.

Schacht, T. E. (1985). *DSM–III* and the politics of truth. *American Psychologist, 40,* 513–521. http://dx.doi.org/10.1037/0003-066X.40.5.513

Schacter, D. L. (2001). *The seven sins of memory: How the mind forgets and remembers.* Boston, MA: Houghton Mifflin.

Schneiderman, N., Ironson, G., & Siegel, S. D. (2005). Stress and health: Psychological, behavioral, and biological determinants. *Annual Review of Clinical Psychology, 1,* 607–628. http://dx.doi.org/10.1146/annurev.clinpsy.1.102803.144141

Schwartz, B. (2004). *The paradox of choice.* New York, NY: HarperCollins.

Schwarz, N., Strack, F., Hilton, D., & Naderer, G. (1991). Base rates, representativeness, and the logic of conversation: The contextual relevance of "irrelevant" information. *Social Cognition, 9*(1), 67–84. http://dx.doi.org/10.1521/soco.1991.9.1.67

Seitz, P. F. (1966). The consensus problem in psychoanalytic research. In L. Gottschalk & L. Auerbach (Eds.), *Methods of research and psychotherapy* (pp. 209–225). New York, NY: Appleton, Century, Crofts. http://dx.doi.org/10.1007/978-1-4684-6045-2_17

Selye, H. (1976). *The stress of life* (Revised ed.). New York, NY: McGraw-Hill.

Shakow, D. (1976). What is clinical psychology? *American Psychologist, 31,* 553–560. http://dx.doi.org/10.1037/0003-066X.31.8.553

Silberschatz, G. (2005a). An overview of research on control-mastery theory. In G. Silberschatz (Ed.), *Transformative relationships: The control-mastery theory of psychotherapy* (pp. 189–218). New York, NY: Routledge.

Silberschatz, G. (2005b). *Transformative relationships: The control-mastery theory of psychotherapy.* New York, NY: Routledge.

Simon, H. A. (1956). Rational choice and the structure of the environment. *Psychological Review, 63,* 129–138. http://dx.doi.org/10.1037/h0042769

Simon, H. A. (1992). What is an "explanation" of behavior? *Psychological Science, 3,* 150–161. http://dx.doi.org/10.1111/j.1467-9280.1992.tb00017.x

Singer, J. L., & Salovey, P. (1991). Organized knowledge structures and personality. In M. J. Horowitz (Ed.), *Person schemas and maladaptive interpersonal patterns* (pp. 33–80). Chicago, IL: University of Chicago Press.

Skinner, B. F. (1953). *Science and human behavior.* New York, NY: The Free Press.

Smith, H. (1991). *The world's religions.* New York, NY: Harper Collins.

Smith, T. B., Rodriguez, M. D., & Bernal, G. (2011). Culture. In J. C. Norcross (Ed.), *Psychotherapy relationships that work: Evidence-based responsiveness* (2nd ed., pp. 316–335). New York, NY: Oxford University Press. http://dx.doi.org/10.1093/acprof:oso/9780199737208.003.0016

Sperry, L., & Sperry, J. (2012). *Case conceptualization: Mastering this competency with ease and confidence.* New York, NY: Taylor & Francis.

Spiegel, A. (2005, January). The dictionary of disorder: How one man revolutionized psychiatry. *The New Yorker,* 56–63.

Spitzer, R. L., Forman, J. B., & Nee, J. (1979). *DSM–III* field trials: I. Initial interrater diagnostic reliability. *The American Journal of Psychiatry, 136,* 815–817.

Spitzer, R. L., Kroenke, K., Williams, J. B., & Löwe, B. (2006). A brief measure for assessing generalized anxiety disorder: The GAD-7. *Archives of Internal Medicine, 166,* 1092–1097. http://dx.doi.org/10.1001/archinte.166.10.1092

Spitzer, R. L., Williams, J. B., Gibbon, M., & First, M. B. (1992). The Structured Clinical Interview for *DSM–III–R* (SCID). I: History, rationale, and description. *Archives of General Psychiatry, 49,* 624–629. http://dx.doi.org/10.1001/archpsyc.1992.01820080032005

Stanovich, K. E. (2009). *What intelligence tests miss.* New Haven, CT: Yale University Press.

Steblay, N. M., & Bothwell, R. K. (1994). Evidence for hypnotically refreshed testimony: The view from the laboratory. *Law and Human Behavior, 18,* 635–651. http://dx.doi.org/10.1007/BF01499329

Steele, C. M., & Aronson, J. (1995). Stereotype threat and the intellectual test performance of African Americans. *Journal of Personality and Social Psychology, 69,* 797–811. http://dx.doi.org/10.1037/0022-3514.69.5.797

Strupp, H. H., & Binder, J. L. (1984). *Psychotherapy in a new key.* New York, NY: Basic Books.

Sturmey, P. (2008). *Behavioral case formulation and intervention: A functional analytic approach.* Chichester, England: Wiley-Blackwell. http://dx.doi.org/10.1002/9780470773192

Sue, D. W., Capodilupo, C. M., Torino, G. C., Bucceri, J. M., Holder, A. M. B., Nadal, K. L., & Esquilin, M. (2007). Racial microaggressions in everyday life: Implications for clinical practice. *American Psychologist, 62,* 271–286. http://dx.doi.org/10.1037/0003-066X.62.4.271

Sue, S. (1998). In search of cultural competence in psychotherapy and counseling. *American Psychologist, 53,* 440–448. http://dx.doi.org/10.1037/0003-066X.53.4.440

Sullivan, H. S. (1953). *The interpersonal theory of psychiatry.* New York, NY: Norton.

Sullivan, H. S. (1954). *The psychiatric interview.* New York, NY: Norton.

Suzuki, S. (2008). *Zen mind, beginner's mind.* Boston, MA: Shambhala.

Swift, J. K., Callahan, J. L., & Vollmer, B. M. (2011). Preferences. In J. C. Norcross (Ed.), *Psychotherapy relationships that work: Evidence-based responsiveness* (2nd ed., pp. 301–315). New York, NY: Oxford University Press. http://dx.doi.org/10.1093/acprof:oso/9780199737208.003.0015

Taleb, N. N. (2007). *The black swan: The impact of the highly improbable.* New York, NY: Random House.

Tarrier, N., & Calam, R. (2002). New developments in cognitive–behavioural case formulation. Epidemiological, systemic and social context: An integrative approach. *Behavioural and Cognitive Psychotherapy, 30*(3), 311–328. http://dx.doi.org/10.1017/S1352465802003065

Thomas, K. (1994, September 30). Roseanne on her 21 personalities. *USA Today,* p. 2D.

Tracey, T. J. G., Wampold, B. E., Lichtenberg, J. W., & Goodyear, R. K. (2014). Expertise in psychotherapy: An elusive goal? *American Psychologist, 69,* 218–229. http://dx.doi.org/10.1037/a0035099

Trull, T. J., & Durrett, C. A. (2005). Categorical and dimensional models of personality disorder. *Annual Review of Clinical Psychology, 1,* 355–380. http://dx.doi.org/10.1146/annurev.clinpsy.1.102803.144009

Tryon, G. S., & Winograd, G. (2011). Goal consensus and collaboration. In J. C. Norcross (Ed.), *Psychotherapy relationships that work: Evidence-based responsiveness* (2nd ed., pp. 153–167). New York, NY: Oxford University Press. http://dx.doi.org/10.1093/acprof:oso/9780199737208.003.0007

Tully, E. C., & Goodman, S. H. (2007). Early developmental processes inform the study of mental disorders. In S. O. Lilienfeld & W. T. O'Donohue (Eds.), *The great ideas of clinical science: 17 principles that every mental health professional should understand* (pp. 313–328). New York, NY: Routledge/Taylor & Francis.

Vaillant, G. E. (1995). *The natural history of alcoholism revisited.* Cambridge, MA: Harvard University Press.

Valsiner, J. (1986). Different perspectives on individual-based generalizations in psychology. In J. Valsiner (Ed.), *The individual subject and scientific psychology* (pp. 391–404). New York, NY: Plenum Press. http://dx.doi.org/10.1007/978-1-4899-2239-7_15

Wachtel, P. L. (1977). *Psychoanalysis and behavior therapy.* New York, NY: Basic Books.

Waldman, I. D. (2007). Behavior genetic approaches are integral for understanding the etiology of psychopathology. In S. O. Lilienfeld & W. T. O'Donohue (Eds.), *The great ideas of clinical science: 17 principles that every mental health professional should understand* (pp. 219–242). New York, NY: Routledge/Taylor & Francis.

Wampold, B. E. (2001a). Contextualizing psychotherapy as a healing practice: Culture, history, and methods. *Applied & Preventive Psychology, 10,* 69–86.

Wampold, B. E. (2001b). *The great psychotherapy debate: Models, methods, and findings.* Mahwah, NJ: Erlbaum.

Wampold, B. E. (2007). Psychotherapy: The humanistic (and effective) treatment. *American Psychologist, 62,* 857–873. http://dx.doi.org/10.1037/0003-066X.62.8.857

Wang, V. O., & Sue, S. (2005). In the eye of the storm: Race and genomics in research and practice. *American Psychologist, 60,* 37–45. http://dx.doi.org/10.1037/0003-066X.60.1.37

Watson, J. C. (2010). Case formulation in EFT. *Journal of Psychotherapy Integration, 20,* 89–100. http://dx.doi.org/10.1037/a0018890

Weiss, J. (1990). Unconscious mental functioning. *Scientific American, 262,* 103–109. http://dx.doi.org/10.1038/scientificamerican0390-103

Weiss, J. (1993). *How psychotherapy works: Process and technique.* New York, NY: Guilford Press.

Wells, K. B., Burnam, M. A., Rogers, W., Hays, R., & Camp, P. (1992). The course of depression in adult outpatients: Results from the Medical Outcomes Study. *Archives of General Psychiatry, 49,* 788–794. http://dx.doi.org/10.1001/archpsyc.1992.01820100032007

Wilder, D. A. (2009). A behavior analytic formulation of a case of psychosis. In P. Sturmey (Ed.), *Clinical case formulation: Varieties of approaches* (pp. 107–118). Chichester, England: Wiley-Blackwell. http://dx.doi.org/10.1002/9780470747513.ch8

Williams, C. L., & Berry, J. W. (1991). Primary prevention of acculturative stress among refugees. Application of psychological theory and practice. *American Psychologist, 46,* 632–641. http://dx.doi.org/10.1037/0003-066X.46.6.632

Williams, J. B. W., Gibbon, M., First, M. B., Spitzer, R. L., Davies, M., Borus, J., . . . Wittchen, H.-U. (1992). The Structured Clinical Interview for *DSM–III–R* (SCID). II. Multisite test-retest reliability. *Archives of General Psychiatry, 49,* 630–636. http://dx.doi.org/10.1001/archpsyc.1992.01820080038006

Wolpe, J. (1958). *Psychotherapy by reciprocal inhibition.* Stanford, CA: Stanford University Press.

Wolpe, J., & Turkat, I. D. (1985). Behavioral formulation of clinical cases. In I. D. Turkat (Ed.), *Behavioral case formulation* (pp. 5–36). New York, NY: Plenum. http://dx.doi.org/10.1007/978-1-4899-3644-8_2

Wood, J. M., Garb, H. N., & Nezworski, M. T. (2007). Psychometrics: Better measurement makes better clinicians. In S. O. Lilienfeld & W. T. O'Donohue (Eds.), *The great ideas of clinical science: 17 principles that every mental health professional should understand* (pp. 77–92). New York, NY: Routledge/Taylor & Francis.

Woody, S. R., Detweiler-Bedell, J., Teachman, B. A., & O'Hearn, T. (2003). *Treatment planning in psychotherapy: Taking the guesswork out of clinical care.* New York, NY: Guilford Press.

Wordsworth, W. (1807). *Poems, in two volumes.* London, England: Longman, Hurst, Rees, and Orme.

World Health Organization. (1992). *International classification of diseases and related health problems* (10th rev.). Geneva, Switzerland: Author.

Worthington, E. L., Jr., Hook, J. N., Davis, D. E., & McDaniel, M. A. (2011). Religion and spirituality. In J. C. Norcross (Ed.), *Psychotherapy relationships that work: Evidence-based responsiveness* (2nd ed., pp. 402–420). New York, NY: Oxford University Press. http://dx.doi.org/10.1093/acprof:oso/9780199737208.003.0020

Wright, J. H., Basco, M. R., & Thase, M. E. (2006). *Learning cognitive–behavior therapy: An illustrated guide.* Washington, DC: American Psychiatric Publishing.

Yalom, I. D. (1980). *Existential psychotherapy.* New York, NY: Basic Books.

Young, J. E. (1990). *Cognitive therapy for personality disorders: A schema-focused approach.* Sarasota, FL: Professional Resource Exchange.

Young, J. E., Klosko, J. S., & Weishaar, M. E. (2003). *Schema therapy: A practitioner's guide.* New York, NY: Guilford Press.

Zeldow, P. B. (2009). In defense of clinical judgment, credentialed clinicians, and reflective practice. *Psychotherapy: Theory, Research, Practice, Training, 46,* 1–10. http://dx.doi.org/10.1037/a0015132

Zoellner, L. A., Abramowitz, J. S., Moore, S. A., & Slagle, D. M. (2009). Flooding. In W. T. O'Donohue & J. E. Fisher (Eds.), *General principles and empirically supported techniques of cognitive behavior therapy* (2nd ed., pp. 300–308). Hoboken, NJ: Wiley.

Zubin, J., & Spring, B. (1977). Vulnerability—A new view of schizophrenia. *Journal of Abnormal Psychology, 86,* 103–126. http://dx.doi.org/10.1037/0021-843X.86.2.103

Zuckerman, M. (1999). *Vulnerability to psychopathology: A biosocial model* (pp. 25–83). Washington, DC: American Psychological Association. http://dx.doi.org/10.1037/10316-002

Index

Jiménez-Chafey, M. I., 157
Johnson, Samuel, 55

Kahneman, D., 33, 34, 38, 40, 48
Kafka, Franz, 4
Kazdin, A. E., 121
Kelly, S. M., 55
Kendjelic, E. M., 170–171
Kendler, K. S., 98
Kind learning environments,
    48, 49, 51
Kirk, S. A., 97, 101
Klein, G., 48
Kluckhohn, C., 54–55
Koerner, K., 74
Kohut, H., 112, 138
Korea, alcohol abuse in, 61
Kraepelin, E., 21
Kroeber, A. L., 54–55
Kuehlwein, K. T., 116
Kutchins, H., 97, 101
Kuyken, W., 129, 171

Lambert, M. J., 69, 77, 78, 80
Learned helplessness model, 18
Learning environments, 48–49, 51
Learning factors, common, 69
Lewinsohn, P. M., 18, 143
Lichtenberg, J. W., 50
Lombardo, E. R., 86, 142
Long-term outcome goals, 161
Long-term process goals, 161–162
Love, psychopathology as gift of, 137
Luborsky, L., 18, 26, 27, 74, 126
Lucas, C. P., 170–171
Lueger, R. J., 77

Mahoney, M. J., 115–116
Maintenance stage of change,
    158, 160
Major depressive disorder
    cultural differences in expression
        of, 60

heritability of, 124
reliability of diagnoses based on
    DSM–5 for, 97
Maling, M. S., 77
Martinovich, Z., 77
Masochistic Personality Disorder, 98
Maximizers, 167
McClain, T., 171
Measurable goals, 162
Medical functioning, problems with, 86
"Medical model" approach, 21, 70
Memories
    false, 32–33, 45
    hypnosis and confidence in, 45
Menninger, Karl, 21
Mental disorder(s). *See also*
        Psychopathology; *specific
        disorders*
    categorical vs. dimensionalist view
        of, 21–23
    cultural differences in expression
        of, 60–61
    definition of, 101–103
    "medical model" view of, 21
Mental set, control of, 130
Messer, S. B., 111–113, 183–184
Meyer, Adolf, 21
Michels, R., 171
Michelson, A., 152
Minnesota Multiphasic Personality
    Inventory, 153
Minority status, 56–57
Mirroring selfobjects, 112–113, 138
Mood, problems with, 87, 89
Musa, M., 171
"My Heart Leaps Up" (William
    Wordsworth), 128

Narrative information, 73–74, 120
Neale, J. M., 110
Neglect of base rates, 44–45
Nelson-Gray, R. O., 26
Nezu, A. M., 86, 116, 142

About the Author

Tracy D. Eells, PhD, is a clinical psychologist, a professor in the department of psychiatry and behavioral sciences, and vice provost for faculty affairs at the University of Louisville. He maintains an individual psychotherapy practice, working with adults presenting with a wide variety of relationship, mood, anxiety, and life problems. He regularly supervises clinical psychology graduate students and psychiatry residents. Psychological assessment is also a major part of his practice. He has taught and conducted research on psychotherapy case formulation for more than 20 years and more recently has researched the role of computer-assisted cognitive–behavioral therapy for treatment of depression. He is a fellow of Division 29 (Psychotherapy) of the American Psychological Association.

Dr. Eells obtained his PhD in clinical psychology at the University of North Carolina, Chapel Hill, in 1989 and completed a postdoctoral fellowship at the John D. and Catherine T. MacArthur Foundation Program on Conscious and Unconscious Mental Processes of the University of California, San Francisco. In addition to publishing many journal articles and book chapters he is the editor of the *Handbook of Psychotherapy Case Formulation*, now in its second edition.

About the Series Editors

Jon Carlson, PsyD, EdD, ABPP, is distinguished professor, psychology and counseling at Governors State University and a psychologist at the Wellness Clinic in Lake Geneva, Wisconsin. Dr. Carlson has served as editor of several periodicals including the *Journal of Individual Psychology* and *The Family Journal*. He holds Diplomates in both family psychology and Adlerian psychology. He has authored 175 journal articles and 60 books including *Time for a Better Marriage, Adlerian Therapy, Inclusive Cultural Empathy, The Mummy at the Dining Room Table, Bad Therapy, The Client Who Changed Me, Their Finest Hour, Creative Breakthroughs in Therapy, Moved by the Spirit, Duped: Lies and Deception in Psychotherapy, Never Be Lonely Again, Helping Beyond the Fifty Minute Hour, Psychopathology and Psychotherapy, How a Master Therapist Works* and *Being a Master Therapist*. He has created over 300 professional trade videos and DVDs with leading professional therapists and educators. In 2004 the American Counseling Association named him a "Living Legend." In 2009 the Division of Psychotherapy of the American Psychological Association (APA) named him "Distinguished Psychologist" for his life contribution to psychotherapy and in 2011 he received the APA Distinguished Career Contribution to Education and Training Award. He has received similar awards from four other professional organizations.

Matt Englar-Carlson, PhD, is a professor of counseling at California State University–Fullerton. He is a fellow of Division 51 of the American Psychological Association (APA). As a scholar, teacher, and clinician, Dr. Englar-Carlson has been an innovator and professionally passionate about training and teaching clinicians to work more effectively with their male clients. He has more than 30 publications and 50 national and international presentations, most of which are focused on men and masculinity and diversity issues in psychological training and practice. Dr. Englar-Carlson coedited the books *In the Room With Men: A Casebook of Therapeutic Change* and *Counseling Troubled Boys: A Guidebook for Professionals* and was featured in the 2010 APA-produced DVD *Engaging Men in Psychotherapy.* In 2007, he was named Researcher of the Year by the Society for the Psychological Study of Men and Masculinity. He is also a member of the APA Working Group to Develop Guidelines for Psychological Practice With Boys and Men. As a clinician, he has worked with children, adults, and families in school, community, and university mental health settings.